D1833003

CORPORATE PHILANTHROPY

CORPORATE PHILANTHROPY
An Instrument of Social and Economic Change

BY

Dr. K. S.V. Menon & Ms. Swapna Menon

KALPAZ

©Author

All rights reserved. No part of this work may be reproduced, stored, adapted, or transmitted in any form or by any means, electronic, mechanical, photocopying, micro-filming recording or otherwise, or translated in any language, without the prior written permission of the copyright owner and the publisher. The book is sold subject to the condition that it shall not, by way of trade or otherwise, be lent, resold, hired out, or otherwise circulated without the prior publisher's written consent in any form of binding or cover other than that in which it is published.

The views and opinions expressed in this book are author(s) own and the facts reported by them have been verified to the extent possible, and the publishers are not in any way liable for the same.

First Published, 2020

Published by

Kalpaz Publications
C-30, Satyawati Nagar,
Delhi – 110052
Ph.: 011-47034999, 9811692060
www.kalpazpublications.com
E-mail: kalpaz@hotmail.com

Printed at: G. Print Process, Delhi

Cataloging in Publication Data—DK
Courtesy: D.K. Agencies (P) Ltd. <docinfo@dkagencies.com>

Menon, K. S. V., 1937- **author.**
Corporate philanthropy : an instrument of social and economic change / by Dr. K.S.V. Menon & Ms. Swapna Menon.
pages cm
Includes bibliographical references.
ISBN 9789353241933

1. Corporations—Charitable contributions—India. 2. Corporations—Charitable contributions—India—Case studies. I. Menon, Swapna, author. II. Title.

LCC HG4028.C6M46 2019 | DDC 658.1530954 23

Dedication

Raghava and Mallika,
Grandchildren of Dr K S V Menon

Contents

Preface

Derived from the Greek "philanthropos" and Latin "philanthropia", the term "philanthropy" literally translates as "love of humanity", or "useful to mankind". First coined by the fifth century BC playwright Aeschylus in Prometheus Bound, the modern concept of philanthropy took shape in the eighteenth and nineteenth centuries, and became a very fashionable activity among British and American traders and entrepreneurs.

Often implemented as a component of corporate social responsibility (CSR) programs, corporate philanthropy (CP) today is a way for businesses to give back to local, national or even international communities, via charitable donations to nonprofit organizations. This "giving back" can take the form of financial (cash) donations or non-cash contributions such as time, expertise, or tangible (in-kind) goods.

In chapter 1 an attempt has been made to trace and discuss various aspects of corporate philanthropy and its varied dimensions. These include the motivations for corporate philanthropy, potential benefits for implementing firms, and examples of societal impacts.

In chapter 2 we have traced various elements which spurred greater interest in philanthropy in India. A number of studies have sought to quantify, analyze and promote such giving. It is a planned intervention that seeks to attain a specific impact over a period of time. The history of giving in India, with a few notable exceptions, has been largely non-strategic and religious in nature.

As stipulated in the Section 135 of the Companies Act, companies having a net worth of INR 500 crore (Cr.) or more, a turnover of INR 1000 Cr. or more, or a net profit of INR 5 Cr. or more in a given financial year are required to spend 2 percent of their average net profit (of previous three years) on CSR programmes. Indian companies responded well to the mandatory CSR with almost INR 8800 Cr. CSR spend in the 1st reporting year of the CSR compliance. The Act heralded a new era for the development of corporate philanthropy in India.

Total number of companies liable for CSR	Rs. 21337Cr.
Total CSR prescribed amount (collect)	Rs. 23247.90 Cr. (57 percent)
Total CSR amount spent	Rs. 13326.69 Cr.

In the budget speech of 2019, Finance Minister has proposed to initiate steps towards creating an electronic fund raising platform — a social stock exchange — under the regulatory ambit of Securities and Exchange Board of India for listing social enterprises and voluntary organisations working for the realisation of a social welfare objective so that they can raise capital as equity, debt or as units like a mutual fund". This will provide further boost to the philanthropic ecosystem.

The authors believe with a growing economy and rising wealth, the role of domestic private philanthropy becomes increasingly important. Both domestic corporations and Indian ultra high net worth individuals need to enhance the level and nature of their giving.

Many resourceful and gracious women in India and globally are coming forward to support philanthropic activities directed at vulnerable sections of society. In the past thirty years women's philanthropy has emerged as a distinct movement using innovative and creative ideas to improve local, national and global communities. Women are engaged in philanthropy from many perspectives – as donors, as professionals, as fundraisers, as nonprofit leaders – in both formal and informal networks. Chapter 3 discusses in detail various aspects of women philanthropists. Some of well known women philanthropies in India and abroad have been listed therein. These include Nita Ambani, Kiran Mazumdar-Shaw, Kiran Nadar, Rohini Nilekani, Melinda Gates, Susan Buffett, Susan Dell, Pam Omidyar etc. These are only indicative not exhaustive of such women donors.

Giving in itself is a noble act regardless of the motivation or approach. It can be one of the most personally rewarding experiences. However, the seriousness, scale and complexity of India's social problems require philanthropists to go beyond personal satisfaction. An appropriate strategy and deeper thinking are required to tackle effectively and systematically varied problems facing the community. Chapter 4 pin points some of the issues and the strategies warranted to mitigate them. Major conclusions and findings have also been presented therein.

It may be mentioned that well before the introduction CSR rules in the company's act many known corporate entities like Tata's were very active and liberal in supporting philanthropic endeavors in different fields like healthcare, education, Rural upliftment, Poverty Alleviation, Farmers welfare etc.

A unique feature of our effort is to bring to focus the role of major corporate philanthropists. They include Tata Trust, Reliance Foundation, Shiv Nadar Foundation, Azim Premji Foundation, ITC Limited, Piramal Foundation, Birla Foundation, Vedanta Foundation, Hinduja Foundation etc. However it may be mentioned that the list is not complete and only indicative. An attempt has been made to discuss their areas of contribution, like education, healthcare, rural development, poverty alleviation etc.

The write up is based on available printed literature and readily available information network. We have liberally drawn from various publications by reputed experts, institutions, particularly consulting firms like Bain & Company, KPMG, E&Y, Deloitte, who bring out periodical reports inter-alia on philanthropy. We thank all of them. The material has been vetted / reviewed by respective organisations whenever found necessary.

We feel the case studies will be found useful to those firms which are moving towards setting up of foundations for philanthropy and academics and others in developing an appropriate corporate philanthropic framework in the country.

Writers have their moments of satisfaction – an occasion to acknowledge their gratitude to all those who have directly or indirectly helped them to complete their work. We have also benefited a great deal from exchange of ideas on the subject with a number of professional friends and experts who are too numerous to mention here. Last but not the least; we are also indebted to Mr. PN Rajan and Ms Prakashini Santhan for computer and secretarial assistance. Thanks are due to Mr. Pankaj Jain & Ms. Sippy Jain of Haryana Leather Chemicals Ltd. for their financial support to take up and complete this work.

However none of them is responsible for probable lapses in the book. The views expressed and the suggestions made are purely personal and have nothing to do with the organisations with which they are currently or in the past associated. We will feel amply rewarded if our humble effort goes some way in the process of transformation under way and making a new India.

Chapter - 1

Conceptual framework

Derived from the Greek "philanthropos" and Latin "philanthropia", the term "philanthropy" literally translates as "love of humanity", or "useful to mankind". First coined by the fifth century BC playwright Aeschylus in Prometheus Bound, the modern concept of philanthropy took shape in the eighteenth and nineteenth centuries, and became a very fashionable activity among British and American traders and entrepreneurs. However, claims that the first American philanthropists were actually Native Americans, as demonstrated by the value placed on concern for the common good within their cultures.

Often implemented as a component of corporate social responsibility (CSR) programs, corporate philanthropy (CP) today is a way for businesses to give back to local, national or even international communities, via charitable donations to nonprofit organizations. This "giving back" can take the form of financial (cash) donations or non-cash contributions such as time, expertise, or tangible (in-kind) goods. Table 1 lists a select number of contemporary definitions of CP.

Morris et al. (2013) suggest that there are two key types of CP: conditional charitable support based on purchases or a percent of pre-tax profits; and an unconditional form of giving in which there is no purchase-based promise or obligation to donate on behalf of the donor, thereby generating a variable charitable support value.

Leisinger & Schmitt (2011) argue that CP should generally address the roots of a social problem, rather than its symptoms (except in cases of humanitarian emergency), to demonstrate the values that a firm stands for.

However, the participation of firms in philanthropic activities remains, for some at least, a source of contention. For example, Friedman (1970) argues that charitablc contributions should be made by individual stockholders, rather than big business, as the latter's solitary social responsibility is to maximize wealth for shareholders.

Tonello (2011) also suggests that some people still oppose CP today on the grounds that it consumes company resources, and is prone to further the goals of management rather than shareholders.

An attempt has been made in the following paragraphs to identify key findings within the literature relating to the motivations for corporate philanthropy, potential benefits for implementing firms, and examples of societal impacts. The motivations or key drivers for corporate philanthropy are presented as a continuum ranging from pure altruism to pure profit maximization or economic/market-based reasons. Altruistic corporate philanthropy is described as the general desire of a firm to do good deeds simply because it is the right thing to do, without any consideration for the benefits that firm might receive in return. Strategic philanthropy is described as a form of impure altruism, in which firms invest in societal programs that are synergistic with their own mission, goals, and objectives. This still results in a direct societal impact, but also generates indirect benefits for the firm's core business objectives, which in the long run impact a firm's bottom line. Pure market-based motivations for corporate philanthropy use the advancement of social interests as a vehicle to directly increase consumption and profits for a firm– for example, by linking the fundraising for a charitable cause to the purchase of a firm's products and services.

- The literature identifies at least six broad categories of benefit for firms engaging in corporate philanthropy. These are:
    - Executive and employee recruitment and retention;
    - Brand building/loyalty and corporate image;
    - New opportunities for innovation;
    - Building trust and influence among government and legislative bodies;
    - Fiscal impact; and
    - Increasing profits and shareholder returns.
- The societal impacts of effective corporate philanthropy programs can extend to:
    - Public health, nutrition, and welfare;
    - Educational and employment opportunities;
    - The development of a stronger climate for doing business;
    - Environmental impacts;
    - International/disaster relief; and
    - Diverse, one-off local issues.

Proponents of increased transparency claim that a company has nothing to fear if the gifts and donations are being made for legitimate business reasons;

but full disclosure can also attract negative scrutiny, and potentially give away insights that could erode a firm's competitive advantage.

Table 1: Select Contemporary Definitions of Corporate Philanthropy

Authors	***Definition***
Campopiano, De Massis & Chirico (2015)	"...the discretionary wealth transfer of net income to stakeholders." (p. 245)
Fontelera (2015)	"...a company's way of giving back to its community -- local, regional, national or international -- through financial donations and non-cash contributions such as time, expertise and tangible goods like computers, medicine, food and textbooks. Companies can donate to charities and nonprofits by giving directly from the company's cash or assets, fundraising through its employees, and fundraising from others."
Gautier & Pache (2015)	"...voluntary donations of corporate resources to charitable causes." (p. 344)
Liket & Simaens (2015)	"...the voluntary business of giving money, time or in-kind goods without any direct commercial benefit, to one or more organizations whose core purpose is to benefit the community's welfare." (pp. 285- 286).
Kabongo, Change & Li (2013)	"...an act of corporations giving a portion of their profits and resources to non-profit organizations." (p. 49).
Morris, Bartkus, Glassman & Rhiel (2013)	"...charitable support not associated specifically with marketing a product or service." (p. 286)
Lähdesmäki & Takala (2012)	"...the charitable transfer of the firm's resources at below market prices. ...a voluntary allocation of a firm's resources to activities that are not business related and for which there are no clear social expectations as to how the firm should perform." (p. 374)
Van Kranenburg & Zoet-Wissink (2012)	"...an extension of corporate social responsibility." (p. 11)
Leisinger & Schmitt (2011)	"...voluntary, active, non-reciprocal efforts (financial, organizational, human resources, etc.) by an entity with the sole purpose of benefiting human beings, or fulfilling an unmet social need, regardless of any specific 'return on investment' for the donor." (p. 4)
Lev, Petrovits & Radhakrishnan (2011)	"...includes direct cash giving, foundation grants, stock donations, employee time, product donations, and other gifts in kind." (p. 2)
Tonello (2011)	"...one component of social responsibility, albeit an important, highly visible component."

The motives for corporate philanthropy

One of the most comprehensive and broad-ranging reviews of CP is provided by Gautier & Pache (2015). Drawing from a review of 162 academic papers published in management, marketing, economics, sociology, and public policy journals, they conceptualize CP along a continuum, ranging from altruism at one end to for-profit at the other.

Gautier & Pache's altruistic extreme focuses on a commitment to the common good. That is, a genuine desire by managers and owners to do good deeds for the sake of it can be an important potential driver for CP. The for-profit end-point emphasizes CP as a purely marketing activity. That is, a firm can also only engage in CP if it can benefit from the investment through the generation of extra returns for shareholders. In addition, Gautier & Pache refer to a midpoint along their continuum in which CP is conceptualized as a community investment. This community investment also indirectly serves the firm's interest through an improvement of brand image, to gain approval and respect from local business elites, or even to counter government intrusions. Almost all of the papers reviewed by Gautier & Pache date from the 1980s onwards, lending weight to the currency of their findings. 75 percent are American in origin, and 87 percent display an Anglo-Saxon bias.

Liket & Simaens (2015) offer three conceptualizations of CP as economic, ethical, and idealized practices; and conclude that the motives are usually highly contextual. Questioning the lack of empirical studies establishing the extent to which CP motives are altruistic or strategic in nature, Liket & Simaens suggest that this is consistent with the conceptual ambiguity and lack of clarity about the objectives of CP.

Ricks and Peters (2013) also identify three key motives underpinning CP. These are:

- A normative motive, encouraging corporate philanthropy on the basis that all stakeholder interests are inherently valuable, even those with no specific financial or contractual arrangements with a firm;
- An enlightened self-interest motive, in which a firm will help others primarily to promote its financial self-interest, without any specific plan and/or way of measuring the extent to which its CP is responsible for financial results; and
- A strategic motive, in which the social and economic goals of a firm and the target recipients of CP are measureable, and can be realized simultaneously and complementarily.

Ricks and Peters, therefore, do not draw a distinction between strategic and economic/for-profit motives.

Drawing from these insights, Seidman recommends that the motivations or key drivers for CP are best conceptualized as a continuum ranging from altruism at one end to pure business/market/economic reasons at the other. This is illustrated in Figure 1. Each key driver will be discussed in turn.

Figure 1: The Corporate Philanthropy Key Motivations Continuum

Altruistic Motivations for Corporate Philanthropy

Altruistically oriented firms chose the object of their philanthropic engagement exclusively on the basis of personal preference and social importance.

Defined by Kerr, Godfrey-Smith, and Feldman (2004) as:

"…behavior that benefits others at a personal cost to the behaving individual" (p. 135), the concept of altruism can be traced back to the nineteenth century French mathematician and philosopher Auguste Comte, who argued in Catéchisme Positiviste that an individual has a moral obligation to renounce self-interest and live for others.

The Online Oxford English Dictionary defines altruism as:

"…the belief in or practice of disinterested and selfless concern for the well-being of others."

Altruism, therefore, is a general desire to do good deeds, not because of an obligation, sense of duty, through loyalty, or for religious reasons, but simply because it is believed to be the right thing to do. Altruistic CP is a form of unidirectional helping behavior. It refers to the making of a charitable gift or donation (in cash or kind) by a firm to a nonprofit with the sole objective of benefiting society.

Consistent with Bowden's (1953) early definition of CSR as the obligation of a businessman to act in a way that will contribute to society's general wellbeing, a firm engaging in altruistically-motivated CP has no thought whatsoever for the benefits they might receive in return for their philanthropic gesture. They are exclusively motivated by an advancement of social welfare. Altruistic CP, therefore, is:

"…a voluntary expression of the firm's commitment to the common good…an expression of a firm's care for the society that surrounds it" (Gautier & Pache, 2015, p. 347).

Godfrey (2005) equates altruism with business citizenship, which he defines as the deep social involvement of a firm's obligations to all citizens, irrespective of any economic gain. During the 1980s and 90s, both Democrat and Republican U.S. administrations called upon businesses to take a greater role in solving societal problems, lending weight to the notion of altruism as a key driver of CP.

One issue with the altruistic approach is that goodness is often in the eye of the beholder, and therefore somewhat arbitrary. History suggests that altruistic charitable management sometimes reflects the fleeting and personal wishes of shareholders or top managers, rather than any interest in the greater good. For example, Lev et al. (2011) state that CP is one potential area where managers have discretion to use a firm's resources independent of business objectives. There is no limit (in theory or practice) placed upon managerial decision making, investments and moral obligations under an altruistic approach; and little-to-no political accountability to check managerial discretion. Directors are less likely to question altruistic CP for fear of being labeled misanthropes. Firms sometimes give more to charity when their top executives and directors have close ties to local business elites (Galaskiewicz, 1997). Urriolagoitia & Vernis (2012) also warn that CP motivated by altruism can be unfairly influenced by local NGOs applying the most pressure within a community.

The biggest problem with a CP strategy based on altruism, though, is its incompatibility with the capitalist concept of the firm, and in particular the primary objective of profit maximization. This issue is succinctly summarized by Friedman (1970), who argues that charitable contributions should be made by individual stockholders, rather than big business. The sole social responsibility of big business, according to Friedman, is to increase profits for shareholders. Tonello (2011) also suggests that CP is still criticized today because it consumes company resources, and far-too-frequently furthers the goals of management rather than shareholders.

Porter and Kramer (2002) identify two implicit assumptions underlying Friedman's objection:

(a) Social and economic objectives are separate and distinct to such an extent that a firm's social spending will come at the expense of its economic results; and

(b) Firms that address social objectives provide no greater benefit than individual donors.

However, they also counter that both of these assumptions only hold true when CP is altruistically motivated, and therefore unfocused and piecemeal.

Concerns about altruistic motives for CP has also encouraged the likes of Kaye (2013) to conclude that a firm today cannot simply cut a check, and claim that they are "doing good". In short:

"...a company needs to do more than sweat out quarterly Wall Street reports, and instead not only look far into the future, but build a strong business and around it, a more just and resilient society." (Kaye, 2013)

Strategic Philanthropic Motivation

An alternative understanding of CP, which attempts to address the profit maximization concerns of critics such as Friedman, is centered on strategic motivations.

The concept of strategic philanthropy was first suggested by Post & Waddock (1995), when they drew a distinction between the orderly methods and procedures that a firm adheres to when making donations ("philanthropic strategy"), and the corporate donations that have meaning and impact for both the giver and the receiver ("strategic philanthropy"). Strategic philanthropy is therefore supposed to guarantee a synergy between the mission, goals, and objectives of the donor firm, and the cause or activity benefiting from the donation. This motivational driver for philanthropy is supported by Lev, Petrovits & Radhakrishnan (2011) who write:

"Acknowledging the economic benefits of corporate philanthropy does not negate its power to alleviate social problems and enhance communities."

Porter & Kramer (2002) disagree with the use of the term "strategic", suggesting that strategic philanthropy in practice is all too frequently reduced to a form of public relations or advertising. The end goal of this public relations or advertising exercise, they argue, is simply the promotion of a corporate image or brand through cause-related marketing or sponsorship. Porter & Kramer conclude that CP will generate the most value for shareholders when a firm:

- Engages in sufficient due diligence to select the best grantees;
- Promotes the donor recipients to suppliers, customers and competitors, thereby maximizing the benefit-cost ratio of their social investments;
- Utilizes their non-monetary skills to improve the performance of CP recipients and social impact per dollar expended; and
- Advances knowledge and practice in the field, finding new solutions to create social value However, subsequent academic studies suggest that a form of strategic philanthropy resembling Porter & Kramer's enhanced bullet-pointed conceptualization does exist.

"Strategic philanthropy is an example of the firm seeking to achieve a synergistic outcome by targeting corporate resources at societal problems or issues that resonate with the core values and mission of the firm. Thus, as an application of the familiar aphorism, "charity begins at home," corporations can contribute to their communities in more meaningful and effective ways by carefully defining what they stand for as corporate organizations."

Godfrey (2005) suggests that firms practicing strategic philanthropy generate intangible strategic assets such as reputational capital, employee commitment, and trust or acquiescence among regulatory institutions and legislative bodies. The extent to which a firm participates in strategic philanthropy is always limited to its strategic interests, thereby ensuring that the primary objective of any business (profit maximization or the generation of shareholder wealth) is adhered to. Godfrey argues that the key determinant of a CP program motivated by strategic reasons is "Does the philanthropic activity of the firm represent a genuine manifestation of underlying intentions, vision, and character, or is the activity simply designed to ingratiate the firm among the impacted community?"

Van Kranenburg and Zoet-Wissink (2012) appear to describe the strategic drivers as "impure altruistic" motives. They suggest that firms that engage in CP for impure altruistic reasons do so for a combination of self-centered and other-centered (societal) motives.

Gautier & Pache (2015) also highlight a broad consensus in the literature that suggests CP serves the firm's interests, albeit indirectly, in terms of reputation, prestige, or employee pride. They refrain from using the label "strategic philanthropy" in favor of a concept of "CP as community investment." However, the core tenets appear very similar. For example, Gautier & Pache suggest that a firm can in the long run benefit from CP based on community investment motives, as the philanthropy will help foster a better environment for business through enhanced social cohesion, safety, education and infrastructure improvements.

Gan (2006) suggests that strategically-motivated philanthropy is symbolic of the conflicts that the managers of contemporary firms must explore, understand, and resolve. The strategic motivation for philanthropy therefore focuses a firm's charitable efforts on a cause or issue that simultaneously provides a direct benefit for society, and indirectly supports a firm's core business objectives. According to the 2015 Edelman Trust Barometer, 84 percent of consumers believe that a firm can pursue its own goals while also acting in a way that is beneficial for society.

Market Motivations for Philanthropy

The academic literature also identifies a third potential driver for philanthropy – that is, for-profit or market motives. Unlike the concept of strategic philanthropy, which can indirectly affect the bottom line of a firm, a market-based approach directly and positively affects profitability or shareholder value. One example is the linking of fundraising for a charitable cause to the purchase of a firm's products and services. Under this latter cause-related example, the firm's "gift" simply amounts to the transfer of money directly collected from consumer purchases. Nickel and Eikenberry (2009) argue that the subtext of consumption, profits, and media celebration intrinsic to the market motivations for CP do not communicate or reflect a desire for society as a whole:

"A discourse of philanthropy in which consumption, profit, and media celebration uncritically narrate money conveys a false message about how the world is and how it could be.... The transformative potential of philanthropy is in its ability to represent the need for social change. A designified philanthropy blurred with consumption, profit, and media celebration fails to signify anything other than consumption, profit, and celebration."

Gautier & Pache suggest that a shift toward CP motivated by market or economic reasons not only creates confusion about the nature of the practice. It also calls into question whether it can even be philanthropic, as:

"...the absence of commercial returns is the cornerstone of philanthropy."

Morris, Bartkus, Glassman & Rhiel (2013) also suggest that consumers are on times suspicious about the primary beneficiary of purchase-based philanthropy. That is, they question who truly benefits – the nonprofit/charity, or the firm producing the product?

Impact of Business Size on Philanthropic Motivations: Most academic studies of CP to dates focus on the motivations of large firms. However, an estimated 90 percent of businesses worldwide are small- or medium-sized enterprises (SMEs); and these SMEs are usually very different in terms of structure and philosophy to bigger firms. The Midmarket Institute also claims that medium-sized enterprises comprise 26 percent of U.S. businesses.

Likert & Simaens (2015) conclude that company size, as well as industry region, internal audiences, and the size of philanthropic budgets can all influence CP. Campopiano, De Massis & Chirico's (2015) study of philanthropic practices at SMEs in Lombardy, Italy, in 2012 concludes that philanthropic engagement increases with family involvement in ownership.

Lähdesmäki & Takala's (2012) empirical study of 25 Finnish SMEs concludes that their philanthropic efforts are more reactive than planned, reflect the ideas and motives of the owner-manager, and are strategic in the sense that they served both societal causes and the economic objectives of their own businesses. The authors also acknowledge that the number of close relationships between a small business and its stakeholders potentially increases the probability of an altruistic motive. It is dangerous to draw generalizations from Lähdesmäki & Takala's small sample study. Nevertheless, they propose a categorization of small business philanthropy, based on two main themes or dimensions, for future research, illustrated in Table 2. One of the themes is motives, which ranges from altruistic to marketing reasons. The other theme is the basis for engagement, ranging from ad hoc decisions to more strategic deliberations.

Van Kranenburg & Zoet-Wissink (2012) also explore a niche aspect of SME CP. This is the extent to which SMEs support international causes. Drawing from a mail survey of 142 SMEs in two cities (Arnhem and Nijmegen in the Netherlands), van Kranenburg & Zoet-Wissink reject the suggestion that SME support for international charities is driven more by the altruistic, rather than the self-interest, motives of managers. They also fail to find a significant difference between the choice of decision-maker (that is, contracted manager or owner) and the propensity to support international charities, or the age of the SME and its propensity to support international causes. Finally, van Kranenburg & Zoet-Wissink suggest that small firms are less inclined to support international causes than medium-sized companies, in part because they focus to a large extent on their own local communities.

Table 2: Potential Classification of Philanthropic Motives in a Small Business Setting

	Marketing Orientation	*Altruistic Orientation*
Ad-Hoc Decisions	Type A CP expected to bring some added value to a business, but targets are random and based on ad-hoc decisions	Type C CP is the moral duty of a business, but targets are random and based on ad-hoc decisions
Strategic Deliberation	Type B CP expected to bring some added value to a business, and the targets are strategically chosen	Type D CP is the moral duty of a business, and the targets are strategically chosen

A survey of 170 executives at medium-sized enterprises conducted by Business4Better in 2013 also found that:

- 75 percent engaged in corporate philanthropy to impact their communities, rather than improve their bottom lines;
- Checkbook philanthropy is being replaced by more meaningful practices such as 40 percent offering employees time-off to volunteer, and 30 percent of companies engaging in pro-bono services;
- Philanthropic plans are usually championed by CEOs;
- Causes tend to be local, business-focused, and targeted at 1-5 nonprofits; and
- Less than 20 percent of employees participate in the philanthropic programs.

The impacts of corporate philanthropy for business: The impact of CP on a firm is dependent in part on their motivations for engaging in philanthropic activity. Nevertheless, the literature identifies at least six ways in which firms can benefit through their implementation of one or more CP programs. This section describes each internal benefit in turn, providing real-world examples where possible.

Executive and Employee Recruitment and Retention: An effective CP strategy can help a company or corporation retain, motivate, and develop the skill sets of existing executives and employees, as well as attract new people to join their workforce.

Turban & Greening (1997), for example, suggest that corporate giving enhances the attractiveness of an employer to prospective employees. Kaye (2013) states that an increasing number of professionals are attracted to employers that are perceived to have a strong social purpose. Integrity Solutions (2013) conclude that employees increasingly want to know that their employer shares their own personal values. The Truist Blog (2013) proposes that millennials want to feel inspired by their work; and a CECP (2006) member survey concludes that employee volunteer programs:

"...increase collaboration, team-building and internal networking, enhance employee retention and provide professional development opportunities for all levels of employees."

The effective implementation of a CP program enables employees to take a pride in both their work and employer, thereby potentially increasing their morale; and engaged employees result in a more productive workforce.

One good example of the employee morale-boosting benefit is State Street's Global Giving Campaign (McGrail, 2013). State Street is an American worldwide financial services holding company. Founded in 1792, it is the second oldest financial institution in the United States. In 2011, State Street launched The Global Giving Campaign to primarily engage and unite its employees worldwide around a single cause over a three-year period. The societal impacts of this campaign were a secondary consideration. A company-wide employee survey chose education as the principal focus of the campaign, and decisions about appropriate educational partners were devolved to three regions (North America, EMEA, and Asia Pacific). During the first year of the campaign, $1.3 million was raised in employee gift contributions and matched on a 1-to-1 basis by the firm. The State Street Foundation also monetized 7,500 employee volunteer hours donated to the educational partners. A survey of employees at the end of the first year concluded that 63 percent of surveyed employees felt engaged as a result of their participation in the campaign; and 59 percent stated that volunteer opportunities helped increase their level of engagement. By the end of the second year, 71 percent of employees participating in the educational philanthropic campaign expressed a stronger commitment to State Street.

The New York Life Foundation's philanthropic focus on childhood bereavement, which strategically aligns with the corporation's mutual insurance business, is reported to have increased employees pride and participation in the foundation's work (Cunniffe, 2013).

Home Depot's Corporate Month of Service, where company employees engage in volunteer projects throughout the U.S, has helped instill a greater sense of corporate pride among 91 percent of the home improvement retailer's workforce (CECP, 2006).

Encouraging employees to participate in nonprofit activities can also prove beneficial for the acquisition of new skills. Higher employee job satisfaction and commitment, and leadership/professional skills are all associated with corporate-sponsored volunteer experiences. Adecco (2015) estimate that 76 percent of staff on pro bono contracts acquire significant job-relevant skills.

Deloitte's volunteer community projects are perceived to develop leadership skills among junior staff, helping them to enhance their communication, delegation, and management skills (CECP, 2006).

IBM's Smarter Cities Challenge – a competitive grant program that sends teams of employees into cities around the world to address community issues – is heralded by Doug Conant, Chairman of the Committee Encouraging Corporate Philanthropy, as:

"...a priceless program for professional development and employee engagement that IBM could not have purchased through the market." (Cunniffe, 2013)

IBM also offers 100 online tools for employees to explore when they volunteer with an organization, encompassing areas such as how to write a business plan, and the role of a board of directors.

Lev et al. (2011) highlight Microsoft's CP program which includes organized group activities, paid leave-of-absence for employees that volunteer matched by a $17 per hour contribution from the corporation, and nonprofit board service training to hone employees' leadership skills. Microsoft implements CP worldwide; and its 2010 corporate citizenship report claims to have increased Egyptian employee satisfaction from 61 percent to 91 percent following the launch of a volunteer program in the country.

Tonello (2011) suggests that company executives can benefit as a result of a CP program in a number of ways. For example, their status can become elevated in elite social circles, through their management of the donation. Executives are sometimes given the freedom to support organizations and causes matching their own ideological agendas; and they can further their careers by gaining favor with board members.

An effective CP program can also help to maintain an ongoing pipeline of future talent for a firm to harvest.

A 2013 Cone Communications/Echo Global CSR Study of 10,287 adults in ten countries found that 81 percent of respondents consider CSR (including philanthropy) when they identify potential employers.

Two examples of recruitment pipeline benefits are provided by Porter & Kramer (2002).

Cisco System's Networking Academy, which began as a form of altruistic giving, has developed into a web-based distance learning curriculum for computer network administrators at 9,900 institutions in 147 countries. In addition to the many social benefits of the program, the Networking Academy has helped alleviate a potential constraint on Cisco's future growth (the lack of suitably-trained future employees), and also provided attractive job opportunities for high school graduates within the IT industry.

DreamWorks' philanthropic supports for an entertainment studies program at LA Community Colleges, which aims to improve the education of and employment opportunities for low income students, has also generated for the studio a pipeline of specialist-trained graduates.

3M's Frontline Talent Initiative which enhanced the sales training of students in colleges has helped to cut in half the amount of time needed for a newly hired frontline employee to be rated as productive by their supervisor.

A March 2013 survey of 173 medium-sized enterprises by Business4Better concluded that less than 10 percent use CSR (including CP) for employee engagement; and CP programs introduced and managed by the CEO or owner do not always attain a high employee participation rate. This has led Scott (2014) to conclude:

"With employee engagement being an area of particular struggle for mid-sized companies, it's important that these organizations better leverage the power of strong volunteer and giving programs to awaken and inspire their employees...and keep the best of them from walking out the door to bigger rivals."

Gautier & Pache (2015) also call for additional research to assess the outcomes of CP on employees. However, there is a significant amount of compelling evidence to suggest a positive relationship between effective CP programs and executive/employee recruitment and retention.

Brand Building/Loyalty and Corporate Image

An effective CP strategy can also help establish or build brand and corporate recognition, generate brand loyalty, offset negative perceptions, and repair damaged consumer relationships.

Gan (2006), for example, suggests that CP can create goodwill, in which public relations can be used to help to cultivate a positive, socially responsible image in the eyes of a sometimes critical consumer. Lev et al. (2011) state that charitable contributions can increase the consumer recognition of either a brand or a company as a whole. Vázquez-Carrasco & López-Pérez's (2013) systemic review of SME CSR also suggests that CP in SMEs can enhance brand image and positioning.

Godfrey (2005) suggests that the reputation of a company or corporation has economic value because it disposes stakeholders to hold beliefs and/or engage in actions that potentially create or destroy shareholder wealth.

Werbel and Wortman's (2000) analysis of 163 corporate foundations between 1988 and 1993 found that the total amount of philanthropic allocations increase following negative media exposure, to help repair damaged relationships.

Patten's (2008) analysis of corporate press releases announcing donations to the 2004 Tsunami in Southeast Asia generated a significant positive 5-day cumulative abnormal return among a sample of 79 U.S. companies.

CECP (2006) found that 35 percent of its members use marketing or advertising to raise awareness of their CP. The key to the success of any CP program is that it must be perceived as a genuine manifestation of the benefactor's underlying social responsiveness. If this is not the case, it is unlikely to have a positive public relations impact or increase shareholder value. Sasse & Trahan (2007), for example, conclude that consumers develop a negative attitude to firms they believe are engaging in "cause-exploitative marketing" – that is, the excessive promotion of CP can create cynicism rather than goodwill.

A study by Ricks (2005) supports the assertion that CP can have an overall positive effect on consumer perceptions, but these effects do not always transfer to brand evaluations, patronage intentions, or by corollary increase sales. He also concludes that a reactive form of CP is often not the most viable way to thwart negative publicity.

ConAgra, a U.S. packaged foods company headquartered in Nebraska, is highlighted by Siu Turner (2015) as a good example of a company connecting its CP to marketing and PR, through its Child Hunger Ends Here campaign. This encouraged consumers to buy specially marked ConAgra brands to trigger a meal donation to Feeding America (a hunger relief organization). Not only was the delivery goal of three million meals achieved in 2014. ConAgra also witnessed a 40 percent increase in awareness, and a 39 percent increase in sales.

The Truist Blog (2013) argues that a well-executed CP program can resonate with customers on a deeply emotional level that goes far beyond even the most creative advertising campaign. That is, CP initiatives lead to greater customer engagement by making the connection between your company, the customer experience, and community building.

Establishing New Opportunities for Innovation

Philanthropic partnerships with universities, non-profits, and foundations, can grant benefactor businesses access to new ideas, technical expertise, invaluable research, and fertile recruitment pipelines.

Cunniffe (2013), for example, suggests that aligning philanthropy with business-related causes has benefits for incubating business ideas based on an interview with the former President and CEO of Campbell Soup and Chairman of CECP.

Recognizing the importance of world-class science and education partnerships, DuPont is a prime example of a corporation attempting to inspire the next generation of scientists, engineers, and innovators through CP. Its emphasis on STEM education programs and science literacy include the DuPont Challenge for students, Ag Ambassadors Academy for teachers, and the Young Professor Program. All three programs are used to stimulate innovation, as well as help develop a highly trained workforce. The Young Professor Program, targeted at universities, has awarded grants in excess of $50 million to 700 young professors in 19 countries. DuPont's website states:

"The hope is that these unrestricted grants will lead to a fruitful relationship beneficial to both parties, and could include future research partnerships, student hiring, etc."

Porter & Kramer (2002) suggest that one primary reason for CP is that businesses cannot flourish in a degraded environment. Philanthropic partnerships with universities can help to rectify this issue. One potential problem with this approach is the sheer number of companies trying to focus their philanthropic activity on education. For example, CECP (2006) found that 77 percent of its members had adopted education as a focus area for their company's philanthropy. However, Kumashiro (2012) claims that philanthropic giving to date has still to surpass 1 percent of total educational funding in the United States.

CECP's Giving in Numbers 2015 Edition suggests that technology companies allocate 45 percent of their philanthropy to K-12 and Higher Education programs. This is consistent with the sector's dual needs of a well-trained workforce and access to innovative research programs.

Clevenger's (2014) doctoral dissertation suggests that little research has been conducted into the corporate-higher education partnerships. Drawing from an ethnographic study of ASU, the ASU Foundation, and six 6 U.S. corporations from 2006 through 2010, Clevenger identifies research as one reason why corporations engage with higher education institutions.

Bereskin et al. (2015) suggest that philanthropic partnerships with research organizations can also expand a company's knowledge, and serve as an outsourcing of research and development. For example, Texas Instruments' Analog Design Contest not only enables students to engage with the corporation's products. The contest rules automatically grant Texas Instruments the exclusive right to exploit the intellectual property rights of contest submissions. As a result, the contest is a mechanism for students to innovate for the corporation.

Quest Diagnostics' partnership with the University of California, San Francisco gives researchers access to its exclusive patient database and opportunities to bid for grants worth up to $500,000 per project. In return, Quest can leverage university expertise to identify new biomarkers for future products.

Corporate Philanthropy as a Means of Buying Influence: An effective CP can be used by a company to help build strong relationships with government officials, community leaders, and other key non-consumer stakeholders. That is, CP can be used by a company or corporation to "buy" influence.

Gan (2006) suggests that establishing direct links between for-profit businesses and non-profit recipients can generate political leverage for business to maneuver around regulation. Van Kranenburg & Zoet-Wissink (2012) suggest that CP helps firms to gain sociopolitical legitimacy, elicit positive stakeholder responses, and gain political access.

Fooks and Gilmore's (2013) analysis of British American Tobacco's CP suggests that tobacco companies primarily allocate charitable contributions according to their political effect potential. These effects are:

- Access to policymakers;
- Constituency building among civil society organizations to build support for policy positions and generate advocacy allies;
- The use of donations to weaken opposing constituencies;
- Enhancement of the donor's status as a source of credible information; and
- Agenda-setting.

One British American Tobacco document unearthed by Fooks & Gilmore suggests the use of philanthropic work to offset the negative effects accruing to the industry from primary health and passive smoking issues. Another document recommends the targeting of charitable contributions to projects demonstrating political priority, to enhance British American Tobacco's ability to build platforms for dialogue with several governments. A good example of this political influence impact is the company's decision to fund urban regeneration projects and City Technology Colleges in the UK during the Thatcher years, based on their proximity and access to the UK government.

Hirschhorn (2004) also suggests that Philip Morris' entire CSR program (not just its philanthropic giving) is designed to burnish the company reputation and deflect lawsuits, based on an analysis of internal documents.

Su & He's (2010) survey of 3,837 Chinese private firms concludes that companies engage in CP to protect their property rights and nurture political connections as a means of maximizing profits.

The ethics of using CP impact to buy government influence might be open to debate; but its existence cannot be questioned.

A more ethical example is The Sutton Trust, which was founded in the UK in 1997 by Sir Peter Lampl to improve social mobility through education.

The Trust today provides multi-year grants to fund new and innovative projects that provide educational opportunities for young people from disadvantaged backgrounds. By funding and publicizing grantee achievements, Ochs (2008) claims that it has been able to attract government attention and influence educational policy change.

Fiscal Impacts of Corporate Philanthropy

The previous section suggested that CP can be used to help create favorable business climates for firms, through government and legislative influence. Neiheisel (1994) suggests that this opportunity to influence government can include protection from higher taxes.

However, an alternative fiscal benefit is also available to implementers of CP. That is, firms can use the available fiscal incentives to deduct the monetary value of their CP from state and federal tax obligations. Charitable contributions are reported on corporate tax returns, but not always disclosed to shareholders unless they are donated via charitable foundations.

Gautier & Pache (2015) conclude that the fiscal impacts of corporate philanthropy to date have not been studied in detail. Arulampalam & Stoneham's (1995) UK study suggests that lower corporate tax rates are positively linked to lower levels of philanthropy. That is, the level of philanthropy declines because companies can offset less of the cost of the philanthropy from their corporate taxes.

Carroll and Joulfaian (2005) have also explored the effects of taxes on corporate philanthropy. Working with a sample of 26,000 C and S corporations, their results suggest that CP declines in accordance with tax prices, and rises with income and advertising. Given the price-sensitivity of corporate charitable contributions, they conclude that a profit maximization model fails to fully explain patterns of CP in the short run.

Maximizing Profits/Increasing Shareholder Returns: A CP program motivated by purely unselfish altruistic reasons seeks only to improve society. However, strategic and marketing-motivated CP programs also seek to maximize corporate profits in the long-run, thereby increasing shareholder returns.

Gautier & Pache (2015), for example, state that there is a widespread belief that firms implementing effective CP programs perform better from a financial perspective. Lev et al.'s (2010) analysis of 251 U.S. firms from 1989 through 2000 estimates that a $500,000 increase in charitable contributions on average could generate an additional $3 million in sales revenues, equating to a $791,500 increase in net income. Their data is sourced from the Taft Corporate Giving Directory, and consists of 1,168 observations. Although the association between contributions and subsequent corporate financial performance is described by the authors as statistically and economically significant, they also note decreasing marginal returns to philanthropy. This means that their estimates of enhanced sales growth are not estimated to continue in perpetuity.

Tonello (2011) suggests that increasing CP expenditure is positively associated with future revenue growth for consumer product companies.

Porter & Kramer (2002) suggest that Safeco's partnership with the nonprofit sector to expand affordable housing and enhance public safety has increased insurance sales by up to 40 percent in four test markets.

Lev et al. (2011) suggest that Crate and Barrel's gift card scheme, in which customers allocate CP to different U.S. educational projects, generated a 16 percent increase in sales for redeemers in 2007-2008, and a 5 percent increase in sales for non-redeemers.

However, other studies question the existence of a positive relationship between the amount of corporate giving and corporate financial performance.

For example, Griffin and Mahon (1997) find no correlation between philanthropic generosity and financial performance for seven chemical industry companies, using multiple sources of data and dimensions of corporate financial performance.

Seifert et al.'s (2003) study of matched pairs of generous and less generous companies fails to find a significant relationship between corporate philanthropy and financial performance.

Working with a sample of 540 firms listed in Bloomberg from 2003 through 2011, Hogan et al. (2014) also fail to find a significant relationship between CP expressed as a percent of EBITDA and excess returns for shareholders.

The literature is therefore at best inconclusive on the relationship between CP and corporate financial performance. This can be explained with reference to at least three limitations.

First, most of the studies consist of multiple industries possessing very different social and environmental concerns and degrees of stakeholder interaction; and this variation could have an impact on the quantitative assessments.

Second, different authors use different methods to measure corporate financial performance, including profitability, asset utilization, liquidity and risk/market measures. This again could impact the calculations.

Third, Kaye (2013) states that the payback for CP is not immediate – it can take 10-15 years. However, it is not clear to what extent (if at all) studies take this delayed payback period into account in their quantifications of the relationship between CP and corporate financial performance.

Given the inconclusive nature of the literature, Lim (2010) calls for a more systematic study of the value of CP for traditional investors. This might also explain why Business 4 Better (2013) concludes that only 20 percent of mid-sized companies measure the success of their CSR (including CP) in terms of financial impact.

Gautier & Pache (2015) ultimately describe the link between CP and financial performance as:

"...one of the most researched and frustrating questions among scholars interested in the business and society relations: many variations appear across firms, industries, and periods." (p. 358)

Competitive Advantage: Each of the individual benefits discussed above can potentially offer a firm some form of competitive advantage. This is a key goal of both strategic philanthropy and a marketing-motivated CP program.

Tonello (2011) suggests that a competitive advantage is only possible when the corporate giving programs are well-designed and carefully executed.

SAP is a good example of a company or corporation using CP to acquire a competitive advantage. A global market leader in enterprise application software, SAP currently donates technologies across the world, with an emphasis on emerging and frontier markets. Their CP is carefully targeted to take advantage of significant future rewards and returns potential in markets currently underserved by the corporation (Kaye, 2013). For example, in 2013, SAP launched a five-year Skill for Africa program tasked with developing information technology skills to boost access to education, and offer critical support for entrepreneurs. SAP's CP programs are always tailored to the specific needs of each market. For example, in Brazil, SAP has established a 3-year Emerging Entrepreneurship Initiative to mentor small businesses short on capital who need help navigating bureaucratic red-tape.

The competitive advantages afforded to SAP through their CP extend far beyond employee engagement. For example, Kaye (2013) suggests that SAP's CP will also help to ensure a long-term future for the corporation through the grooming and development of local talent. It will also build a strong business climate critical for the development of SMEs as future SAP customers and suppliers, and ultimately benefit the corporation's bottom line.

The societal impacts of corporate philanthropy

Liket & Simaens (2015) suggest that there's been very little academic research investigating the social outcomes of CP. Nevertheless, a number of general observations can be made, supported where possible, with real-world evidence.

Educational and Employment Prospects: CECP's Giving in Numbers 2015 Edition estimates that education (both K-12 and Higher combined) is the most popular cause among U.S. companies in 2014, attracting 30 percent of annual philanthropic allocations.

Tonello (2011) argues that technology companies are often the largest funders of educational institutions, which is consistent with their need for a well-trained workforce and their desire to access university programs.

Lev et al. (2011) suggest that corporate philanthropy can stimulate innovation through grants to universities and other organizations. Universities are often required to source corporate matching money for research activities in state or federal grants; and universities leverage corporate dollars to grow their research endeavors and programs. For example, the Global Institute of Sustainability at Arizona State University, which offers transdisciplinary degree programs to create practical solutions to social, economic and environmental problems, was initially established with a $50 million philanthropic donation by the Julie Ann Wrigley Foundation. University of Arizona President Ann Weaver Hart also describes corporate philanthropic partnerships as one important way for public universities to improve outcomes in teaching, research, and public engagement.

Improved educational outcomes by corollary can result in enhanced employment prospects within a community. Some examples of educational and employment societal benefits associated with CP are as follows:

The APS Foundation supports STEM education programs to educate Arizona's future leaders, to help maintain a strong and prosperous economy. Foundation grants are awarded on a biannual basis to programs that help teachers not only increase knowledge in STEM subjects, but also transfer this knowledge effectively to students.

The Bill and Melinda Gates Foundation works with public, private, and nonprofit partners in Washington State to improve educational outcomes for children and families. Their Education Pathways program focuses on five key areas:

- Improved transitions from preschool to college;
- Data-driven decision making focusing on student success;
- Quality instruction and leadership in early-learning programs;
- Increased innovation to boost student achievement; and
- Alignment among health, housing and social service systems.

Goldman Sachs' 10,000 Women initiative fosters economic growth by providing female entrepreneurs worldwide with a business and management education, mentoring and networking, and access to capital. To date, over 10,000 women from 43 countries have participated via a network of 90 academic and nonprofit partners. Thirty months after completing the program, 82 percent of program graduates surveyed have increased their revenue, and 71 percent have created new jobs. Women use their income and skills to support both their families and communities.

Intel Teach is a professional development course for K–12 teachers to integrate technology effectively into classrooms and promote student-centered approaches, engaging students in learning and preparing them with critical skills for success in the digital world. Over 15 million teachers have received training in 70 countries. To gauge the success of their program, Intel measures and holds itself accountable for changes in the way that teachers use information and communications technology in the classroom.

75.4 percent of participants apply new plans for integrating technology into the classroom at least once after completing the program. Negative evaluations and feedback from the program is also used by the corporation to help improve future designs.

In 2013, JPMorgan Chase launched New Skills at Work, one of the largest private sector programs addressing workforce readiness. The $250 million five-year initiative seeks to tackle the skills gap and help workers compete in the global market. In the first year, JPMorgan Chase implemented the program in Houston, Louisiana, Miami, Columbus, New York City, the U.K., and France to identify opportunities for each respective workforce. The banking and financial service company's philanthropic support is used to produce innovative, data-driven analysis of skills demand and supply gaps in local markets, develop effective workforce programs tailored to the employment needs of each community, and encourage collaboration with like-minded stakeholders.

Motorola Solutions is attempting to combat low academic achievement and high truancy rates in Chicago Schools through a philanthropic association with the Chicago Vocational Career Academy. Over 100 Motorola employees serve as mentors and skills-based volunteers at the Academy; and they completed more than 70,000 hours of service in 2013.

SAP strives to enact positive social change through economic growth, job creation, and innovation. In 2014, the global market leader in enterprise application software contributed approximately €22 million in cash donations to non-governmental and non-profit organizations. To help secure employment for people with autism in technology-oriented jobs, SAP has worked closely since 2013 with Specialisterne in the U.S., UK, Denmark, Ireland, Austria, Switzerland, Germany, Norway, Iceland and Poland. SAP's CP efforts also include a partnership with Emprego Ligado, a blue-collar employment site in São Paulo connecting unskilled workers to jobs closest to their homes, thereby reducing commuter time and money. Part of SAP's Emerging Entrepreneurs Initiative, Emprego Ligado was selected from more than 500 candidates to receive philanthropic support which includes software, exclusive mentorship and participation at SAP events.

Shell has also donated more than $24.8 million to the University of Texas at Austin, including a 5-year $7.5 million collaboration to address worldwide oil and gas issues. Most of this money is devoted to research in the Department of Petroleum & Geosystems Engineering and Bureau of Economic Geology. However, $470,000 is used to support University of Texas at Austin student activities and recruitment programs.

Walmart and the Walmart Foundation have committed $40 million, 2011 through 2019, to help veterans and their families via employment and transition programs. An estimated one million service members are expected to exit the military over the next five years, and San Francisco's Swords to Plowshares, the American GI Forum's National Veterans Outreach Program, and the Institute for Veterans and Military Families all benefit from the corporate philanthropy.

Health, Nutrition, and Welfare

CECP's Giving in Numbers 2015 Edition estimates that health and social services is the second most popular cause among U.S. companies in 2014, attracting 26 percent of annual philanthropic allocations.

Some examples of CP being used to generate health and welfare benefits in the U.S. and/or overseas are as follows:

Coca-Cola's flagship philanthropy program, the Replenish Africa Initiative (RAIN), is a sustainable approach to improve access to clean water for up to 2 million Africans by 2015, reduce preventable waterborne illnesses, and empower women through clean water access and entrepreneurship. Drawing from a six year $30 million Coca-Cola commitment, and in partnership with 140 organizations, RAIN:

- Improves access to water and sanitation, and promotes improved hygiene behaviors for positive impacts on health and development;
- Establishes or enhances sustainable water management practices, improving environmental stewardship and community health; and
- Promotes efficient and sustainable use of water for economic development.

The societal impacts of RAIN to date include:

- Clean, sustainable water access for 1 million people (target 2 million);
- Access to sanitation for 180,000 people (target 350,000);
- 35 benefiting countries (target 55);
- 34 watersheds positively impacted by RAIN, covering 65 percent of Africa; and
- 2 billion liters of water replenished each year to nature and communities.

Heasman (2009) claims that an additional non-societal benefit of the program are that it enables Coca-Cola to return to the communities and nature an amount of water equivalent to the water used in all their beverages and their production.

The ExxonMobil Foundation supports programs targeted at global health issues, as a springboard to future opportunity, achievement and development. One example is the ExxonMobil Malaria Initiative, which supports a wide range of prevention, treatment and advocacy programs. ExxonMobil has committed over $133 million to help fund malaria programs in Africa and the Pacific Rim since 2000, primarily in locations in which they have a business interest. This has paid for 13.6 million bed nets, 2.1 million doses of antimalarial treatments, and 2.2 million rapid diagnostic kits. It has also been used to train 426,000 health workers.

Glaxo Smith Kline's five-year partnership with Save the Children aims to bring much-needed medicines and vaccines to some of the world's poorest children, train thousands of health workers, and develop child-friendly medicines. Launched in 2013, the program extends beyond traditional charity corporate fundraising, and utilizes GSK's R&D capabilities to help save up to 1 million children's lives. Countries currently benefiting from the program include the Democratic Republic of the Congo (which is ranked 168 out of 169 countries in the Human Development Index), and Kenya.

In addition to the 10,000 Women initiative, Goldman Sachs' innovative International Finance Facility for Immunization (IFFIm) is a great example of strategic philanthropy. The investment banking company offers a small group of bankers on a pro-bono basis to issue bonds secured against national government pledges for developing and delivering children's immunization programs. This enables the charity GAVI to plan better, accelerate R&D, reduce vaccine prices, and increase the speed of delivery. In 2013, the bonds were credited with saving at least 3 million lives – a major social impact, which indirectly has also generated commercial benefits for Goldman Sachs as a seller of the bonds.

The Hershey Company has developed Cocoa Link, a free mobile technology platform, to educate 45,000 rural cocoa farmers in 1,800 Ghana communities about agricultural practices. The program also offers child safety and welfare information. Results to date include a:

- 46 percent increase in farmers' yields;
- 70 percent increase in farmers' incomes;
- 68 percent participation rate by farmers in literacy training; and
- 90 percent participation rate by farmers in basic business and conservation training.

The Kellogg Company and Kellogg's Corporate Citizen Fund have provided local and national support to Feeding America for over 30 years. In 2009, Kellogg announced that it would donate an entire day's worth of cereal production (equivalent to 55 million cereal servings) to the hunger relief network of more than 200 food banks in the U.S. The 2009 donation was worth $10m at retail value prices, and was intended to help address more than 36 million Americans at that time facing hunger. The campaign was supported by employee food drives, a 3-month online donation program that offered consumers $5 of Kellogg's coupons in return for a donation of $5 or more, and a social media campaign with Ashton Kutcher's Katalyst Media. Through their global Breakfasts for Better Days initiative, Kellogg's has also donated more than 900 million servings of cereal and snacks since 2013.

The Nike Foundation's Girl Effect program, run in partnership with the NoVo Foundation, the World Bank, DFID and the United Nations Foundation, is a multi-million dollar program that aims to empower adolescent girls around the world and help reduce global poverty. Adopting a holistic approach, the program focuses on five key assets: education; health; economic security; safety; and voice and rights. Launched in 2008, the CP program aims to reach 250 million girls living in poverty across the world by 2030, giving them the tools and access to the critical assets they need to achieve their full potential.

In 2009, Pepsi's employees launched the Food for Good program. This aims to make healthy food physically and financially available for low-income families through sustainable, business-driven decisions. Over 4 million meals have been served in the U.S. since 2009, including 1.4 million meals in 2014.

Develop a Stronger Climate for Doing Business: CECP's Giving in Numbers 2015 Edition estimates that 15 percent of U.S. CP allocations in 2014 focused on community and economic development causes.

CP can help to develop a stronger business climate, assist new entrepreneurs, build a strong infrastructure for SMEs, foster the development of business clusters, and strengthen supporting industries. Investing in community and development causes can also help to foster a healthier environment for donor firms to do business. Some examples include:

American Express' Travel and Tourism Academies in secondary schools, which train students for careers at airlines, hotels, and restaurants, have helped to foster the development of clusters and strengthen supporting industries. For example, 80 percent of U.S. students graduating from the program have gone on to college, and 25 percent have embarked on careers in the travel industry after graduation.

APS offers a Focused Future program to help leaders from less-populated areas in Arizona develop community and economic development plans and strategies, to lay the foundations for future economic growth. This nine to twelve month step-by-step process helps community leaders define economic goals, and create action plans to make those goals become a reality.

Freeport McMor Ran partners with NGOs, foundations, and institutions to support community development initiatives via a General Social Investment Program. Two Arizona-specific examples are implemented in Ajo and Bisbee. The types of community benefit Freeport expect as a result of their philanthropy include: increased economic activity in each community; improvements to the business and recreational infrastructure to attract new business, residents and tourists; and an expansion or improvement in local housing options.

In 2014, JP Morgan Chase launched Small Business forward, a $30 million five-year initiative to support the formation, growth and success of sector-specific small business clusters by helping nonprofit owners provide small business owners with access to investors, managerial training, skilled workers, supply chains, facilities and new markets. Small businesses are perceived by JPMorgan Chase to be the cornerstone of local communities, creating jobs and encouraging innovation.

Environmental Issues: CECP's giving in Numbers 2015 Edition estimates that environmental programs attracted 4 percent of U.S. CP in 2014, rising to 10 percent in the utilities sector. The environmental benefits of CP include investments in programs that reduce pollution and waste, and the sustainable use of natural resources.

ConocoPhillips' Water Conservation program is a great example of environmental CP. With nearly two-thirds of the world's population predicted to be living in severe water-stressed conditions by 2025, ConocoPhillips is partnering with communities and institutions to sustainably protect and manage water resources, and ensure that vital ecosystems are able to deliver the services essential to human wellbeing.

There are three core strands to their philanthropy. Conoco Phillips preserves and manages habitats in the greatest need of conservation and of most importance to its business operations. The program strengthens individuals' and organizations' ability to manage water and biodiversity resources effectively. It also fosters innovation and multi-sector solutions to water-quality and accessibility challenges. Each approach enables the multinational energy corporation to serve community needs, and also complement business objectives.

In addition to donating 1 percent of its annual sales to environmental causes, the winter and outdoor clothing company Patagonia has invited other companies (including its supply chain) to do likewise. Patagonia has also asked consumers to refrain from buying products they do not really need (known as the Common Threads Initiative Pledge). As a result, over 1,200 companies in 48 countries now donate 1 percent of their sales to more than 3,300 nonprofits.47 They also operate a Worn Wear blog, to share stories about the longevity of their clothing. This is a good example of strategic philanthropy, linking concern for the environment with the longevity of Patagonia's core product line.

Toyota Financial Services is currently donating $5 to the Boys and Girls Clubs of America (BGCA) for every customer that signs up to their paperless billing services. The campaign has raised over $200,000 for BGCA, as well as dramatically reducing the corporation's paper and printing costs.

Disaster Relief: CECP's giving in Numbers 2015 Edition estimates that disaster relief attracted 2 percent of total U.S. CP allocations in 2014.

For example, the U.S. Chamber of Commerce lists total pledges of $59.1 million from U.S. based firms in response to the Philippine Typhoon Haiyan. This includes grants awarded to the likes of CARE, Direct Relief and the Philippine Red Cross to deliver immediate relief to affected communities, in-kind donations of antibiotics and medical supplies, and the transportation of water purification systems. Accenture donated over $2 million in cash and pro-bono contributions to support relief and reconstruction efforts as part of this CP.

Patten (2008) investigated the market reaction to corporate press releases announcing disaster relief donations to the December 2004 Southeast Asian tsunami. Drawing from a sample of 79 U.S. companies, he identifies a statistically significant positive 5-day cumulative abnormal return. He also concludes that companies making larger donations realize more positive market reactions than others making smaller gifts. The potential societal benefits are far bigger than any impact on market prices for contributing companies; and Patten also lacks a control group of non-contributing companies. However, this again demonstrates the indirect strategic value of CP.

Other Examples: CP can also enhance cultural and arts opportunities within communities, address civic and public affairs issues, or address a wide range of other social issues. CECP's Giving in Numbers 2015 Edition estimates that cultural and arts initiatives and civic and public affairs programs each attracted 5 percent of total U.S. CP in 2014. An estimated 13 percent of total U.S. CP in 2014 is devoted to diverse, unclassified social campaigns.

One good example of an unclassified social campaign is FedEx's Moment of Silence. This was launched in 2013 to bring attention to the number of teens who are killed each year crossing roads due to the distraction of electronic devices such as ipods and cell phones. During the first two years of operations, FedEx had shared the message with 580,000 students at 907 schools in 241 cities.

Another example is Wells Fargo's Principal Forgiveness program, which is targeted at financially challenged borrowers who live in a home worth less than their outstanding payments on their Wells Fargo-owned loan. This CP program has benefited 218,000 customers since 2009. The total value of the principal forgiveness is $8.4 billion.

Conclusions and organisational considerations: This study has offered a number of insights into CP based on a comprehensive literature review and, where possible, real world examples.

Describing CP as a component of CSR in which firms typically make cash and in-kind gifts and donations to society-based programs, the study has suggested that philanthropic gestures were initially left to the whims and preferences of individuals. However, they have increased in popularity among firms following a 1954 Supreme Court ruling (Smith Manufacturing v Barlow) in which the legal restrictions for CP were removed.

An effective CP strategy can help a firm retain, motivate, and develop the skill sets of existing executives and employees, as well as attract new people to join their workforce.

It can also help establish or build brand and corporate recognition, generate brand loyalty, offset negative perceptions, and repair damaged consumer relationships.

Philanthropic partnerships with universities, non-profits, and foundations, can grant benefactor businesses access to new ideas and intellectual property rights, technical expertise, invaluable research, and even fertile recruitment pipelines for talented graduates.

An effective CP program can be used by a firm to help build strong relationships with government officials, community leaders, and other key non-consumer stakeholders. That is, it can be used "buy" influence.

Firms can use the available fiscal incentives to deduct the monetary value of their CP from state and federal tax obligations.

Finally, strategic and marketing-motivated CP programs also offer firms the potential to maximize profits and increase shareholder returns. Evidence of this latter benefit is at best inconclusive for at least three reasons:

(a) Most academic studies consist of multiple industries possessing very different social and environmental concerns and degrees of stakeholder interaction.

(b) Corporate financial performance is measured in diverse ways.

(c) The payback period for CP is not immediate. It can take 10-15 years.

Nevertheless, there are several studies and anecdotal examples where a relationship between effective CP and bottom line benefits can be identified. For example, Lev et al.'s (2010) analysis of 251 U.S. firms from 1989 through 2000 estimates that a $500,000 increase in charitable contributions on average could generate an additional $3 million in sales revenues, equating to a $791,500 increase in net income.

Safeco's partnership with the nonprofit sector to expand affordable housing and enhance public safety allegedly increased insurance sales by up to 40 percent in four test markets; and Crate and Barrel's gift card scheme, encouraging customers to allocate CP between different educational projects, generated a 16 percent increase in sales for redeemers and a 5 percent increase in sales for non-redeemers in 2007-08.

Examples of Societal Impact: CECP (2015) estimates the most popular causes among U.S. companies in 2014 as follows:

Education (K-12 and Higher)	30 percent
Health and Social Services	26 percent
Community and Economic Development	15 percent
Arts and Culture	5 percent
Civic and Public Affairs	5 percent
Environment	4 percent
Disaster Relief	2 percent
Other	13 percent

Likert & Simaen (2015) suggest that there has been limited research into the social outcomes of CP.

Nevertheless, examples of societal impact can be found on a program-by-program bias in several areas.

CP programs such as the Exxon Mobil Malaria Initiative and Kellogg's Breakfasts for Better Days initiative make significant improvements in public health, nutrition, and welfare.

Enhanced educational and employment opportunities are generated by the likes of APS' STEM initiative or JP Morgan Chase's New Skills at Work program.

Concluding Remarks: Effective CP is a long-term commitment which, if implemented effectively, can result in both corporate and societal benefits.

To minimize objections and maximize impacts, a firm's CP should ideally be driven by strategic considerations. This is not to dismiss the other motivations for CP. Altruistic motives, in particular, which expect nothing in return for return for a philanthropic gift other than social advancement, are noble and can dominate thinking in smaller enterprises. Likert & Simaens (2015) also call for a detailed empirical study to establish the extent to which CP motivations are altruistic or strategic.

Nevertheless, the alignment of CP with the mission, goals, and objectives of a firm can not only reduce skepticism about motives, increase employee participation, and reduce stakeholder suspicions about ingratiation. It can also enable the firm to make a meaningful and direct social impact, while simultaneously indirectly benefitting its own bottom line in the long run through reputational capital, employee commitment, and trust or acquiescence among regulatory institutions and legislative bodies.

Lev et al. (2011) recommend that directors and top executives should oversee the CP program to ensure a good fit with other business activities and signal a strong commitment to community involvement; and appropriate resources must be identified from the outset to implement the program.

To establish CP as a source of pride, cohesion, and productivity among existing employees, Gautier & Pache (2015) recommend adherence to a clear set of guidelines to stop executives from advocating favorite causes.

There is also widespread support within the literature for continuously evaluating CP, and estimating an overall social return-on-investment. One such framework is already offered by the CECP.

Given the inconclusive nature of the literature, additional insights are also required to establish the nature of the link between CP and corporate financial performance. If a link does exist, is it industry-specific, in terms of sector or size; or is the inconclusive nature of the findings to date simply a reflection of the effectiveness (or ineffectiveness) of the CP programs studied?

Studies of CP within larger organizations currently appear to dominate. However, 90 percent of the world's companies are SMEs, employing 1-49, or 50-250 staff. There are unique characteristics associated with SMEs, including closer ties with owners, and increased family participation. The motives, organizational structure, and operating philosophies of SMEs can be very different to larger organizations; and there is a clear need for more detailed analysis of CP within an SME setting.

Indian Corporates in CP: We have tried to identify a few major corporates who have initiated philantorphic activities in India over the years. It may be admitted however no specific methodology has been deployed to name these institutions / corporates but is based on overall perception in the country their contribution in the field of philanthrophic activities in various fields like poverty alleviation, healthcare, education, basic infrastructure improvement like sanitation, water supply, energy conservation, gender parity etc. The presentation has been prepared on the basis of available material readily available in print and other forms of literature which have been vetted by the respective institutions covered in the study.

Chapter - 2

Emerging Philanthropy in India

Rapid economic growth, wealth creation and recent large gifts by wealthy individuals in India have spurred greater interest in philanthropy in India. Over the past five years, there has been increasing media coverage of philanthropic gifts and a number of studies have sought to quantify, analyze and promote such giving. It is a planned intervention that seeks to attain a specific impact over a period of time. The history of giving in India, with a few notable exceptions, has been largely non-strategic and religious in nature.

High Networth Individual (HNI) Philanthropy

For HNIs sought to explore trends in their giving through combining two methods. Firstly, it looked at the list of the 20 wealthiest Indians and sought to explore publicly available information on their philanthropic giving. Secondly, it polled a number of development practitioners to find individual and family foundations that were set up in the previous five years. It found that, of a total of 26 instances of HNI philanthropic giving, 20 give through a foundation structure; and 17 of those seem to conflate giving through their linked company foundation with individual giving. One of the plausible reasons for the conflation of individual and linked company giving is the relatively high degree of promoter control over many of the leading Indian companies. Often, a spouse or other family member was found to play a leading management role in the linked company's foundation. Where both individual and family foundations existed, there were often porous boundaries between the two with shared management staff and infrastructure.

There was a strong preference for operational foundations over grant-making foundations. According to the study commissioned by National Foundation for India, of 20 HNIs giving through individual or linked company foundations, 16 were operational foundations directly implementing programs, three had both operational and grant-making components and only two were purely grant-making foundations. The strong preference for direct operations versus support to non-profit organizations seems to be based on two factors: a lack of confidence that donations made will benefit intended beneficiaries if routed through NGOs, who are often perceived as inefficient or corrupt; and the lack of successful example of NGOs scaling up their work to reach large populations.

Philanthropic giving by family and linked foundations reviewed is disproportionately directed at four areas: education, health and livelihood initiatives, and seems to leave out a large number of other development challenges. Selection of focus areas for philanthropic giving was primarily based on personal experience and beliefs of the donor rather than a detailed analysis of gaps, strategic fit and potential intervention strategies. A review of geographic area of operations reported by family foundations also seems to suggest that certain regions – particularly the North East and Jammu and Kashmir – are underrepresented.

The corporate social responsibility rules, which came into force from April 2014, make it mandatory for large Indian firms to set aside at least 2 percent of their average net profit for socially responsibsle expenditure.

The Companies Act, 2013 brought in many changes in the corporate landscape of India, ranging from introduction of one-person company (OPC) to rules for better corporate governance, from the mandatory women director on boards of listed firms to the provision of the mandatory CSR. Introduction of CSR rules was the most debated and talked-about point since the Draft Companies Bill was presented in the Lower House of the Parliament in 2011. Technically, with the new Companies Act, India became the leading country to make companies invest a part of their profits for communities as compliance.

As stipulated in the Section 135 of the Companies Act, companies having a net worth of INR 500 crore (Cr.) or more, a turnover of INR 1000 Cr. or more, or a net profit of INR 5 Cr. or more in a given financial year are required to spend 2 percent of their average net profit (of previous three years) on CSR programmes. Indian companies responded well to the mandatory CSR with almost INR 8800 Cr. CSR spend in the 1st reporting year of the CSR compliance. The Act heralded a new era for the development sector in India which was under resource-crunch due to decreasing foreign-funding (read 'grants') to Indian non-profits, shift in strategic focus of large grant-making organizations from India to other low-income countries and tightening of noose on Foreign Contribution Regulation Act (FCRA), a compulsory government-nod for non-profits to obtain foreign-funding.

If we look at the overall CSR ecosystem in India, the total CSR fund investment by companies in India would cross INR 50,000 Cr. by 31st March 2019, since the applicability of the mandatory CSR. A large chunk of this is towards education and skills development projects, followed by healthcare and sanitation initiatives, both of which are top priorities for the central government as well.

If we dig-deeper in the reported and projected CSR data, it is largely the big 500 companies that define the CSR landscape of the country. These big

500 companies command more than 90 percent of the total CSR pool of the country. Making it more specific, it's only the top 20 companies that command more than 45 percent of India's total prescribed CSR fund year after year, the total prescribed CSR spend for these 500 companies between FY 2014-15 and FY-2018-19 is INR 49537Cr. If we look at the whole CSR ecosystem in India and all the companies under the CSR mandate the numbers add up to INR 56000 Cr.

NGOBOX has been analysing CSR data of companies from FY 2014-15 and publishing analytical reports 'India CSR Outlook Report' since 2015. Based on the reported CSR data of companies, we have tried to look at theme-wise CSR trajectory from 2014-15 to 2018-19. Here, the data for the first three financial years is the actual reported data of the company while the data for 2017-18 and 2018-19 is projected data based on the trends of previous three years' trends and a few sample data-analyses done for the FY 2017-18. These 500 companies are the ones that were required to spend INR 1Cr or more in FY 2017-18.

This is indicative of the potential spend on philantorphic activities in the country by the Corporate India.

A booklet brought by PWC for Confederation of Indian Industry has succinctly spelt out the steps and the role of SMEs in popularisation of CSR in the country which are highlighted in the following paragraphs.

The global context: While there may be no single universally accepted definition of CSR, each definition that currently exists underpins the impact that businesses have on society at large and the societal expectations of them. Although the roots of CSR lie in philanthropic activities (such as donations, charity, relief work, etc.) of corporations, globally, the concept of CSR has evolved and now encompasses all related concepts such as triple bottom line, corporate citizenship, philanthropy, strategic philanthropy, shared value, corporate sustainability and business responsibility. This is evident in some of the definitions presented below:

The European Commission (EC) defines CSR as "the responsibility of enterprises for their impacts on society". To completely meet their social responsibility, enterprises "should have in place a process to integrate social, environmental, ethical human rights and consumer concerns into their business operations and core strategy in close collaboration with their stakeholders"

The World Business Council for Sustainable Development (WBCSD) defines CSR as "the continuing commitment by business to contribute to economic development while improving the quality of life of the workforce and their families as well as of the community and society at large."

According to the UNIDO, "Corporate social responsibility is a management concept whereby companies integrate social and environmental concerns in their business operations and interactions with their stakeholders. CSR is generally understood as being the way through which a company achieves a balance of economic, environmental and social imperatives (Triple-Bottom-Line Approach), while at the same time addressing the expectations of shareholders and stakeholders. In this sense it is important to draw a distinction between CSR, which can be a strategic business management concept, and charity, sponsorships or philanthropy. Even though the latter can also make a valuable contribution to poverty reduction, will directly enhance the reputation of a company and strengthen its brand, the concept of CSR clearly goes beyond that."

From the above definitions, it is clear that:

- The CSR approach is holistic and integrated with the core business strategy for addressing social and environmental impacts of businesses.
- CSR needs to address the well-being of all stakeholders and not just the company's shareholders.
- Philanthropic activities are only a part of CSR, which otherwise constitutes a much larger set of activities entailing strategic business benefits.

CSR in India

CSR in India has traditionally been seen as a philanthropic activity. And in keeping with the Indian tradition, it was an activity that was performed but not deliberated. As a result, there is limited documentation on specific activities related to this concept. However, what was clearly evident that much of this had a national character encapsulated within it, whether it was endowing institutions to actively participating in India's freedom movement, and embedded in the idea of trusteeship.

As some observers have pointed out, the practice of CSR in India still remains within the philanthropic space, but has moved from institutional building (educational, research and cultural) to community development through various projects. Also, with global influences and with communities becoming more active and demanding, there appears to be a discernible trend, that while CSR remains largely restricted to community development, it is getting more strategic in nature (that is, getting linked with business) than philanthropic, and a large number of companies are reporting the activities they are undertaking in this space in their official websites, annual reports, sustainability reports and even publishing CSR reports.

The Companies Act, 2013 has introduced the idea of CSR to the forefront and through its disclose-or-explain mandate, is promoting greater transparency and disclosure. Schedule VII of the Act (see Apendix), which lists out the CSR activities, suggests communities to be the focal point. On the other hand, by discussing a company's relationship to its stakeholders and integrating CSR into its core operations, the draft rules suggest that CSR needs to go beyond communities and beyond the concept of philanthropy. It will be interesting to observe the ways in which this will translate into action at the ground level, and how the understanding of CSR is set to undergo a change.

CSR and sustainability: Sustainability (corporate sustainability) is derived from the concept of sustainable development which is defined by the Brundtland Commission as "development that meets the needs of the present without compromising the ability of future generations to meet their own needs". Corporate sustainability essentially refers to the role that companies can play in meeting the agenda of sustainable development and entails a balanced approach to economic progress, social progress and environmental stewardship.

CSR in India tends to focus on what is done with profits after they are made. On the other hand, sustainability is about factoring the social and environmental impacts of conducting business, that is, how profits are made. Hence, much of the Indian practice of CSR is an important component of sustainability or responsible business, which is a larger idea, a fact that is evident from various sustainability frameworks. An interesting case in point is the National Voluntery Guidelines (NVGs) for social, environmental and economic responsibilities of business issued by the Ministry of Corporate Affairs in June 2011. Principle eight relating to inclusive development encompasses most of the aspects covered by the CSR clause of the Companies Act, 2013. However, the remaining eight principles relate to other aspects of the business. The UN Global Compact, a widely used sustainability framework has 10 principles covering social, environmental, human rights and governance issues, and what is described as CSR is implicit rather than explicit in these principles.

Globally, the notion of CSR and sustainability seems to be converging, as is evident from the various definitions of CSR put forth by global organisations. The genesis of this convergence can be observed from the preamble to the recently released draft rules relating to the CSR clause within the Companies Act, 2013 which talks about stakeholders and integrating it with the social, environmental and economic objectives, all of which constitute the idea of a triple bottom line approach. It is also acknowledged in the Guidelines on Corporate Social Responsibility and Sustainability for Central Public Sector Enterprises issued by the DPE in April 2013. The new guidelines, which have replaced two existing separate guidelines on CSR and sustainable development, issued in 2010 and 2011 respectively, mentions the following:

"Since corporate social responsibility and sustainability are so closely entwined, it can be said that corporate social responsibility and sustainability is a company's commitment to its stakeholders to conduct business in an economically, socially and environmentally sustainable manner that is transparent and ethical."

Benefits of a robust CSR programme

As the business environment gets increasingly complex and stakeholders become vocal about their expectations, good CSR practices can only bring in greater benefits, some of which are as follows:

Communities provide the licence to operate: Apart from internal drivers such as values and ethos, some of the key stakeholders that influence corporate behaviour include governments (through laws and regulations), investors and customers. In India, a fourth and increasingly important stakeholder is the community, and many companies have started realising that the 'licence to operate' is no longer given by governments alone, but communities that are impacted by a company's business operations. Thus, a robust CSR programme that meets the aspirations of these communities not only provides them with the licence to operate, but also to maintain the licence, thereby precluding the 'trust deficit'.

Attracting and retaining employees: Several human resource studies have linked a company's ability to attract, retain and motivate employees with their CSR commitments. Interventions that encourage and enable employees to participate are shown to increase employee morale and a sense of belonging to the company.

Communities as suppliers: There are certain innovative CSR initiatives emerging, wherein companies have invested in enhancing community livelihood by incorporating them into their supply chain. This has benefitted communities and increased their income levels, while providing these companies with an additional and secure supply chain.

Enhancing corporate reputation: The traditional benefit of generating goodwill, creating a positive image and branding benefits continue to exist for companies that operate effective CSR programmes. This allows companies to position themselves as responsible corporate citizens.

Global principles and guidelines: A comprehensive guidance for companies pertaining to CSR is available in the form of several globally recognised guidelines, frameworks, principles and tools, some of which are discussed below. It must be noted that most of these guidelines relate to the larger concept of sustainability or business responsibility, in keeping with the fact that these concepts are closely aligned globally with the notion of CSR.

UNGC: UNGC is world's largest corporate citizenship initiative with the objective to mainstream the adoption of sustainable and socially responsible policies by businesses around the world. The 10 principles of the UN Global Compact have been derived from various UN conventions such as the Universal Declaration of Human Rights, ILO's Declaration on Fundamental Principles and Rights at Work, the Rio Declaration on environment and development, and the UN Convention against Corruption. These prin-ciples cover four broad areas:

Human rights (support and respect the protection of international human rights and ensure that business is not complicit with human rights abuses)

Labour rights (uphold the freedom of as-sociation and effective recognition of the right to collective bargaining, elimination of all forms of forced and compulsory labour, effective abolition of child labour and elimination of description in respect of employment and occupation)

Environment (supports a precautionary approach to environmental challenges, undertake initiatives to promote greater environmental responsibility and encour-age the development of environmental friendly technology)

The UN Guiding Principles on Business and Human Rights: The UN guiding principles provide assistance to states and businesses to fulfil their existing obligations towards respecting and protecting human rights and fundamental freedoms and comply with the existing laws. These principles act as global standards for addressing the risk of human rights violation related to business activity. In circumstances when these laws are breached or the guidance is not adhered to, suitable remedies have also been recom-mended. The primary focus is on the protec-tion of human rights by both, the state and the business enterprises, and the principles broadly outline the manner in which the framework can be implemented.

ILO's tripartite declaration of principles on multinational enterprises and social policy: This is another voluntary declaration whose adoption by governments, employers and mul-tinational organisations is encouraged, with the intention of further ensuring labour and social standards. This is particularly for organisations that operate across multiple countries. Focus is on core labour standards such as (i) freedom of association and the right to collective bargain-ing (prohibition of discrimination, bonded and forced labour) (ii) industrial relations (no trade union restrictions, regular discussions between management and labour, and the provision of a forum to lodge complaints in case of labour standard violation) (iii) employment opportu-nities (creation of job security, improved living and working conditions and ensuring that wages are on par with those of other enter-prises in the same country).

OECD Guidelines: Multinational enterprises

OECD Guidelines for multinational enterprises elaborate on the principles and standards for responsible business conduct for multinational corporations. These guidelines were recently updated in 2011. They cover areas such as employment, human rights, environment, information disclosure, combating bribery, consumer interests, science and technology, competition and taxation. They contain defined standards for socially and environmentally responsible corporate behaviour, and also pro-vide procedures for resolving disputes between corporations and communities or individuals adversely impacted by business activities.

OECD CSR policy tool: The OECD CSR policy tool aims to help companies gain insight into their current CSR activities, assess its value and determine other CSR activities that can be employed. This policy tool is based on the OECD Guidelines and the ISO26000 implementation guidelines. The re-sult of the policy tool is a complete CSR policy, including an action plan with tasks, responsibilities and a communication strategy plan.

The SROI Network: The SROI Network is a framework based on social generally accepted accounting principles (SGAAP) that can be used to help manage and understand the social, economic and environ-mental outcomes created by an organisation or a person. In order to increase the social value or impact of a task, SROI helps in understanding, managing and communicating the social value that a particular task creates in a clear and consistent way with customers, beneficiaries and funders. It also helps in managing risks and identifying opportunities and raise finances. It flags potential improvements to services, information systems and the way to govern the businesses. By forecasting the value a company expects to create using SROI, one can identify the areas where changes are required and a comparison of performance against forecasts will help create additional value.

National Voluntary Guidelines on Social, Environmental and Economic Responsibilities of Business: These guidelines rolled-out by the Ministry of Corporate Affairs in India, were developed through an extensive consultative process with the objective of providing a distinctive India-centric approach for Indian businesses to un-derstand the nuances of responsible business, applicable to large and small businesses alike. They are easy to comprehend and implement, and encourage businesses to adopt the triple bottom line approach. These guidelines consist of nine principles which relate to ethics and transparency, product life cycle sustainability, employee well-being, stakeholder engagement, human rights, environmental stewardship, responsible policy advocacy, inclusive develop-ment and consumer well-being. Each principle consists of core elements that further articulate the purpose and sense of each principle. It also provides an approach for adopting these guidelines.

CSR: Planning and strategizing: The first step towards formalising CSR projects in a corporate structure is the constitution of a CSR committee as per the specifications in the Companies Act, 2013, clause 135.

This is an excellent starting point for any company new to CSR. In case a company already practices CSR, this committee should be set up at the earliest so that it can guide the alignment of the company's activities with the requirements of the Act.

For effective implementation, the CSR committee must also oversee the systematic development of a set of processes and guidelines for CSR to deliver its proposed value to the company, including:

- one-time processes such as developing the CSR strategy and operationalising the institutional mechanism.

- Repetitive processes such as the annual CSR policy, due diligence of the implementation partner, project development, project approval, contracting, budgeting and payments, monitoring, impact measurement and reporting and communication

A set of such enabling processes, their inter-relationships and the sequence in which they need to be developed have been identified below:

CSR processes

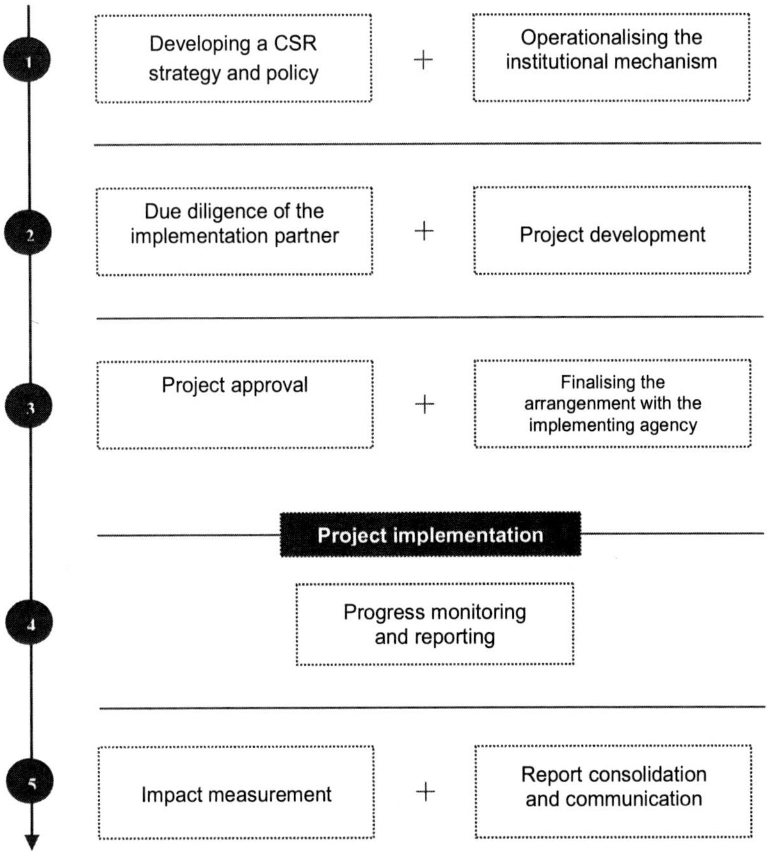

While developing these processes, no standard set of recommendations exist for all companies. However, an overview of the required details, the activities required to be completed for each of these processes along with some additional guidance on critical issues has been provided below:

Developing a CSR strategy and policy

Purpose: The Companies Act, 2013 requires every company to put out its CSR policy in the public domain. The guidance provided in the Act and the draft rules on what constitutes a CSR policy are that it should:

- exclude normal business activities of the company
- contain a list of the CSR projects or programmes which the company plans to undertake during the implementation year

While specifying the annual report requirements, the draft rules go on to say is that the company must provide:

- a brief outline of its CSR policy, including 'the statement of intent reflecting the ethos of the company, broad areas of CSR interest and an overview of activities to be undertaken'
- a web link to the CSR policy including 'the full list of projects, activities and programmes proposed to be undertaken by the company'

Since most of the development requires long-term commitments and their impact often takes a while to accrue, a good CSR practice requires that a company that is serious about its CSR should develop a long-term (three to five years) vision and strategy which is reviewed annually and the activities and budgets are planned on an annual basis. The latter will comply with the CSR policy requirements of the Companies Act, 2013.

To avoid confusion regarding terms like policy, strategy, project and programme, a brief explanation has been provided here:

- CSR strategy refers to what the company expects to achieve in the next three to five years and incorporates the vision, mission and goals on a broader level. It also entails how it plans to achieve these in terms of organisation and approach.
- CSR policy refers to what the company expects to achieve over the next year. This is aligned with the requirements of the Companies Act, 2013.
- Programme refers to a sector or an issue that the company proposes to address through its CSR. This can, for instance, be 'education of the girl child' or 'agriculture development'. Programmes will be clearly outlined in the company's CSR strategy.
- Programme goals will be achieved through a series of individual projects and, a project refers to a set of interventions, typically in a specific geography and addressing a specific stakeholder group, with a definite set of goals, beginning and end and a budget attached to it.

- Each project in turn will consist of a number of activities. All of which contribute towards the project goals.

Frameworking CSR strategy

An effective CSR strategy should articulate:

- who it wishes to address i e the target group
- where it wishes to work i e the geography
- what sectors or issues it wishes to address

A brief understanding of these terms is outlined below:

Target group: While development and welfare programmes in India address all the citizens, the focus is on the disadvantaged, marginalised and excluded. Marginalisation in India is primarily on the basis of gender, disability, ethnicity and location. This leads to social and physical exclusion of such groups from all kinds of development. Engaging the marginalised in India is further complicated due to language and literacy variances, information asymmetry, infrastructure constraints, geographical challenges and cultural barriers to name a few. The CSR strategy should ideally indicate which of these marginalised groups it proposes to target.

Geography: The Companies Act, 2013 encourages companies to target their CSR interventions in their local region. While this is an obvious choice for companies that are in manufacturing, those in the services sector (like banking and telecom) with a wider footprint have no concentrated local region. Companies must decide whether their CSR activities will be focused on a few geographies (this can be around their plants or in specific backward districts) or whether they will prefer to particularly work anywhere in India.

Sector and issue: Sector refers to the development area that the company wishes to focus on; typically, health, education, livelihood, environment, and so on. Issue refers to a specific aspect of a sector for example, primary education in the education sector, skills development or social enterprise in the livelihoods sector. It is important for a company to determine which sector and issues it will focus on to ensure significant positive impact. Also, the reporting format in draft rules of the Companies Act, 2013 requires that the company report against the sector making it all the more important.

Process

Objective: Developing the CSR strategy and policy.

Process owners: The CSR committee

Inputs:

- Guidance from the board
- Companies Act requirements

- Corporate business strategy, plan and supply chain
- Development priorities: both, national and wherever the company has business interests

Output(s): the CSR policy document and an indication of sectors and issues, geographies and a profile of the beneficiaries.

Activities

- Reviewing the past as well as the current CSR activities and examining their alignment with Schedule VII of the Companies Act, 2013.
- Studying the publicly available information on national and local development priorities.
- Meeting development experts in the government as well as the NGOs to understand priorities and identifying potential areas of intervention.
- Conducting internal meetings with business leaders to establish the relevance of potential CSR activities to the company's core business.
- Studying the good CSR practices of other companies and their achievements.
- Developing a CSR strategy that defines for the next three to five years, what the company's CSR activities will cover in terms of:
  - vision and mission
  - sectors and issues
  - geographies: states and districts
  - beneficiaries
  - KPIs
- Determining the implementation mechanism:
  - grant-making or direct implementation
  - institutional mechanism: in-house department, corporate foundation, partnerships with other NGOs
- Annually developing a CSR policy in line with the Companies Act, 2013 rules that defines programmes, geographies and budgets for the following financial year, aligned with the strategy and ensuring that the 2 percent requirement of funds allocation is met
- Establish methods for monitoring and reporting

Operationalising the institutional mechanism Purpose

In order for a corporate to gain the greatest leverage and a strategic advantage through the investment of intellectual and financial resources, they are required to select their implementation mechanism. In terms of implementation mechanism, a company has several options, which are permitted under the CSR draft rules:

- Self-execution through:
  - an in-house CSR department
  - a company foundation with execution capabilities
- Making grants to an independent implementation partner (which has a track record of at least three years).
- The grants can be made:
  - directly by an in-house CSR department
  - through the company's grant-making foundation

The factors that a company needs to consider while deciding between in-house execution and grant-making (whether by the department or the company foundation) are as follows:

Decision criteria	*Grant making*	*Self execution*
Availability and access to implementation partner	Preferred when there is an easy availability and access to the implementation partners (in the target geography working on identified sector and issue) who can work towards the objective that the company wants them to pursue.	Preferred when there is a lack of availability and access to the implementation partners (in the target geography working on identified sector and issue) who can work towards the objective that the company wants them to pursue.
Customisation	The flexibility of customising a CSR project to suit the company needs is low to medium.	The flexibility of customising a CSR project to suit the company needs is high.
Cost of implementation	Implementation partners are more likely to have lower costs due to their concentrated focus in pursuing development activities, cumulative time spent on the field, cost of human resources deployed and in general operational efficiencies. Fixed costs are usually averaged down as the implementation partners usually try to tap multiple sources of funding including government assistance.	Overheads are usually higher and economic efficiencies lower (at least during inception and growth phases). Higher fixed costs are involved.
Control	Low to medium levels of control over day to day activities, efficiencies and outputs.	High levels of control over day to day activities, efficiencies and outputs.
Building expertise	Project management know-how is sufficient and in-depth domain knowledge of development issues is not expected.	Project management know-how is required along with in-depth domain knowledge of development issues.

Project development Purpose

The CSR strategy of a company will be implemented through a series of projects which will have definite beginnings, ends, expected outputs and outcomes as well as budgets associated with it. These projects may be of a short duration (a few months) or multi-year.

A company may choose to implement projects through its in-house teams or in partnership with other agencies or a combination of both. Whatever path it takes, it is important for the project to be developed clearly with distinct baselines, defined activities, 'monitorable' targets and budgets. In the case of multi-year projects, it is important to include a provision to undertake annual reviews which can form the basis to revise the project.

Process

Objective: Developing a feasible project proposal.

Process owners: The implementation agency (the CSR department, company foundation or the NGO partner)

Inputs:

- the CSR policy
- institutional mechanisms
- information from the government sources, previous studies done in the area, etc
- information on programs targeting similar geographies and beneficiary groups or strategies
- monitoring impact measurement reports from any earlier projects

Output(s):

A project proposal that details:

- a project context including the roles of other development actors
- key needs of the target beneficiaries
- project goals, KPIs, baselines and expected end lines
- project milestones for progress monitoring purposes
- activities and timelines to achieve the stated project goals
- budgets along with the basis for estimation
- risks and mitigation strategies
- progress reporting: content, frequency

Activities:

- Developing a framework to identify key stakeholder groups including the local community, the local government or bodies, academia and research institutions, investors, etc.
- Conducting a needs assessment (if required) to assess development priorities. The methodology for this can be participatory processes, surveys or a combination of the two.
- Studying and adopting good practices to address similar challenges based on prior experiences or lessons available from other practitioners and develop the approach.
- Detailing the project: the objectives, the beneficiaries and the impact on the beneficiaries, the assumptions, the expected outputs and outcomes, detailed activities, potential to influence public policy and practice.
- Identifying the indicators of success with the means of verification and establish the baseline for each. This can be commissioned as a separate study or can even be included in the needs assessment stage.
- Estimating the budget and how it will be funded specifying the community contributions, leveraging of the government schemes and contributions from the other donors.
- Indicating the monitoring and evaluation methodologies for impact measurement.

Project approval Purpose

Every project, whether developed by the in-house team or an external agency, must be formally examined and approved. This is to ensure that each project is in line with the CSR strategy and policy, the monitoring indicators are clearly defined and relevant and there is an adequate budget available. Projects that go on for longer durations or demand a larger amount of resources must be scrutinised more carefully than the others.

The CSR committee is ultimately the one responsible for every project. It can, however, choose to delegate authority to a project approval committee consisting of company staff and outside experts with clearly defined roles and responsibilities.

Process

Objective: Approve the project based on the CSR policy objectives, principles and guidelines.

Process owners: The CSR committee or the delegated project approval committee.

Inputs:

- a project proposal
- a due diligence report

Output(s): An approved project proposal including a monitoring process and reporting and responsibility for this.

Activities:

- Determining the delegation of power for the project approval.
- Establishing an evaluation framework for the appraisal of the project concepts and implementing agencies that ensure complete alignment with the CSR policy.
- Establishing tests for the theory of change; whether the concept will be able to deliver the intended results. Establishing tests for the value for money, economy, effectiveness and efficiency.
- Reviewing risks and mitigation measures.
- Identifying resource availability and any specific organisational requirements and constraints.
- Laying down organisational supervision and oversight requirements.

Finalising the arrangement with the implementing agency

Purpose

While working with an external agency, it is very important to enter into a formal arrangement which is referred to here as a Memorandum of Understanding or MoU. It defines the roles, responsibilities, deliverables, commitments and consequences in case of any breach. This is essentially a formal acknowledgement that all the partners have voluntarily consented to work together to achieve an agreed outcome that requires each one to play their respective roles.

The term MoU is used more generically here to refer to the arrangements between partners which can range from a formal, legally enforceable contract on the one hand to a simple exchange of written documents on the other. However, what is important for the company to keep in mind is that it is entering into an arrangement with a partner, not a supplier and there is a greater sense of mutuality in this relationship.

It may also be noted that the MoU is relevant only if the project is being implemented by a legal entity other than the company's own CSR department.

It must also be executed if the project is being implemented by the company foundation if it is a separate legal entity.

Disbursement scheduling: For a project to deliver the desired results, it should have sufficient funds to carry out the planned activities. At the same time, having excess funds in the bank account is not prudent financial management. Thus, the scheduling of disbursements is important both for the company (to plan its cash flows from the CSR budget) and the implementing agency and hence needs to be detailed in the MOU.

A good practice suggests that the scheduling of disbursements should be linked with the activities planned for the each period; this can be a quarter, six months or a year depending upon the administrative convenience and budget sizes. Thus, the project budget needs to be broken up accordingly and the funds required for the subsequent period should be made available in advance.

Actual disbursements have to then be linked to the progress on the ground. The MoU should also specify the conditions that the implementing agency should fulfil and the documentation it should provide in support of a disbursement request. Typically, these include the status of:

- activities originally planned in the period
- changes and the reasons thereof
- planned and required funds for the period
- utilised funds and bank balances
- net funds required

Process

Objective: Agree upon and sign the MoU with the partner.

Process owners: The CSR department or company foundation

Inputs:

- an approved project proposal
- a due diligence report

Output(s): MoU with the implementing agency including the disbursement schedule.

Activities:

- Developing template MoUs based on the context. Specify the outputs and outcomes, the approach and methodology, the KPIs, key parameters to be monitored and reported, the mode of communication, contract management team, scope of change in management procedures, dispute or conflict resolution mechanisms, inspection and audit requirements, contract closeout requirements, time-lines, milestones and deliverables, budgets, process of invoicing and release of payments, etc

- Establishing a process for negotiation of the MoU with the implementing agency.
- Negotiating, agreeing upon and signing the MoU

Progress monitoring and reporting

Purpose

Routine progress monitoring serves the following three important purposes:

- It highlights any slippages and helps to determine a corrective action that must be taken if need be.
- It provides an excellent opportunity for learning: what worked and what did not. This can then be immediately applied to other projects.
- This is an essential part of the directors' report as per the CSR clause of the Companies Act, 2013.

To ensure objectivity, it is critical that the monitoring is done by someone other than the people directly engaged in the project implementation. In cases where the implementation is done by a partner or corporate foundation, this role can either be outsourced or played by the company's CSR department. In case the CSR department itself is implementing a project, then monitoring should either be outsourced to a third party or the department structure should include an independent monitoring cell. This decision should be taken by the CSR committee.

Process

Objective: Monitoring progress, distilling lessons and forming the basis for reporting.

Process owners: The CSR committee

Inputs:

- The approved project proposal
- Previous monitoring reports

Output(s):

Determining mid-course corrections

Recommendations for future project designs

Project monitoring reports to the CSR committee

Activities:

- Determining the monitoring schedule for each project based on the approved project proposal.
- Obtaining all relevant progress reports from the project, studying them and making a note of the gaps.
- Holding discussions with the implementation team on reasons for slippages (if any) and agreeing on a corrective action. This may be done through a field visit or remotely, based on what has been agreed in the MoU.
- Holding discussions with the implementation team regarding what lessons are emerging and how they can be applied within the project as well as outside.

Impact measurement

Purpose

Impacts of the development projects typically take a while to manifest. For instance, a girl child education programme can show an increased enrolment and retention of girls and on a monthly basis, but further impacts such as improved learning levels will take at least a year. So, impact measurement studies have different objectives from project monitoring and typically have to be undertaken after providing sufficient time for them to manifest.

Impact measurement is often quite specialised and needs to be undertaken by an independent team with specific skills depending upon project design. For instance, if a girl child education programme has a strong component for mobilising communities, then the members of the evaluation team must not only understand education but also have knowledge of gender and the community in order to assess the impact.

There are several tools and frameworks for measuring impact. Each has its pros and cons depending upon the nature of interventions, time and budgets available for the study and the availability of people. Thus, selecting the impact measurement methodology is important.

Thus, impact studies have to be carefully planned in terms of team composition, timing and methodology. The process must be driven by the CSR committee which can delegate the day-to-day management of the process to an appropriate structure within the company.

Process

Objective: Measuring the outcome and impact of the projects.

Process owners: The CSR committee

Inputs:

- resource planning
- the project MoU

Output(s):

- impact measurement report
- recommendations for the future project designs

Activities:

- Identifying methods for conducting the impact assessment and outcome measurement suited to the context and the size of the project and budgets available.
- Identifying the skills set required for the impact measurement team and accordingly identifying, selecting and appointing the team.
- Assisting the team to prepare the methodology for selecting a sample, conducting surveys, focus group discussions collecting information on the identified indicators.
- Making the provisions for the site visits by the team, involvement of the agency involved during the baseline and needs assessment.
- Undertaking the impact measurement exercise and preparing the report.
- Identifying the lessons for future interventions.

Report consolidation and communication

Purpose

Reporting and communication closes the loop between intent and achievement and is hence a crucial element of the CSR process. In the context of the Companies Act, 2013 this is also a mandatory requirement as it provides crucial inputs to preparing the directors' report.

Project-level reporting forms the base and hence getting it right is critical. Project reports have to be consolidated in programme related reports, aligned with the CSR policy stated by the company as a requirement under the Companies Act, 2013. The report has to conform to the requirements of CSR rules under the Companies Act, 2013 in terms of form and content as non-compliance attracts penalties. This report will also form a key input into the company's SEBI Business Responsibility Report and sustainability report. The CSR committee may choose to go beyond the requirements of the Companies Act, 2013 and issue a stand-alone CSR report.

Process

Objective: Reporting the CSR at an individual project level, consolidated at a programme level and aligned with the requirements under the Companies Act, 2013 and the CSR committee.

Process owners: The CSR department

Inputs:

- CSR strategy and policy
- the project MoU
- monitoring reports from individual projects

Output(s):

- consolidated CSR reports
- external stakeholder communication

Activities:

- Identifying the recipient of the report: the board of directors, investors, government agencies, beneficiaries, etc.
- Selecting the appropriate reporting framework that is aligned with the requirements of the Companies Act, 2013 and the global best practices.
- Consolidating project reports into programme reports and an overall CSR report.

Chapter - 3

Women and Philanthropy

Women's Involvement in Philanthropy

In the past thirty years women's philanthropy has emerged as a distinct movement using innovative and creative ideas to improve local, national and global communities. Women are engaged in philanthropy from many perspectives – as donors, as professionals, as fundraisers, as nonprofit leaders – in both formal and informal networks. This glossary identifies the kaleidoscope of approaches - audiences, methods, process, and purpose – and celebrates the characteristic common to all approaches within the women's philanthropic movement – many women working across the globe to improve the lives of others and to make a difference in their communities.

Women's Roles in Philanthropy

Women have long served as volunteers in the community, sharing their time and talent to improve their community and/or the world. Exceptional women in 17th-19th century American life contributed financial resources for specific projects. Notable among them are Lady Anne Mowlson (Anne Radcliffe), Mary Lyon, Mary Garrett, Mrs. Russell Sage and others who saw a need and met it with boundless energy and enthusiasm.

Today as women make strides in business, government and the nonprofit sector, they have created multiple, overlapping opportunities to be involved with philanthropy, giving time, talent and treasure for the common good. Women are:

- Volunteers
- Professionals
    - o In corporations driving corporate philanthropy
    - o In nonprofits directing change
    - o In foundations setting policy and serving as executives
- Fundraisers

- Members of family foundations
- Donors
    - Individual donors
    - Members of formal collectives
    - Members of informal collectives

And, sometimes they are all of these at once.

The Work Women Do in Philanthropy

The Center on Philanthropy's 2005 symposium, "Women and Philanthropy: Gaining Momentum," drew attention to perceived tension between women funding women and girls' programs and women funding all causes. Attendees posed the questions: Which do women and which should women do? What is the way to maximize impact? If we don't fund women and girls' programs, who will? Is there one right approach for women's philanthropy?

The main strength of the women's philanthropy movement is its *multi-faceted, kaleidoscopic approach* to changing how women actualize philanthropy. The myriad ways for women to be engaged in philanthropy expands exponentially the number of women across generations who seek the niche best suited to them to put their values into action. In the case of the women's philanthropy movement, one size does not fit all nor are there absolutely pure models to follow.

Models and Examples

Listed below are examples of the range of programs in which women are actively involved in raising and allocating money to meet community needs.

Women funding women and girls' programs

Women funding all causes

Women's initiatives in higher education

Women's programs in local United Way organizations

Giving Circles

Women funding women and girls' programs

In this model the focus is programs for women and girls. Some organizations strongly emphasize social justice and/or equity issues in their grantmaking; some focus directly on grassroots programs for women and girls. These organized grantmaking agencies, all with charitable organization status 501(c)3 may fund programs that are local, regional, national, or international in scope.

- Examples:
    - **Ms. Foundation for Women** was created in 1972 with an emphasis on supporting the efforts of women and girls to

govern their own lives and influence the world around them. The Ms. Foundation is a fundraising and grantmaking organization.

- o **Women's Funding Network** was founded in 1985. WFN is an international organization with over 160 member funds dedicated to improving the status of women and girls around the world.
- o **Global Fund for Women** was founded in 1987 with an emphasis on equality and social justice for women and girls around the world. Since then, the Global Fund for Women has granted more than $85 million to 4,200 women's groups in 171 countries, enabling each organization to apply the funds to best address the specific needs of women in their communities.
- o **New York Women's Foundation** was founded by Helen LaKelly Hunt and several other women as a 501(c)3 organization in 1987. The foundation is a voice for women and a force for change. The foundation combines hands-on philanthropy with community-driven projects to change the lives of low-income women and girls. They offer funding in five issue areas: community organizing and advocacy, economic security, girls' positive development, violence against women and girls, and women's health and reproductive rights.
- o **Women's Funds at Community Foundations** *may* fund only women and girls' programs. The Women's Fund of Central Indiana, a special interest fund of the Central Indiana Community Foundation, raises money from women in the community and allocates grants to local nonprofits that support programs for women and girls. Grantmaking at A Fund for Women at the Madison (WI) Community Foundation focuses on education, employment, and self-esteem.

Women funding all causes

In this model women raise funds and/or allocate resources for all causes, regardless of gender.

- Examples:
  - o **Washington Women's Foundation** began in 1995 with 116 women committed to address the broad philanthropic needs of their community. With more than 500 members in 2012,

WWF functions as an organized, sophisticated giving circle in which each member has a vote on how the pooled funds will be allocated.

- **Women Donors Network** was founded in 1991 and now has more than 100 women philanthropists who each donate $25K or more a year to progressive social justice causes. WDN functions as an organized, sophisticated giving circle with emphasis on strategic philanthropy, education, and information sharing.

Women's programs in higher education

Women's philanthropic initiatives in higher education are generally housed in the advancement office and staffed by a development officer. Program emphasis ranges from strictly fundraising to financial literacy, leadership, and networking and more. Some programs direct funds for scholarships (University of Mississippi) or other specific projects. In some cases, the women's philanthropy initiative takes the form of a giving circle in which participating members contribute a designated amount and then decide collectively how to allocate those dollars (Ball State University, Southern Illinois University at Edwardsville).

Women's programs in local United Way organizations

At United Way Worldwide, the United Way's Women's Leadership Council mobilizes the power of women to advance the Common Good in their communities. With more than 50,000 members in 120 communities around the country, the council energizes and inspires women to make a difference – by advocating for issues important to them, taking a leadership role in advan-cing the United Way's work, and making a personal financial commitment.

The emphasis of this initiative is to raise new or additional dollars from women donors to improve the lives of individuals in local communities. More than 120 of the 1350 local United Way agencies around the country sponsor some form of a women's leadership council.

Giving Circles

Giving circles are one of the fastest growing and most varied of the women's giving models. Giving circles can range from extremely informal settings such as four or five women seated around a kitchen table deciding how to allocate their "coupon money" to extremely sophisticated, structured and formal programs such as the Women Donors Network.

The concept behind giving circles, no matter what the composition or disposition, is that pooled giving has greater impact on making a difference in the community. Impact 100 groups are another model of giving circles in which donors raise major funds ($100,000 or greater) from $1,000 or larger contributions. Each donor has one vote in determining how the collected funds will be distributed.

The aforesaid chapter is based mainly on a research study by Women's Philanthropy Institute, Center on Philanthropy at Indiana University.

Given below are the names of a few global and Indian women philanthropists

Melinda Gates
Susan Buffett
Patricia Harris
Marilyn Simons
Susan Dell
Pam Omidyar
Risa La Visso-Mourey
Jennifer Buffett
Carol Larson
Laurene Powell Jobs
Laura Arrillaga-Andereessen
Laura Arnold
Priscilla Chan
Margaret Cargill
Cathy Catalyst
Nita Ambani
Kiran Mazumdar-Shaw
Kiran Nadar
Rohini Nilekani
Rajashree Birla
Anu Aga
Shriya Saran
Daya Bai
Sulajja Firodia Motwani
Janaki Venkataraman
Kalamandalam Radhika
Shobhana Ranade
Shukla Bose

Chapter - 4

Potential Strategic Givers

Giving in itself is a noble act regardless of the motivation or approach. It can be one of the most personally rewarding experiences. However, the seriousness, scale and complexity of India's social problems require philanthropists to go beyond personal satisfaction. Between 2004 and 2015, India recorded 2.24 million crimes against women, and 1.08 million children died before their fifth birthday in 2017 alone. These ongoing problems underscore the need for individuals not only to contribute greater resources but also to ensure that their contributions are strategic enough to have a marked effect on key social development indicators.

Fortunately, a growing number of philanthropists in India are beginning to act upon this need. The philanthropists who have already begun their giving journeys and are now strategically exploring or revisiting questions such as: How has my giving made a difference? How can I achieve the desired change? Whilst there is no single right way to give, philanthropists can achieve their full potential by contemplating those questions and seeking a path to answering them.

Current landscape: Understanding the mindsets of strategic givers

Bains & Company (BC) interviewed 33 Indian donors to understand the behaviours and mindsets that allow givers to move forward in their philanthropic journey. This group includes philanthropists at different stages of their giving journey, mostly involved in entrepreneurial or family ventures (see Figure 1). Donors interviewed contribute on average USD 15,000 to 75,000 per annum to philanthropy, with some contributing more than USD 765,000. This spectrum was chosen to highlight examples that are relatable to givers who are only beginning to think about or practice strategic philanthropy.

The interviews revealed four mindsets that, if adopted, can enable full philanthropic potential:

- Embracing not only a "today forward" approach but also a "future back" lens to planning one's philanthropic journey;

- Appreciating the importance of both the heart and the mind in making philanthropic decisions;
- Focusing not only on inputs but also outcomes to assess the effectiveness of one's philanthropy; and
- Going beyond a funding-only role to becoming an active and collaborative investor.

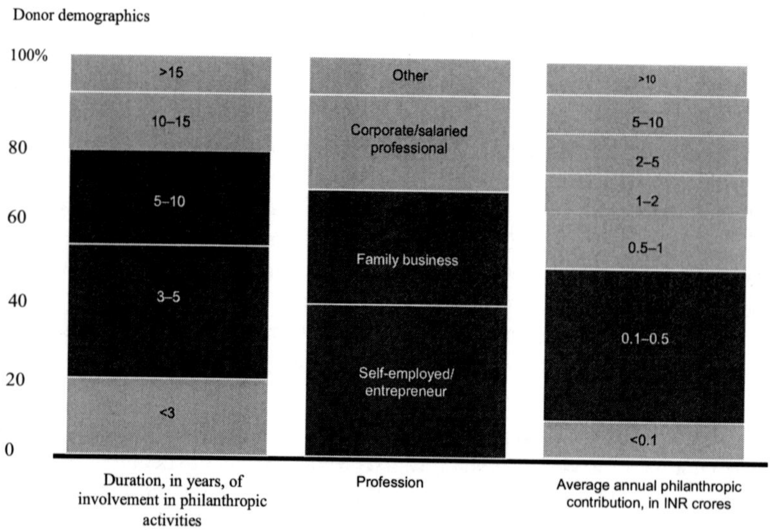

Figure 1: Demographics of the donors we interviewed

Note: INR 0.1 Cr=USD 15,000 and INR 10Cr=USD 1.5M approximately, at an exchange rate of 1 USD=65.1 INR.

Source: India Philanthropy Report 2018 Survey (n=33).

Embracing a "today forward" and "future back" viewpoint

"Today forward" is a step-by-step approach that starts with the status quo and builds incrementally from there. By contrast, the "future back" approach starts with a vision of the future state and works backward. Several of the interviewees expressed a strong commitment to certain causes and spoke about their monetary contribution as a key element of their philanthropy. However, only a few were able to articulate a clear and bold vision that guides their philanthropic plan.

Whilst donors in India largely tend to adopt a "today forward" approach, the "future back" approach of setting an ambitious goal and working backward is relatively uncommon. Consider the following:

- Fewer than 50 percent of interviewed donors felt comfortable rating how ambitious their own goals (see Figure 2).
- Moreover, only one respondent to this question assigned a rating higher than 6 out of a possible 10 (with 0 being unambitious and 10 being highly ambitious).

This may indicate an inclination towards more achievable and incremental goals over bold and aspirational ones. The purpose of the analysis is not to suggest that any one approach is right or wrong. Instead, we believe that a combination of "today forward" and "future back" mindsets would enhance the effectiveness of the donors in the long run, benefiting the philanthropic ecosystem as a whole.

"How ambitious is your philanthropic goal, on a scale of 1 to 10 (with 10 being the highest)?"

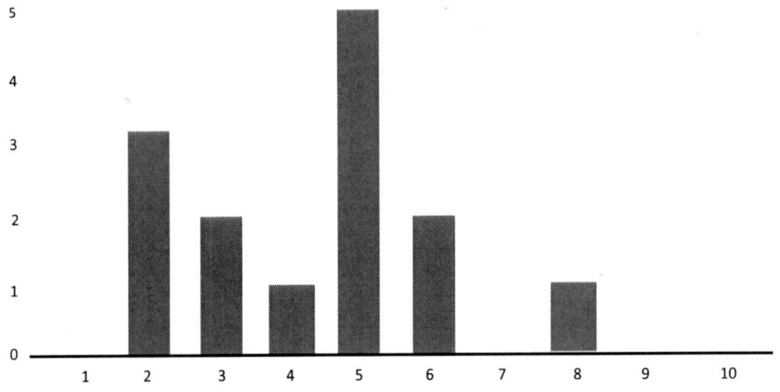

Figure 2: Donors do not feel that their goals are ambitious

Call to action: In the next 30 days, define your own pragmatic "future back" statement and share it with three confidants (peers, family, nongovernmental organisation (NGO) partners).

Case study Ranjit & Anjal Malkani

Having guided companies like SOTC Travel Limited and later Kuoni Travel Group through exceptional growth as CEO, Ranjit Malkani is now putting his business acumen into play in the world of philanthropy. Along with his wife, Anjal, he is setting up his own philanthropic foundation, which he views as a different kind of entrepreneurial endeavour. Whilst the Malkanis have been giving to various causes and nonprofits for several years now, in the last year they have paused and taken a step back to create a clear vision for their philanthropy and a plan to achieve it.

Inspired by the teachings of Buddhism, the Malkanis' vision for their foundation is to help people overcome their suffering. Based on the Buddhist belief that no suffering is greater than another, they have not limited their focus to any particular sector or cause. Instead, they are concentrating on creating extensive and sustainable change by supporting and enabling early-stage nonprofits to scale and improve their systems and processes. In practice, this could mean helping a nonprofit that is running schools to expand its work nationwide or to adopt technology and offer courses online to increase its reach and improve learning outcomes.

They also brought their experience in business to bear in planning their future giving in a structured way. This involved creating a brief purpose document that captures not only the what and how of their philanthropy but also how much funding they could commit to the sector as well as the internal functioning of their foundation over the next decade. This clarity served as an important guide for their giving decisions. In these ways, the Malkanis have merged a future back and today forward mindset by detailing the change they want to see and what they can do today to work towards it.

To this end, over the next seven years the Malkanis plan to invest in building the capacities of a handful of nonprofits, to be selected with Dasra's assistance. The foundation will help these organisations reimagine their capabilities through a structured goal-setting process. It will then involve philanthropy advisers and provide the resources necessary to implement these goals. Ultimately, the foundation aims to fund these nonprofits for five to seven years—and propel them to create greater long-term change and become self-sustaining.

The Malkanis' understanding of the value in adopting a "future back" approach stems from their belief that philanthropy warrants the same rigour as a business. Guided by the knowledge that any successful business begins by clearly defining its product or its market before going on to develop a strategy, the Malkanis understand the importance of beginning philanthropy with a strong vision for change. They set out to elucidate their vision with the help of what they call the "four Ps": the purpose of the work, the process to get there, the people who will partake in the journey and the principles that will guide interactions with the nonprofits and the sector. The Malkanis will launch their foundation's work later this year and are excited to see their vision slowly but surely come alive.

Acknowledging the importance of both heart and mind: Strategic philanthropy is both an art and a science in which the heart and mind work in synergy to make philanthropic decisions. However, donors today don't always conduct their philanthropy through a healthy balance of these two dimensions.

About 40 percent of the responses confirm that areas of personal interest or experience play a pivotal role in the selection of a focus area for one's philanthropy, attesting to the significance of the heart in motivating and guiding such critical philanthropic decisions (see Figure 3).

It cannot be denied that an emotional connection to philanthropy sustains one's giving over time. However, the scale and complexity of developmental challenges in India underscore the urgent need for donors to make certain philanthropic decisions based on an objective analysis and deep understanding of the needs and realities on the ground. Building a strategic plan for one's philanthropy, evaluating the portfolio and creating simple measurement mechanisms to solve for a given cause are examples of areas that can be approached in a structured and analytical manner.

"How did you narrow your focus area?"

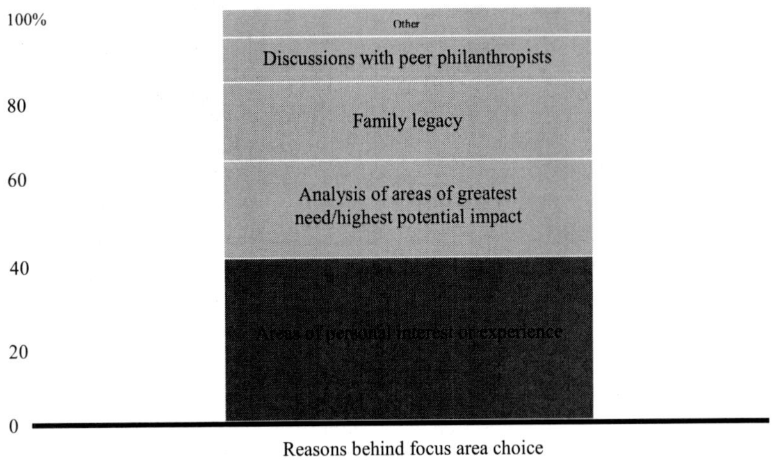

Figure 3: Respondents most often select a cause based on their personal interest or experience

It is also critical to adopt this "mind-driven" approach when reviewing one's giving portfolio so that a clear link between activities and outcomes is established. Conducting reviews is uncommon, though. Less than 50 percent of those interviewed stated that they conduct a portfolio review at least once a year, and only 30 percent do it more than once a year. The irony is that several donors attest to the value of the review process in assessing effectiveness, learning about what is and is not working and correcting course where necessary. In fact, about 70 percent of the donors who perform portfolio review mention they rely on the process to take corrective actions (see Figure 4).

In the future, it will be imperative to strengthen the portfolio review process: Make it more regular and thorough so it can promote corrective action and maximise the value of one's giving—at both the individual and aggregated levels.

Call to action: In the next 30 days, outline a plan for reviewing your giving portfolio. This plan should include defining which aspects of your philanthropy you would like to assess (e.g., distribution of grantees, quantum of funding) and how you will go about doing this (e.g., involving a philanthropy adviser or private wealth manager).

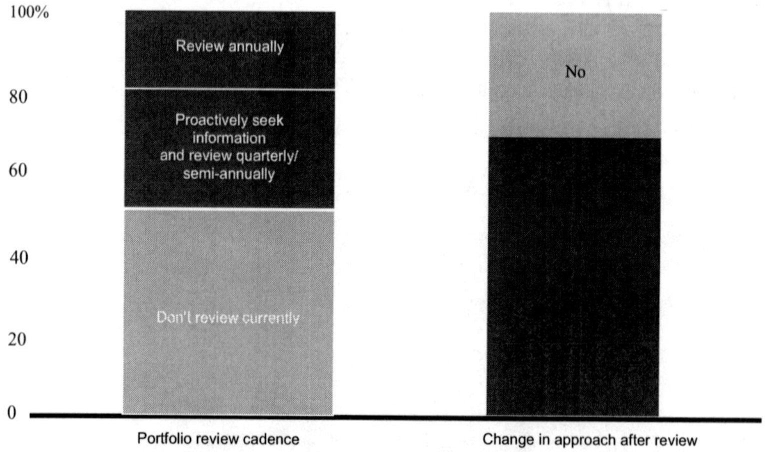

Figure 4: Fewer than half of donors review their portfolio at least once a year, and about 70 percent of those who do it take corrective actions

Case study Sapphira Goradia

Motivated by a strong connection to the country that provided her parents with opportunities to pursue their goals, Sapphira Goradia, a second-generation Indian-American based in Washington, DC, leads her family foundation's efforts to improve health and educational outcomes in India.

Early in her life, Sapphira's parents instilled the importance of giving back and embodied this value through their actions, both large and small. Outside of their significant involvement with Pratham USA, their philanthropy largely took the form of writing cheques to organisations that they felt strongly about. Over the years, they began to question the social returns on their investment, which led them to eventually formalise their giving through the creation of the Vijay and Marie Goradia Foundation. Sapphira joined the foundation in 2013 with the goal of strengthening the strategic focus and scaling the organisations it supports to bring about large-scale change.

The first step in Sapphira's journey was to reflect with her family on some key questions; the answers laid the groundwork for developing a strategy that aligned with their personal values and enabled them to enhance their philanthropic effectiveness. The reflection exercise included personal questions designed to revisit the family's values and motivations: Why do you feel philanthropy is important? What opportunities in your lives were crucial to your own success? The exercise also included more analytical questions such as: What do you believe is fundamental to creating opportunities for others? This reflection exercise, combined with thorough sector research, informed the Goradia family's decision to focus their philanthropy on health and education initiatives in India.

Soon after joining the foundation, Sapphira participated in a philanthropy education programme and built a strong network of peer philanthropists through which she learned more about the concept of strategic giving. She grew to more deeply understand the importance of scale, systems change and risktaking in philanthropy. This knowledge helped inform the foundation's strategy to fund and provide capacity-building support to early-stage organisations with the potential to achieve scale across India. Another principle that guided the foundation's strategy was the desire to give in a manner that creates opportunity for the end beneficiary rather than reinforcing dependency on the foundation or grantee organisations. Specifically, it was important that its philanthropy provide beneficiaries with access to quality healthcare and education so that they have the opportunity to lift themselves out of poverty and pursue their own goals.

Ultimately, Sapphira used both her heart and her mind to arrive at a giving strategy that aligned with her family's values and motivations and set the foundation on a path to transformational social change.

Thinking about inputs *and* outcomes: The focus on philanthropic inputs—time, funds or expertise—is vital; however, on its own it may be insufficient to have a lasting effect on deep-rooted social issues. A keen understanding of how these inputs translate or lead to outcomes on the ground is also necessary. Adopting such a lens not only keeps impact at the centre of one's philanthropy but also serves as a feedback mechanism for enhancing the effectiveness of future philanthropic investments.

A focus on outcomes can help donors better understand where funds are needed—and in doing so, tackles the problem in a holistic way and ensures that the solutions are sustainable. For example, investing in building toilets alone would be an incomplete attempt to solve India's sanitation problem; focusing on strategies to change behaviour regarding open defecation is equally important.

Although this outcomes-driven thinking is catching on with this group of philanthropists, it is still nascent. When asked to define their philanthropic goal post for 2020, only 40 percent of responses related to the scale and impact of giving. However, the majority defined their goalposts in terms of increasing their philanthropic contributions (see Figure 5).

Equally telling is that only half of the respondents rated the effectiveness of their giving in terms of outcomes for beneficiaries. Even among respondents, the average rating was 5 out of 10 (see Figure 6).

A powerful way to reframe one's approach is to identify the tangible outcomes one aspires to achieve through giving, and then work back to outline the inputs to achieve them. It is important to note that it may be difficult to find an existing accurate and measurable key performance indicator (KPI). If so, it makes sense to start with the outcome KPI that fits best, and then work to improve it.

"How do you define your 2020 philanthropic goals for your chosen cause?"

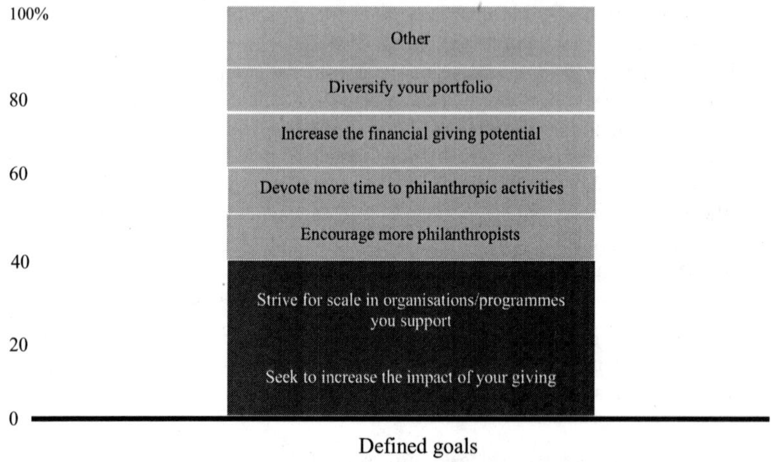

Figure 5: Only 40percent of responses define 2020 goals in terms of outcomes rather than input

"How would you rate the impact of your current giving to the end beneficiary on a scale of 1 to 10 (with 10 being the highest)?"

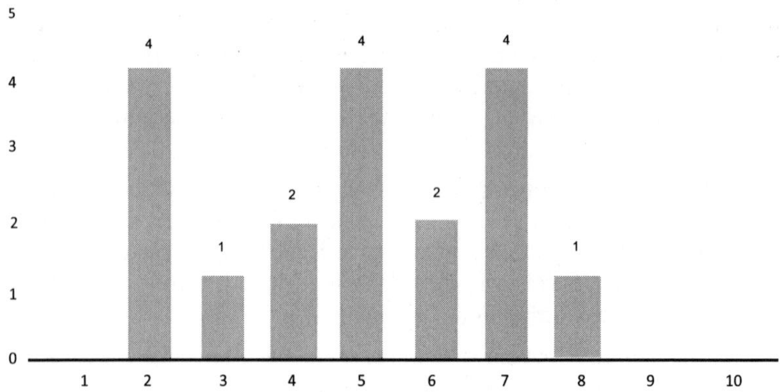

Figure 6: Donors gave low ratings to the outcome of their philanthropic effort

Call to action: In the next 30 days, define your quarterly goalposts both in terms of inputs and outputs as well as in terms of outcomes for the end beneficiary. Involve nonprofit partners who are close to the action on the ground to help strengthen the definition of these goalposts.

Case study Nitin Nayar

With more than 15 years of experience in financial services and private equity, Nitin Nayar, former managing director of Warburg Pincus India, has carried his strong focus on outcomes and results from the business world to his philanthropy. Adopting a sector-agnostic approach, Nitin began his philanthropy with the goal of improving the lives of communities across India. This led him to select high-performing nonprofits with strong and reliable leadership. It also led him to use his professional expertise to help organisations achieve the desired outcomes faster and more effectively.

In 2012, Nitin collaborated with nine peer philanthropists as part of Dasra's giving circle4 in support of the Society for Nutrition, Education and Health Action. Deeply invested in the outcomes resulting from the nonprofit's work on the ground, he devoted a significant amount of his time to understanding the mechanics of SNEHA's programme, its methodology of impact assessment and its vision for the community. Over time, his beyond-capital involvement and relentless focus on outcomes led SNEHA to refine its impact evaluation framework and unearth opportunities to strengthen its programme design.

Nitin recently joined SNEHA's board of trustees and hopes to continue to provide strategic support as the organisation works towards increasing its reach and making a significant difference on key outcome indicators on the ground.

Going beyond a funding-only role to becoming an active and collaborative investor: When it comes to active participation in philanthropy, Indian donors are increasingly diversifying their modes of engagement and appreciating the activities that go beyond cheque writing—a trend that truly reflects the maturity and immense promise of philanthropy in India. This is reflected in the fact that approximately 80 percent of the interviewed donors are engaged in activities to amplify the impact of their philanthropic work beyond contributing funds (see Figure 7). Active participation not only adds value to the nonprofit grantees but benefits the donors themselves, who feel more satisfied with and invested in the outcomes of the initiatives they support.

Additionally, donors are increasingly interested in meeting other stakeholders to share their philanthropic experiences and enhance their overall effectiveness. In fact, meeting with nonprofit leaders and engaging with external advisers were the two most common actions donors took in the last 12 months to improve the effectiveness of their giving (see Figure 8)..

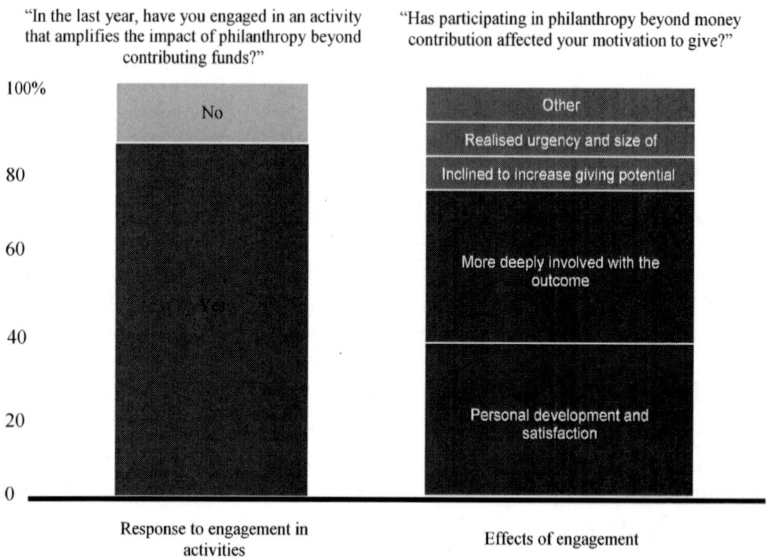

Figure 7: The majority of donors do more than contribute funds, leading to a positive impact on their motivation to give

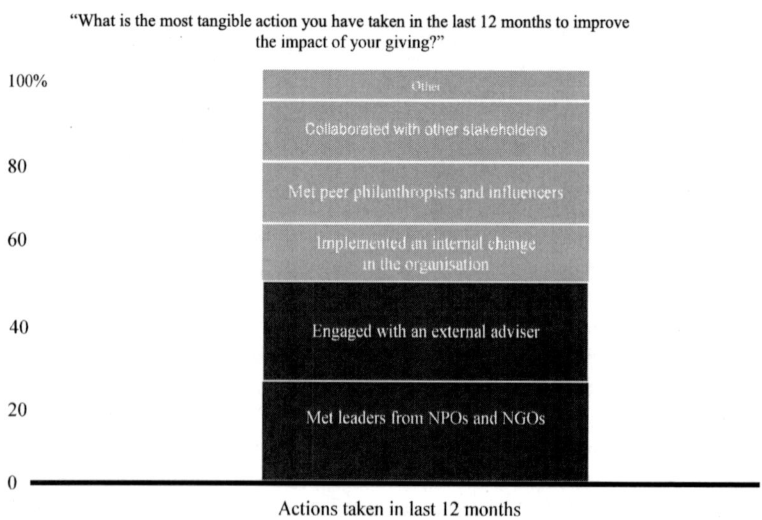

Figure 8: The most common activities that improve the philanthropic impact include interactions with other sector participants

Whilst several donors have begun to interact with others in the sector to pool their expertise to support the growth of nonprofits, there remains a strong opportunity to translate such interactions into more formal forms of collaboration between stakeholders. Given the complexity and scale of developmental challenges in India, the significance of such collaboration has never before been so pronounced.

Call to action: In the next 30 days, work with your nonprofit partners to define one pressing issue challenging the organisation. Treat it as a personal project you want to solve by collaborating with others and using your own expertise. This could relate to creating a fund-raising process, setting up a government partnership or even building a technology platform.

Case study Sean and Jodie Sovak

As a cofounder of Lighthouse, a leading mid-market private equity fund, Sean Sovak has a deep understanding of what it takes to identify potential and empower entrepreneurs to "dream, dare, scale and care." Sean strongly believes that many of the same organisational principles relevant to for-profit organisations also hold true for nonprofits. This insight has been the gateway to his "capital plus expertise" engagement with Muktangan, an NGO that provides education for low-income schoolchildren using a sustainable, community-led model. It also serves as an open resource centre that shares its experiences with schools and teacher education programmes.

Whilst Sean began his philanthropic journey with a focus on the arts, his move to India more than a decade ago shaped his and his wife, Jodie's, approach to giving. Sean and Jodie were deeply affected by the scale and severity of disparity and recognised the urgency for action. Introduced by a colleague to Dasra, their participation in giving circles with peer philanthropists helped educate them about areas of need and innovative, high-impact solutions to address these problems. Over time, a process of selfreflection led the Sovaks to narrow their philanthropic focus to education, with a specific interest in empowering girls and women.

At Muktangan, the Sovaks began by making multiyear financial contributions and regularly meeting with founders Elizabeth and Sunil Mehta to better understand the organisation and its challenges. Over time, they realised that, similar to the business world, the nonprofit sector is made up of many passionate and intelligent founders who are struggling to institutionalise culture, processes and leadership transitions within their organisations. This led to their recognition that capital alone was not enough to enable Muktangan to scale its work.

Today, whilst Sean engages with Muktangan on multiple levels, he hopes that his most meaningful contribution will be his support for a successful, lasting leadership transition for the organisation. Citing philanthropy as one of the most rewarding experiences of his life, Sean finds fulfilment in seeing the effectiveness of capital coupled with time. Although he will continue to focus on education and seek opportunities for collaboration, innovation, growth and deeper impact, he is also thinking about sharing what he and Muktangan have learned with other philanthropists and nonprofit organisations.

Whilst embracing the four mindsets is not easy, many philanthropists in India are already beginning to incorporate them into their philanthropic practices, as demonstrated through the interview findings and case studies. The following sections highlight some practical steps needed to embed the four mindsets into a philanthropic plan and to identify the resources readily available to help propel donors on this fulfilling journey of discovering their full potential.

Practical actions towards strategic giving

The following sections provide actionable guidance on how to absorb these mindsets by encouraging philanthropists to focus on the four key aspects of their giving (see Figure 9).

1. Gauge the effectiveness of your current giving

Philanthropists are often confronted by an important enquiry: "Am I making a difference?" However, most givers soon realise that it is difficult to gauge the effectiveness of individual grants to organisations, let alone the aggregated performance of their philanthropic portfolio. Yet this process of reflection is an important step in learning what is and what is not working, making corrections where necessary and ensuring that the philanthropist's resources are being put to good use.

With the goal of instilling clarity and focus in one's philanthropy, the first step is to conduct a review of the current philanthropic portfolio. For philanthropists who have already been giving and are looking to steer themselves in a more strategic direction, a portfolio review can help them recognise and learn from inefficiencies and successes. Similar to reviews of for-profit investment portfolios, the insights generated from this period of reflection can pave the way for a more catalytic strategy. Whilst many philanthropists have cited monitoring, learning and course correcting as an ongoing process, it is worth considering a formal portfolio review at least once every five years. Philanthropists can consider the following steps as they gauge the effectiveness of their current giving.

Determine your giving potential

Philanthropists often make a financial commitment without a precise understanding of their financial giving potential. As they look to devote a

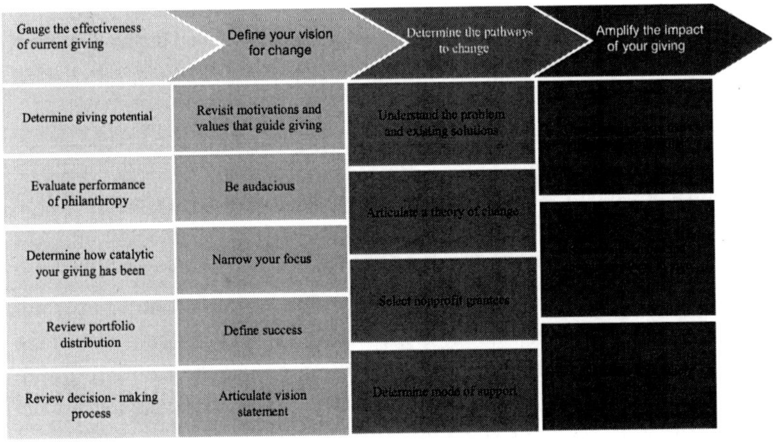

Figure 9 Steps to strengthen the four mindsets

larger proportion of their wealth to philanthropy, it is recommended that they intentionally evaluate their current and projected wealth against their personal and family requirements, investments and savings to ultimately provide clarity into their financial giving potential. Several notable philanthropists have said that asking and answering the question, "How much is enough to live the life I desire?" has been transformative for their philanthropy. Thinking about how this philanthropic capital can be disbursed over time is also useful. Engaging with private wealth managers can be helpful in navigating this exercise.

Evaluate the performance of your philanthropy so far

One of the most important aspects of the review process is assessing the gap between what philanthropists planned to solve for and what they have achieved through their giving so far. If there is a gap, an assessment can be an important inflection point, prompting them to either define their objectives more clearly or revisit their portfolio for better alignment with the desired objectives.

A variety of frameworks can measure the progress of each investment. The metrics used to measure performance could be qualitative or quantitative in nature, although most organisations benefit from a hybrid to mirror the organisation's nuanced work. The Balanced Score card is a tool that measures organisational performance on a number of indicators—beneficiaries, internal processes, financials and learning and growth—to provide a holistic view of the organisation. By evaluating performance across these parameters, the scorecard increases focus on strategy and results, aligns the organisation's strategy with day-to-day work and prioritises projects and initiatives.

It is important to note that this performance assessment is part of a retrospective portfolio review and, therefore, may be constrained by the extent of data already available with the portfolio organisations. Even then, the process will expose the additional data an organisation needs for similar activities in the future.

Assess how catalytic your giving has been

With a broad understanding of the change that one's giving has enabled, it is important to consider how to multiply the effectiveness of philanthropy. The two streams to consider when reflecting on the catalytic nature of giving are:

- **How catalytic was the grant for the organisation?** A careful diagnosis of the grantee organisation's needs can help determine the size and approach by which the grant can be catalytic for an organisation. For instance, the grant size could be weighed against the organisation's stage in its life cycle. A relatively small grant for a promising organisation in its infancy can be catalytic compared with the same grant to a mature one. Other examples of catalytic grants include supporting the institutional needs of a growing organisation. A grant to build organisational leadership in support of a fund-raising officer, for instance, may have a multiplier effect with regard to the ongoing grants that the officer may raise for future work. The timeline and flexibility of philanthropic funding—programmatic vs. institutional, short term vs. long term, restricted vs. unrestricted, or seed vs. growth—are other aspects to consider when thinking of the most catalytic use of philanthropic funds. It is important to note that the most catalytic use of one's funding should not be predetermined but decided in relation to the needs of the organisation and the context of the sector at hand.
- **How catalytic was the philanthropist for the organisation?** Donors are often able to contribute beyond cheque writing in ways that can multiply the opportunities available to an organisation. For example, they can direct their skills and business acumen towards providing strategic direction, mobilise more funds through their peer networks or help facilitate collaboration with critical players like the government. Philanthropists who take the time to carefully match their expertise and resources to the most pressing needs of the nonprofit are able to add the maximum value to the organisation.

Review the distribution of your portfolio

During the review process, it is critical to visualise the breakdown of the philanthropic portfolio across various parameters. Philanthropists may consider the breadth of the portfolio or the depth of engagement with each organisation. For example, given finite resources, is it better to give smaller amounts to multiple organisations or give more to just a handful? Another aspect to consider may be the composition of one's portfolio across emotional and strategic investments. Reviewing one's portfolio distribution can help uncover imbalances and growth opportunities.

Review the mechanism for making philanthropic decisions

In many philanthropic families, important elements such as time commitment, accountability and decision making often are not discussed or articulated. Clarity around decision-making mechanisms is critical not only to ensure smooth execution of these decisions but also to enable grantees to engage effectively with philanthropists with minimal conflict or confusion. This process of review should allow a family to recognise any existing impediments in effective decision making and consequently give shape to a formal structure or at the very least a mutually agreed-upon process of decision making.

Tips and tools to help you gauge the effectiveness of your giving

- Engage philanthropy advisers to conduct a portfolio review.
- Conduct a financial planning session with a private wealth manager.
- Enlist monitoring and evaluation specialists to evaluate the performance of portfolio organisations.

Case study Donald Lobo

Moving from Mumbai to the US in the early 1990s to pursue a post-graduate degree in computer science, Donald Lobo subsequently joined Yahoo's founding team as the "Technical Yahoo." As he began to accumulate wealth early in his life, he also began thinking about giving it away. His philanthropic journey started 15 years ago when he founded the Chintu Gudiya Foundation. Understanding pressing and neglected issues on the ground and taking big bets on organisations with the most effective solutions are integral parts of Donald's philanthropy. He does this by reading articles in academic journals and newspapers, having in-depth conversations with social entrepreneurs and speaking with beneficiaries during three weeks of volunteering every summer with his wife and children. The exposure and exploration helped him test, learn and improve his approach to philanthropy. Today, besides contributing funds, Donald uses his skills and helps organisations strengthen their programmes by using low-cost, open-source technology solutions to collect and analyse data.

In addition to hands-on engagement with philanthropy, a review of his portfolio helped Donald refine his philanthropic strategy. Specifically, it helped him recognise trends and insights into the performance of his grantee organisations, the sector-wide mix of his portfolio, the number of beneficiaries reached and how his support has helped build the capacity of these organisations. Engaging a philanthropy adviser to conduct this portfolio review enhanced its rigour, professionalism and objectivity.

A balance of what he refers to as "Wall Street–type" reports and qualitative voices from the ground helped Donald connect the mind with the heart in his philanthropy. The writings of leaders such as Suparna Gupta of Aangan Trust and numerous conversations with Pratima Joshi of Shelter Associates opened a window into the complex reality of implementing development programmes and the innovative, sometimes frugal ways they overcome grassroots challenges.

Ultimately, the combination of a portfolio review and on-the-ground insights has been a positive reinforcement for Donald, allowing him to assess his years of philanthropy, understand the impact of his giving, expand his sectors of interest, evaluate the right balance between the heart and the mind and eventually pave the path for future giving.

2. Define your vision for change

A better understanding of the effect of their current giving sets the stage for philanthropists to shift their focus and start looking ahead. It is important to clearly articulate what change they wish to see through their giving. Most philanthropists may already have a broad idea of where they want to direct their giving, but it is important to revisit and refine the focus area to ensure that the vision for change is aligned with their values and the needs on the ground. It is only with such alignment that the philanthropist's giving will be sustained over a long period and create maximum impact for the end beneficiary. Here are the avenues that philanthropists have used to define their vision for change.

Revisit the motivations and values that guide your giving

Philanthropists who have already begun their journey have specific motivations and values that have determined their propensity to give and guided the direction of their giving thus far. These could range from personal beliefs and experiences, individual and family values as well as cultural traditions to external factors such as corporate goals and government priorities. Donors tend to make the most sustained and successful contributions when their philanthropic vision and the issues they focus on connect directly to their motivations and convictions. Thus in order to ensure that their contribution consistently and meaningfully bolster progress towards their desired end result, it is imperative to clearly define that philanthropic vision.

A philanthropist's "vision" is an inspirational, long-term view of the kind of world he or she would like to see. It serves as the foundation for adding a more strategic element to giving. At this stage, givers may also consider whether their vision aligns with the broader development goals of the country committed under the United Nations' 2030 Agenda for Sustainable Development. The agenda includes a set of 17 sustainable development goals (SDGs) to end poverty, fight inequality and injustice and tackle climate change by 2030. Contributing to building the country's momentum towards achieving these goals and furthering national aspirations could be another motivating factor for some philanthropists.

Be audacious

Most Indian philanthropists are naturally inclined to give back to society, and they believe in uplifting those who are less privileged. This inclination stems from long-standing ideals and cultural values, including the Gandhian principle of trusteeship and a belief that we are simply custodians of our accumulated or inherited wealth. These philanthropists, therefore, take their responsibility to use their capital in a meaningful way very seriously and have large-scale ambitions of how they can influence change to benefit society. Such "think big" philanthropy goes beyond treating the symptoms of social issues and instead tackles their roots and causes. Givers are encouraged to be audacious and think along these lines when defining their vision. "Audacious" in this context entails creating sustainable impact by effecting systemic change, which yields the most powerful and enduring social returns on investments.

Being audacious begins with an appreciation of all the different aspects and players in the sector or issue at hand. With the big picture in mind, givers can set an audacious goal for their philanthropy and ensure that it contributes to sector-wide efforts targeting the crux of the issue. The audacity of the vision could stem from multiple factors, including the scale of interventions supported; the size and duration of funds committed; or an ambitious longterm outcome, such as policy-level change.

Some donors at this stage may tend to feel overwhelmed by the sector and experience an initial paralysis due to concerns about whether a single philanthropist can effect systemic change. However, givers can always bring in additional partners to deal with aspects of the problem that they may not have the resources to tackle alone. It is important to keep this in mind and not let limited resources become the primary factor constraining the pursuit of an audacious vision.

Narrow your focus

It is important for philanthropists to strike a careful balance between being audacious in what they hope to achieve and having a focused, actionable vision. Tackling the problems in the education space as a whole, for instance, can be considered too Herculean an undertaking for a single donor. To bring about meaningful and lasting social change, philanthropists may narrow their area of focus to a particular aspect of the larger sector.

Givers can narrow their focus area based on several factors:

- **Cause.** Selecting a facet of the larger problem to concentrate on, such as quality of education or mental health
- **Demography.** Focusing on a particular vulnerable population, such as women or religious minorities
- **Geography.** Tackling the challenges faced by a particular community or state
- **Institutions.** Focusing on a certain type of organisation to support, such as a think tank or museum
- **Leadership.** Supporting organisations with strong, inspiring leaders who have the capability to use the philanthropic support to elevate and scale their work.

It is important to note that the focus need not be limited to a single area; it could also be a combination of complementary yet distinct issues. In practice, this means a philanthropist who has chosen to focus on primary school education might go one step further to define the vision as solving the issue of "quality education in urban primary schools in Mumbai"—and, in doing so, create a vision that is both audacious and focused.

Define what success looks like

Whilst the vision for change lays out the desired result, it is important to have a clear-eyed view of the milestones—the smaller goals that indicate progress. This entails listing the tangible outcomes philanthropists want their contributions to create and defining what constitutes successful giving for them. For instance, the specific outcomes for a philanthropist who focuses on primary school education could be higher rates of attendance; improved literacy rates; or, ultimately, more college admissions. Whilst all three outcomes are complementary, they will each occur at different stages and require unique approaches to be achieved. It is therefore critical to plan for each stage and decide when to concentrate efforts on each of the specific outcomes.

To narrow their area of focus and define appropriate metrics of success, it is crucial that philanthropists gain insight into the realities on the ground related to the sector in which they are giving or looking to give to. One of the most important learning experiences for philanthropists trying to define success is conducting field visits and meeting communities. This immersive experience enables philanthropists to create a bottom-up vision—one that addresses the reality of the situation and results in an accurate understanding of what success will look like.

Articulate a well-defined vision statement

The final step in defining a vision for change is to lay out a concise and clear vision statement that can then guide the future giving strategy. The effort of trying to convey a vision in a few words pushes philanthropists to consider all the relevant underlying factors that define their giving and, in turn, frame a succinct vision statement.

There are several benefits to a clearly articulated vision statement, the first of which is the sense of purpose it fosters and constant source of inspiration it provides. If there is more than one decision maker (e.g., other family members, executive members of the trust/foundation), it allows everyone to be in agreement on the direction of the philanthropy and act in accordance with it. The vision statement is thus the foundation for outcome-oriented philanthropy, translating aspirations into concrete outcomes and spelling out the unique definition of success for each philanthropist.14 Philanthropists may consider conducting a formal exercise to outline a vision statement for their giving in consultation with a philanthropy adviser. They may also attend donor education training such as The Philanthropy Workshop or Dasra Philanthropy programme to help them with the same.

Tips and tools to help you define your vision for change

- Conduct visioning exercises with the help of philanthropy advisers.
- Engage with sector experts and nonprofit leaders to better understand needs on the ground.
- Study research reports and relevant articles to assess areas of need.
- Visit communities to better understand ground realities.

Case study | Leena Dandekar

A dynamic, successful entrepreneur with more than 25 years of experience working with the Camlin Group across multiple businesses, Leena Dandekar recently set out to embark on a new journey—that of philanthropy. What began as a search for volunteering opportunities at local NPOs led her to realise that she had the time and potential to contribute in a much larger, more focused manner. She recognised that a bold and clear vision was a prerequisite for bringing alignment within her family, creating a structured philanthropic plan and eventually bringing about meaningful change.

Over the next few months, Leena spoke to seasoned Indian philanthropists and engaged players like Dasra and EdelGive to better understand the philanthropy landscape in India and effective methods for building a strong vision for one's giving. She and her children also visited several nonprofit programme sites to witness first-hand challenges and recognise specific issues that especially resonated with them.

These experiences have culminated in Leena and her children defining a strong vision for their philanthropy, which entails strengthening rural economies whilst restoring the environment. Today, she understands that the process of arriving at a vision requires a fine balance between the head and heart. Having come so far in just 10 months, both Leena and her children acknowledge that they still have a lot to learn. They are looking forward to their first steps in this exciting journey to realise their philanthropic vision.

Determine your pathway to change

With a clearly defined vision for change, it is time to understand how to go about creating this change. Carefully thinking through desired goals and the most appropriate pathways to accomplish them is vital to creating a strategy with the potential to generate impact at scale. Here are some key approaches and actions philanthropists must consider as they move through this phase.

Understand the problem and existing solutions to address it

Before attempting to address a problem, it is important that philanthropists develop a sound understanding of it. This may involve identifying relevant stakeholders such as the government, businesses, philanthropists, nonprofits and the communities that influence the problem; exploring critical gaps and barriers to progress; and outlining the evolving political, economic, physical and cultural environment affecting the problem.

With this understanding, philanthropists may look to identify solutions currently being implemented to address the issue, including building awareness, creating new infrastructure or training frontline workers. Most often, there is no single pathway to solving a given problem. Given the complexity and scale of development problems in India, it is also often indirect and intangible interventions that have the potential to create the deepest and most systemic change. For example, within secondary education, the need today is not to build schools but rather to improve the quality of education in existing schools. That requires philanthropists to support strategies such as policy advocacy and teacher training. Providing such support requires patience along with an understanding that it may not yield visible or measurable impact in the philanthropist's lifetime.

Clearly articulate a theory of change

Ultimately, one must understand the problem before one can identify solutions. This can be articulated with a theory of change—a framework that depicts the path from inputs to outputs to short- or mid-term results to longterm impact. Theories of change also depict the assumptions that underlie a giver's reasoning and the evidence backing these assumptions. A good theory of change can reveal:

- Whether a philanthropist's activities make sense, given his or her goals;

- Whether there are approaches the philanthropist is currently taking that are not directly contributing to achieving the desired goals;
- Whether additional inputs are necessary to achieve the desired goals; and
- Which activities and outcomes the philanthropist can and cannot achieve alone.

Articulating an appropriate and effective theory of change means considering several factors, including research, needs of the community, one's own philanthropic values and available resources.

Carefully select nonprofit grantees based on a set of well-thought-out criteria

With a sound understanding of the most effective solutions to the problem at hand, philanthropists can now determine if they need to establish a new organisation to tackle the problem. It is ideal if philanthropists support existing efforts or partner with other stakeholders through collaborative vehicles such as giving circles, unless forming a new organisation fills a critical gap that cannot be bridged otherwise. Applying the expertise and experiences of existing organisations is a smarter and quicker method of bringing about meaningful change than investing additional time and resources to create a new entity. However, as India is home to millions of NPOs, selecting the right grantee partners can be overwhelming. In these cases, it is useful to consider the following parameters when evaluating organisations and assessing the fit with one's philanthropic plan:

- Presence of appropriate registrations and legal compliance;
- Strength of the organisation's programmes and demonstrated effectiveness;
- Strength of institutional systems and processes;
- Capability and vision of the organisation's leadership;
- Alignment of the organisation's work to one's own vision and values; and
- Growth stage and capacity of the organisation to absorb the grant amount.

Determine your mode of play

Besides the selection of specific interventions to support, there are other considerations that play a role in determining the eventual effectiveness of one's philanthropy. Specifically, as philanthropists look to become more strategic in their giving, they must consciously consider the following:

- **The structure of the giving vehicle.** Giving through a family foundation or a company's corporate social responsibility (CSR) fund, giving directly to organisations or giving through some combination of these vehicles all have differing implications for philanthropists and must be carefully considered as they formalize their giving.
- **The flexibility and purpose of the grant.** The value of supporting an organisation's management capacity and capability is often underestimated in philanthropy. Philanthropists may consider funding not just specific programmes but also organisations' institutional building needs to enable them to carry out their work effectively.
- **The time period of engagement with grantees.** Given the complexity, seriousness and scale of India's development challenges, sustained efforts over a long period of time are necessary to create true change. What's more, long-term engagement with grantees creates the space and infrastructure for them to learn, adjust and—at times—fail, thus enabling them to bring about faster and deeper change.
- **The level of depth and breadth across one's portfolio.** Philanthropists must consider the degree to which their philanthropic investments are spread across multiple organisations or focused on a smaller set of organisations. In general, when high-potential nonprofits are adequately supported, they have the ability to create sustainable impact for a large number of beneficiaries. Placing big bets on a few organisations and their leadership has been a powerful approach to maximising philanthropic effectiveness.

Tips and tools to help you define pathways to change:

- Engage with sector experts and nonprofit leaders to understand the problem and create effective solutions.
- Study research reports and relevant articles to identify evidence-based practices.
- Engage with an intermediary organisation to conduct due diligence on organisations.
- Visit programme sites to evaluate the work of potential nonprofit grantees.
- Engage with philanthropy advisers and participate in donor education training to reflect on the chosen approach.

Case study | Amira Shah Chhabra

The daughter of first-generation entrepreneurs who founded Signet Chemical Corporation, one of India's leading pharmaceutical raw materials distribution companies, Amira Shah Chhabra spends a significant portion of her time guiding and shaping her family's philanthropic efforts through the Harish and Bina Shah Foundation. It was her research for a public policy think tank that ignited her interest in the social sector and propelled her to spend three years at Dasra, working to build the capacity of high-potential nonprofits to scale their impact. Equipped with the knowledge and skills from these experiences, Amira decided to join Signet and develop the business skills she believed necessary to effectively navigate the development world.

Today Amira, along with her parents, sister and husband, is deeply involved in growing the foundation's team and building a robust strategy for generating impact across areas such as women's empowerment, governance, education, health, anti-sex trafficking and menstrual hygiene. The family's involvement in several giving circles served as an important mode of engagement with nonprofits that helped them understand the value and meaning of adopting a strategic approach to scaling impact.

Long-term support and a healthy balance of programmatic and institutional funding based on the needs of the organisation guide the strategy of the Harish and Bina Shah Foundation today. Additionally, based on a nuanced understanding of what it takes to empower women and girls, the foundation places a significant emphasis on nonprofits' willingness to engage men and boys in their programmes.

As a driving force of the foundation, Amira has ensured that philanthropy forms a core part of the work at Signet. Having selected top talent from the company to spend time on the foundation's activities, she ensures that site visits are a fundamental component of the experience. She believes that conducting site visits is key to developing independent thinking, understanding the realities and needs on the ground and ultimately adopting a solution that is closely aligned with them. Her foundation team shares this view and sees these visits as transformative experiences that changed their approach to the work.

Over the next year, the foundation plans to deepen its engagements with grantees and continue to strengthen the strategic principles that guide its approach to creating greater and faster impact.

Case study | Bharat Sheth

Great Eastern Shipping (GE), led by Bharat Sheth, embraced CSR in the wake of the amended Companies Act of 2013. Bharat did not know that what began as a mandate would soon get the top slots in his schedule and become an emotionally rewarding journey. What he did know, however, was that giving back is important and needs to be done well. Thus, by early 2015, GE had a functioning CSR Foundation (GECSRF).

GECSRF constituted an internal CSR committee, led by Bharat and composed of other senior GE leaders, to expedite decision making around grants. Whilst Bharat meets with nonprofit leaders and conducts exploratory meetings with the CSR team, this committee also meets every month to provide an interface with other senior leaders, share experiences from the ground, address questions and allow for quick and effective decision making. Above all, these meetings encourage alignment between GE's leadership and CSR arm, allowing greater agency to the latter.

Today, GECSRF aligns its work with the Sustainable Development Goals, adopting a focus on improving education, healthcare and livelihood across geographies that receive limited funding from corporations. Additionally, long-term, programmatic and institution-building support to early-stage organisations is key to guiding the foundation's strategy. Given these approaches, Bharat's personal investment and the rigour with which the foundation's CSR activities are carried out, it is no surprise that over the last two years, GECSRF has touched more than 40,000 lives in and around Maharashtra and continues to scale and further strengthen its work.

4. Amplify the impact of giving

Whilst contributing funds is no doubt a critical aspect of philanthropy, it is certainly not the only one. Increasing the quantum of funds will only go so far in enhancing impact. Most givers are restricted in the amount of capital they are able to give. A valuable step for philanthropists looking to heighten the effectiveness of their giving is to move beyond providing funds to applying their skills, networks and time to benefit nonprofits. Involving one's family in the philanthropy journey can also be a rewarding experience and play an important role in sustaining one's giving over time. Here are some steps givers can take.

Give time in a way that aligns with one's skills

More effective givers understand that funds alone are limited in the change they can bring about. Such philanthropists look beyond cheque writing to contribute other forms of capital they may have in a manner that achieves synergy with the skills and networks they have to offer.

Resourceful nonprofits are always looking for relevant experience and skills to minimise their overhead costs. Moreover, nonprofits aren't always able to fully and effectively use money that comes their way because they lack a sustainable plan that takes into account strategy, information technology (IT), infrastructure, organizational structure and research and development, among other things. Philanthropists who provide guidance in these areas make an invaluable contribution. For example, several philanthropists with strong business backgrounds sit on the boards of nonprofits and provide strategic direction and advice on organisational development. Philanthropists can provide other forms of assistance and guidance, from supporting talent recruitment to using their technology skills to build and test effective systems.

Philanthropists' relationship capital—their network of employees, board members, clients and the people they know—is another valuable alternative or supplement to monetary giving. It facilitates nonprofits' access to a pool of new, prospective donors and, more importantly, allows them to connect with experts they would otherwise have had to hire at potentially high costs. Highly skilled resources with extensive expertise in technical fields like IT, law and finance are hard to come by in the development sector. Connecting nonprofits to such expertise at low or no cost and engaging with them more deeply has the potential to multiply the philanthropic impact.

Share what is learned and encourage greater giving

Peer interactions provide philanthropists with an opportunity to share their experiences and influence greater and smarter participation in philanthropy. Many Indian donors said they have peers who are their philanthropic role models and who inspired them to begin giving, increase the quantum of their giving and be more strategic whilst doing so.

Beyond inspiring others to give, philanthropists should share with their peer philanthropists what they learned from successes, failures, challenges and effective approaches. This can be a powerful way to replicate effective practices and avoid duplication of efforts or repetitive mistakes. In fact, according to a recent study commissioned by the William and Flora Hewlett Foundation, 92 percent of funders cited their peers and colleagues as their primary source of knowledge on philanthropy.

Platforms to share and learn may take the form of intimate gatherings with one's own networks but can go beyond that to include, for example, philanthropy events, social media, newspaper and magazine articles or a philanthropist's own website. Philanthropists may also look for platforms that promote expertise from within the group. For instance, if topics such as grantee management, monitoring and evaluation or tax and regulatory compliance are of interest, philanthropists can find platforms that are curated to match their learning requirements.

Collaborate with other stakeholders

No one philanthropist alone has the resources and influence to solve India's complex and intractable development issues. Complexity means that solutions cannot be static and single-pronged approaches; they need to be dynamic and concerted efforts led by multiple stakeholders. Philanthropists can thus collaborate with other stakeholders to make significant change within the sector. Other stakeholders can include the government and state institutions, civil society, the private sector, academic institutions and other funders.

Collaboration is a complex process and requires investing considerable thought and effort into building healthy, trustful relationships among the key players. However, the advantages are numerous: Philanthropists benefit from collaboration by accessing greater resources, building knowledge and learning best practices, and achieving a wide variety of goals whilst effectively managing their own time and resources. The change that comes from a collaborative, all-round approach is also deeper and often more scalable than results from separate, siloed initiatives.

The government is one of the most significant stakeholders with which philanthropists can collaborate. Regardless of the cause, government funding and policy are bound to affect the results and are critical to creating powerful and systemic social change. Collaborating with the government can introduce an element of unprecedented scale for nonprofits. Advocating with the government and legislators is also the only way to ensure necessary changes in the law to achieve lasting change.

Partnering with other funders is another important way to amplify the effectiveness of one's philanthropy. The benefits of collaborating with other donors include learning opportunities, dilution of risk and increased impact through larger or longer-term grants. The most tangible example of collaborative giving is a giving circle, which allows for larger contributions, building a community of givers and creating new leaders in philanthropy. Engaging with other givers can become a catalyst for more thoughtful giving, in turn ensuring that the impact on the end beneficiary is maximised.

Tips and tools to help amplify the impact of giving:

- Host gatherings to expand the community of givers.
- Join philanthropy peer networks.
- Share information about philanthropy through events or media platforms.
- Engage with nonprofit leaders to understand nonmonetary needs of the organisation.

Case study | Aparna Piramal Raje

Aparna Piramal Raje, columnist and writer on business, design, urbanisation and workplaces, focuses her philanthropy on organisations with strong leadership and the potential to scale their work, regardless of the sector they serve. However, from the very beginning of her giving journey, she viewed her role as going beyond cheque writing to fostering a community of givers in India and influencing greater and smarter participation in philanthropy.

She believes that a strong network of philanthropists not only serves as a platform for cross-learning but is also a way of sharing and spreading the joy of giving. This led her to mobilise seven other families from her apartment complex in Mumbai to give collaboratively to a nonprofit named ARMMAN in support of their innovative technological solution to improve maternal and child health in the city's urban slums. This action was also guided by her belief that collaborating with other philanthropists and jointly committing funding has the potential to create far greater and more meaningful change than any one individual is capable of creating through a single contribution.

Beyond spearheading a giving circle with her neighbours, Aparna has hosted gatherings at her home, shared documented impact studies and brought potential funders on site visits to stir interest in and eventually commit funding to ARMMAN, Magic Bus and other nonprofits she supports. Applying her background in journalism, she also regularly publishes articles related to the Indian development sector as a way to increase awareness around social issues and encourage greater participation in philanthropy.

Today, the idea of amplifying effectiveness beyond monetary contributions forms the foundational principle guiding Aparna's philanthropy. Over time, she plans to involve her children in her journey, increase the amount of capital and time she contributes to philanthropic activities and ultimately serve as an active proponent of strengthening the philanthropy movement in India.

Case study | Dhruv Khaitan

A serial entrepreneur, Dhruv Khaitan has helped conceptualise, create and scale high-technology ventures in India and has strategically mentored these companies through their inception, growth and eventual divestment. Over the last year, he began to consider how his expertise can help create catalytic growth for organisations in the nonprofit sector. Whilst he had already been funding midsized organisations to help them scale, he now believes that he can multiply the effect of every rupee he contributes by directly engaging with nonprofits and providing them with strategic direction and guidance.

With this goal in mind, Dhruv is building a Strategic Support Group (SSG), which brings together professionals, experts, business people and donors who are interested in giving their time to build the capacities of the nonprofits they support. These individuals, including Dhruv himself, use the skills they developed in their professional practices to bring new capabilities to organisations in areas such as strategy, technology, marketing, financial planning, process excellence, scaling, unit economics, innovation and government relations.

The SSG also facilitates synergistic partnerships between nonprofits that have complementary strengths. The idea behind bringing partners together is to provide access to and encourage them to share best practices, skills, knowledge and experiences. Nonprofits working together can also fulfil their strategic objectives of scaling and expanding to new geographies rather than attempting to reinvent the wheel alone.

Providing strategic support along with capital amplifies the impact of Dhruv's philanthropy, enabling nonprofits to scale efficiently and effectively and achieve better and faster outcomes. Over the next few years, he aims to build a sector-agnostic portfolio of 10 to 15 organisations that the SSG can support in a meaningful way.

Conclusion

Engaging in philanthropy itself is an honourable act, regardless of the quantum, nature and approach of the giving. Yet, given the magnitude and urgency of India's development challenges, the need for philanthropists to adopt a strategic approach is now more pronounced than ever before

Adopting not just a "today forward" but also a "future back" mindset can be achieved by defining a clear philanthropic vision. The steps may involve revisiting the motivations that guide giving and articulating an audacious yet focused vision statement. Similarly, evolving beyond contributing funds to become a trusted collaborator can be done by utilising relevant skills, sharing findings and involving other stakeholders.

Chapter - 5

Conclusion and Findings

To sum up, according to India Philanthropy report 2019 by Bain & company, India has maintained a strong philanthropic momentum with the social sector funding growing steadily at 11 percent in the last 5 years, between 2014 and 2018. Private funding grew at a rate of 15 percent per year in India during the same period while public funding increased at a pace of about 10 percent per year. Funding by individual philanthropists grew the most- by 21 percent between 2014 and 2018.

However, India's social sector requires a significant funding ramp up if it is to achieve the 2030 UN Sustainable Development Goals (SDGs). The SDGs 2030 are global goals, locally owned by 193 countries across the world, including India. Even if India sustains its current funding growth rate and channels all philanthropic capital into these SDGs it will face an annual shortfall of Rs 4.2 lakh crore ($60 billion) if it is to achieve even 5 of the 17 SDGs by 2030.

While the government continues to be the largest contributor to social sector funding in India, hovering at about 6 percent of GDP, private philanthropy is expanding and has outpaced public funding growth. Despite a slowdown in foreign funding in recent years, private funding grew at a rate of 15 percent per year between FY2014 and FY2018, while public funding increased at a pace of about 10 percent per year.

Foreign contributions declined by about 40 percent during the period under review amid a government crackdown on non-governmental organisations (NGOs) for violation of the Foreign Contribution Regulation Act (FCRA) of 2010. According to data from the Ministry of Home Affairs, more than 13,000 NGO licences have been cancelled under the FCRA in the past three years, including approximately 4,800 in 2017 alone. NGOs need to comply with government regulations, including timely filing of annual returns and validation of bank accounts receiving foreign funds, to allow for a larger influx of foreign funds and thereby increase the social sector's wallet size.

Corporate Social Responsibility (CSR) budget outlays of the domestic corporations and contributions of corporate charitable trusts, combined, have grown at a rate of 12 percent between financial year 2014 and 2018, and they contributed approximately Rs 13,000 crore to social sector funding in financial year 2018.

Philanthropic funding from individuals remained the brightest spot growing at 21 percent per year in the past five years. Tthese individuals currently contribute about 60 percent of the total private funding, estimated at Rs 43,000 crore. A significant portion of this comes from a few established figures who continue to lead individual giving, as they have in the past.

"With a growing economy and rising wealth, the role of domestic private philanthropy becomes increasingly important, regardless of how foreign contributions evolve. Both domestic corporations and Indian ultra high net worth individuals need to enhance the level and nature of their giving."

In the budget speech of 2019, Finance Minister has proposed to initiate steps towards creating an electronic fund raising platform — a social stock exchange — under the regulatory ambit of Securities and Exchange Board of India for listing social enterprises and voluntary organisations working for the realisation of a social welfare objective so that they can raise capital as equity, debt or as units like a mutual fund". This will provide further boost to the philanthropic ecosystem.

Under this mechanism, social welfare and volunteer organisations would be listed on a platform operating under the Securities and Exchange Board of India (SEBI), similar to how companies on stock exchanges like the Bombay Stock Exchange are listed. This would allow infusion of capital into these organisations from investors.

Similar social stock exchange models already exist in some countries. For instance, Canada has Social Venture Connexion (SVX), which connects investors with impact funds and ventures. Similarly, South Africa has the South African Social Investment Exchange (SASIX), which lists organisations that are achieving a "measurable social impact" and allows investment in their projects. Other countries with social stock exchanges include the UK and Singapore.

It would help social enterprises/ NGOs to raise funds through equity, debt or as units like a mutual fund to meet social welfare objectives. This step would clearly stimulate governance in the social sector."

"It will serve as a platform for fund mobilisation for ventures which may have an overriding social purpose, which is sustainable and reflective of the changing social attitudes towards impact investing," said Emkay Wealth Management head of research Joseph Thomas. Social stock exchanges promote socially valuable objectives and a reasonable financial return.

Case Studies

Major corporate philanthropists include Tata Trust, Reliance Foundation, Shiv Nadar Foundation, Azim Premji Foundation, ITC Limited, Piramal Foundation, Birla Foundation, Vedanta Foundation etc. However it may be mentioned that the list is not complete and only indicative. An attempt has been made below to discuss their areas of operation, specific contribution in the field of philanthropy, their unique contribution to select sectors of the economy, their impact on the community etc. The write up is based on available printed literature and readily available information network. The material has been vetted / reviewed by respective organisation.

Tata Trust

Tata Trusts are amongst India's oldest, non-sectarian philanthropic organisations. The Trusts own two-third of the stock holding of Tata Sons, the apex company of the Tata group of companies. The wealth that accrues from this asset supports an assortment of causes, institutions and individuals in a wide variety of areas. In this manner, the profits that the Tata companies earn go back many times over to the communities they operate in. These funds have been deployed towards a whole range of community development programmes across the country, for over 100 years now.

Since its inception, Tata Trusts have played a pioneering role in transforming traditional ideas of charity and introducing the concept of philanthropy to make a real difference to communities. Through grant-making, direct implementation and co-partnership strategies, the Trusts support and drive innovation in the areas of healthcare and nutrition; water and sanitation; energy; education; rural livelihoods; natural resource management; urban poverty alleviation; enhancing civil society and governance; media, arts, crafts and culture; and diversified employment. The Trusts engage with competent individuals and government bodies, international agencies and like-minded private sector organisations to nurture a self-sustaining eco-system that collectively works across all these areas.

Tata Trusts continue to be guided by the principles of its Founder, Jamsetji Tata. With the Founder's vision of proactive philanthropy and his approach to 'giving', the Trusts catalyse societal development while ensuring that initiatives and interventions have a contemporary relevance to the nation. In addition to promoting and facilitating initiatives in elementary education, Tata Trusts also award fellowships and merit scholarships to students pursuing higher studies. It grooms social scientists, cancer specialists, nuclear scientists and distinguished institutional administrators, who in turn have striven to make the country a power to reckon with in various fields, including science and technology. The Trusts also support causes and initiatives that provide disaster relief and aids in rescue work in case of calamities. The Trusts not only assist by providing grants and helping to mobilise funds, they also offer on-ground support directly as well as in partnership with other stakeholders.

In order to enhance impact and ensure that interventions are sustainable, the Trusts have adopted a cluster-based approach, supporting multiple interlinked activities in identified clusters of contiguous villages across select geographies across India. Coupled with this, is the Trusts' strict adherence to ensuring that robust financial systems are put in place with all partner organisations. Today, spread over 17 states and 170 districts across the country, programmes supported by the Trusts reach out to millions of households through an efficient network of 450 plus partner organisations. Additionally, the Trusts' projects and initiatives, especially in the area of educational attainment, significantly contribute to building intellectual capital in the country.

Tata Sons is the principal investment holding company and promoter of Tata companies. Sixty-six percent of the equity share capital of Tata Sons is held by philanthropic trusts, which support education, health, livelihood generation and art and culture. The revenue of Tata companies, taken together, is ~$100 billion. These companies collectively employ over 695,000 people.

Each Tata company or enterprise operates independently under the guidance and supervision of its own board of directors and shareholders. There are 29 publicly-listed Tata enterprises with a combined market capitalisation (India) of about $144.79 billion (as on March 28, 2018). Tata companies with significant scale include Tata Steel, Tata Motors, Tata Consultancy Services, Tata Power, Tata Chemicals, Tata Global Beverages, Tata Teleservices, Titan, Tata Communications and Indian Hotels.

Many Tata companies have achieved global leadership in their businesses. For instance, Tata Communications is the No1 international wholesale voice provider and Tata Motors is among the top ten commercial vehicle manufacturers in the world. Tata Steel is among the top 10 best steelmakers and TCS is the second-largest IT services company in the world by market cap and profit. Tata Global Beverages is the second-largest tea company in the world and Tata Chemicals is the world's third-largest manufacturer of soda ash. Employing a diverse workforce in their operations, Tata companies have made significant local investments in different geographies.

With its pioneering and entrepreneurial spirit, the Tata group has spawned several industries of national importance in India: steel, hydro-power, hospitality and airlines. The same spirit, coupled with innovativeness, has been displayed by entities such as TCS, India's first software company, and Tata Motors, which made India's first indigenously developed car, the Tata Indica and the smart city car, the Tata Nano. Pursuit of excellence has similarly been manifested in innovations like the SilentTrack technology developed by Tata Steel Europe and the next-generation Terrain Response, including infrared laser scanning to predict terrain and Wade Aid to predict water depth, by Jaguar Land Rover.

The Tata Trusts, majority shareholders of Tata Sons, have endowed institutions of science and technology, medical research, social studies and the performing arts. The trusts also provide aid and assistance to non-government organisations working in the areas of education, healthcare and livelihoods. Tata companies themselves undertake a wide range of social welfare activities, especially at the locations of their operations, as also deploy sustainable business practices.

Going forward, Tata companies are building multinational businesses that seek to differentiate themselves through customer-centricity, innovation, entrepreneurship, trustworthiness and values-driven business operations, while balancing the interests of diverse stakeholders including shareholders, employees and civil society.

Regional spread

North India: The northern region of India includes the states of Punjab, Jammu & Kashmir, Haryana, Himachal Pradesh, Uttar Pradesh and Uttarakhand. The developmental issues that plague the region vary from one end of the spectrum to another. The Central Himalayan states of Uttarakhand and Himachal Pradesh have been witnessing rapid depletion of natural resources due to environmental degradation. Loss of forest cover has led to widespread soil erosion, loss of soil fertility, decreased agricultural production and migration of population.

While in Punjab, Haryana, and Uttar Pradesh, the over use of new technology such as high-yielding seeds chemical fertilisers, pesticides and farm mechanisation as part of the Green Revolution has led to multiple problems related to agriculture.

The Tata Trusts have initiatives operational in the region that are designed to tackle issues specific to each state:

Programmes	*Key interventions*	*States*
Reviving the Green Revolution	Livelihood	Punjab
Eastern Uttar Pradesh Initiative	Livelihood, Education, Media, Arts, Craft and Culture, and Health	Uttar Pradesh
Himmothan Pariyojana	Livelihood, Water and Sanitation, and Education	Himachal Pradesh, Uttarakhand
Tata Water Mission	Water and Sanitation	Uttarakhand

North East India: The north-east region of India is considered one of the biodiversity hotspots in the world. A far-flung frontier region connected to the rest of India by a narrow 22-km corridor in Assam, it is consists of the eight states of Arunachal Pradesh, Assam, Manipur, Meghalaya, Mizoram, Nagaland, Sikkim and Tripura.

The Trusts launched the North East Initiative in 2008 to address developmental issues in the region through the provision of enhanced livelihood opportunities, improved agricultural practices and sustainable use of natural resources. It aims to create an effective channel for the dissemination of knowledge and expertise in the region.

Subsistence agriculture forms the main occupation with about 80 percent of the population engaging in it. While settled cultivation is practiced in the plains, shifting cultivation, locally known as jhum, is the predominant agricultural practice in the hilly regions. Unchecked practice of jhum has put pressure on the fragile ecosystem and led to food scarcity. Rising unemployment, health issues, etc. pose a serious threat to the social and economic stability of the region.

Since 2008, the Tata Trusts have been working for the development of the region through the following programmes:

Programmes	*Key interventions*	*States*
North East Initiative	Enhancing livelihoods through agriculture, horticulture, and piggery. education	Arunachal Pradesh, Mizoram, Nagaland
Centre for Microfinance and Livelihood	Enhancing livelihoods through skill building in agriculture, fisheries, dairy, etc	Tripura, Assam, Manipur, Meghalaya
Tata Water Mission	Drinking water and sanitation	Nagaland
Assam Cancer Care Foundation	Cancer care	Assam

Central India: The central India belt is rich in natural resources, yet the poorest region of the country, and home to many tribal populations. Agricultural practices followed by the tribals, who form 90 percent of the population, are quite primitive and productivity is low. This has resulted in the tribal populations progressively slipping deeper into poverty.

The Tata Trusts interventions in the region to improve the quality of life focus on fighting poverty through water and land resources management and a livelihood-centred approach, besides education and health initiatives. They are spread across the states of Jharkhand, Odisha, Chhattisgarh, West Bengal, Madhya Pradesh, Maharashtra, Gujarat and Rajasthan.

South India: The Southern region of India comprises the states of Andhra Pradesh, Karnataka, Tamil Nadu, Telangana and Kerala. The Tata Trusts interventions in the South are focused in the areas of education, enhancing livelihoods, health, water issues and agricultural productivity.

Programmes	***Key interventions***	***States***
Tata Water Mission	Water and sanitation	Odisha, Jharkhand, Gujarat, Rajasthan
South Odisha Initiative	Health, education, skill building, natural resource management	Odisha
Central India Initiative	Livelihoods	Chhattisgarh, Jharkhand, Odisha, Madhya Pradesh, Maharashtra, Gujarat
Madrasa Initiative	Education	West Bengal
Sukhi Baliraja Initiative	Education, livelihoods, health	Maharashtra
Kharash Vistarotthan Yojana	Education, water and sanitation, natural resource management, health	Gujarat
Sakh Se Vikas	Livelihoods, education, health, nutrition, skill building	Rajasthan

The Trusts support research initiatives that seek solutions to water-related issues through the Tata Water Mission in South India. Building and enhancing livelihoods of small and marginal farmers is the Trusts objective in the initiation of the Reviving the Green Revolution programme in Tamil Nadu, with agricultural and allied interventions tailored to suit local conditions. In Karnataka, Kalike Samruddhi Upakram targets overall human development through health, livelihoods, skill development, and education as the core.

Programmes	***Key interventions***	***States***
Tata Water Mission	Drinking Water and Sanitation	Andhra Pradesh, Karnataka, Telangana
Kalike Samruddhi Upakram	Education, Livelihoods, Health, and Skill Building	Yadgir (Karnataka)
Reviving the Green Revolution	Livelihoods	Tamil Nadu

Healthcare: The health situation in the country today is an evolving canvas. With 1.8 million deaths among children (age <5 years) and 68,000 deaths among mothers every year, and 52 million children who are stunted, India's burden of reproductive health, and child health and nutrition is greater than that in any other country.

While there is development, the pace is slow and falls short of national and MDG targets. Chronic diseases like cardiovascular diseases, mental health disorders, diabetes, cancer and injuries are the leading causes of death and disability in India, and are projected to have a pronounced increase in their contribution to the burden of disease during the next 25 years.

Although the burden of infectious diseases has decreased as a result of overall socioeconomic progress and increasing use of vaccines and antimicrobials in the past 60 years, they still contribute about 30 percent of the disease burden in India. While the control of HIV and leprosy seems to be successful, control of diseases such as tuberculosis and malaria is a concern. Underlying all this is the fact that India has a severe shortage of human resources for health with the available workforce being concentrated in urban areas. The health system has limitations in planning, financing, human resources, infrastructure, supply systems, governance and monitoring.

For decades now, Tata Trusts have been engaged in the field of public health, developing and supporting initiatives to address some of the major issues.

The broad areas of engagement of the Trusts' health portfolio fall into the following domains:

- Women and child health focused primary care and nutrition.
- Non-communicable diseases with a focus on mental health, detection and early intervention for developmental disabilities in children (under the age of 6), and cancer care.
- Human resources for health.

Nutrition initiatives: Addressing the malnutrition challenge in the Indian context is one of the key focus areas for the Trusts. Tata Trusts, under the leadership of Mr Tata, have prioritised malnutrition because of the alarming statistics that we have in the country and the inter-generational consequences the problem has. Malnutrition is believed to be the underlying cause of over 45 percent of under-five mortality. India has a high prevalence of childhood stunting and maternal and childhood anaemia. These can have long-term effects on cognition and overall productivity. There is evidence that malnutrition can result in potential Gross Domestic Product (GDP) losses of 2-3 percent and a more than 10 percent potential reduction in lifetime earnings for each malnourished individual.

Given the multi-factor and complex nature of the issue, Tata Trusts have adopted a multi-pronged approach to be able to address the issue of malnutrition effectively and at scale. Tata Trusts will make strategic investments that will play a gap filling or a catalytic role in the ecosystem and engender better health outcomes. The effort broadly, has been to look for existing and emerging 'platforms' to deliver enhanced nutrition. To address the challenge of stunting, Tata Trusts are taking an intense multi-sectoral approach looking at maternal care, water and sanitation, behavioural change communication and poverty alleviation in an integrated way. To address the challenge of micronutrient deficiencies, Tata Trusts are looking at fortification of staple food vehicles such as flour, salt, oil, and milk.

Some of the key initiatives undertaken by the Trusts are:

- Community based Management of Acute Malnutrition (CMAM) in Nandurbar, Maharashtra - a three arm trial run using existing Government machinery.
- Centralised kitchens for Tribal schools - hygienic, nutritious food reaches 15,000 children everyday through these kitchens.

- Promotion of double fortified salt- ensuring availability and affordability through demand and supply aggregation. In addition, Tata Trusts have created 'The India Nutrition Initiative' with a panel of leading experts, in order to develop and advocate an informed stand on policy relating to nutrition. Tata Trusts are also investing in the development of a rapid survey tool for effective programming and planning of a multi-sectoral approach towards nutrition and a data portal to access nutrition data on a click of a button.

Education

Technology in Education: The Technology in Education initiative focusses on appropriate use of technology to improve teaching and learning processes by working with both teachers and students. This initiative aims to bridge the digital divide between rural and urban areas by providing access to technology in rural and remote areas and creating an open source content.

Integrated approach to Technology in Education: Initiated in 2012, the Integrated Approach to Technology in Education (ITE) is a pedagogical framework to improve teaching and learning processes. It fosters 21st century skills and quality learning through projects in middle school children and adolescents in some of the most underprivileged geographies (91 percent rural). Students, mostly first-time computer users, create learning artifacts like weather charts and comparative charts on jute production or population density to deepen their learning of the subject matter. All the projects assigned are carefully selected by the teachers and matched with the curriculum.

The main objectives of the programme are:

- Bridge the digital divide and foster digital citizenship.
- Increase interest in learning.
- Improve learning and higher order thinking skills.
- Improve teaching and learning processes.
- Build teacher capacities through professional development.

Technology is embedded in the teachers' lesson plans and pedagogy. The teacher designs learning activities and students use technology to construct their own learning. Technology is used as a tool, rather than as an end in itself.

ITE is implemented in eight states, which includes Assam, Gujarat, Jharkhand, Maharashtra, Odisha, Uttarakhand, Uttar Pradesh and West Bengal. It is channelised through NGO partners and associate organisations of Tata Trusts. ITE is also being layered with the education plans directly implemented under the Eastern Uttar Pradesh Initiative and education activities in ashramshalas under the South Odisha Initiative. In 2015, the Trusts formed state and district partnerships with the governments of Assam and West Bengal under ITE, which covers 225 government schools and madrasas in these states. The master teachers' cadre in these schools mentor teachers from approximately 600 schools in their catchment areas in West Bengal and Assam. The capacity building (training and research) of partners, teachers and school administrators is undertaken by the Centre for Education Innovation and Action Research at Tata Institute of Social Sciences. The Centre offers a certificate course for teachers in 'ICT in Education for School Teachers', which has been completed by 100 teachers.

Currently, ITE is practiced in about 275 schools, which includes independent learning centres and madrasas. It reaches out to 22,000 children as on December 2017 and has impacted 26,000 children since inception. Over the years, about 2,500 teachers, which includes community facilitators and teachers training faculty in a cascade model, have been trained in the ITE approach and skills.

Connected Learning Initiative: Secondary education in India has progressed to near universalisation. Curricular and pedagogic reforms are in process to prepare youth to acquire, demonstrate and apply deep conceptual understanding and skills, which will help them avail opportunities in a modern, technology-driven society. However, only 40 percent students perform well at recall level in mathematics and science, and only 20 percent reach higher order problem-solving (according to National Assessment Survey 2012) level. Challenges, especially in underprivileged areas, include teacher shortages and lack of quality education, limited resources in Indian languages, and absence of a culture of active, hands-on learning.

To tackle the challenge, the Connected Learning Initiative (CLIx), a bold and innovative programme, offers a scalable model with global relevance for quality teaching and learning. It harnesses modern technology to improve the academic prospects of high school students in underserved communities of India. CLIx is currently being implemented in the states of Mizoram, Rajasthan, Chhattisgarh and Telangana.

By integrating educational technology in pedagogical design and professional development of teachers, CLIx aims to provide high-quality learning experiences in Hindi, Telugu and English, focusing on authentic, hands-on, conceptual learning and the development of values, skills and competencies.

The programme seeks to impact and enhance the quality of learning and teaching in government high schools. The target groups are students in grades 8 and 9 and teachers of mathematics, science and English.

Khan Academy: The five year collaboration of Tata Trusts with Khan Academy will provide free high quality educational resources for use in both online and offline modes. Breaking the "One size fits all" policy of traditional classrooms, the personalised learning platform being offered will allow each child to learn at his/her pace and take ownership of their own learning. Building teacher competency in subject areas and allowing for teachers to use dashboards to identify students and areas that need attention, will maximise outcomes. With quality and equity for the entire education system as a goal, this programme hopes to reach learners not just through schools across the country but also through tutoring centres and common service centres.

Tech learning

Children learning lessons through a Skype call: Tata Trusts conceptualised the integrated approach to Technology in Education (ITE) with a view to improve the pedagogical system for schools that cater to underprivileged students. Through the approach, the Trusts aim to bridge the digital divide, enhance learning and improve the dwindling attendance.

Sports: Tata Trusts have a cherished history of making contributions to the development of sport in India. Sir Dorabji Tata was a pioneering spirit, a man deeply appreciative of the power of sport in transforming lives. He was the first President of the Indian Olympic Committee, established in 1927 and an active leader in shaping the Indian Olympic movement. He made personal contributions to fund the participation of India in the Antwerp (1920) and Paris (1924) Olympics.

The Trusts continue to build on its rich heritage, with sports as a means and accelerator for meaningful engagement with young children from marginalised sections of the society. Sports can serve as a catalyst for development, raising aspirations, improving health and strengthening the education and development of children.

The cultural ethos of India suffered significant damage during the centuries of foreign rule, as its people were relegated into situations of disadvantage by imperialist forces. In the aftermath of Independence, vast sections of society, especially in urban areas, took to education as a means to extricate themselves from the various constraints that undermined their existence.

As a result, India suffered from severe imbalances in physical and intellectual development, with the former neglected for the sake of academic progress. Over the past few decades, families have actively discouraged children from the pursuit of sport. However, the growth of cricket and the success of the country's Olympic heroes have turned the focus back to sport.

Several of the country's heroes from the *akharas* of Haryana or rickety gymnasiums in Tripura have emerged from humble backgrounds, underlining the power of sports as a tool for social transformation. Tata Trusts are focused on strengthening this shift in momentum by actively working in underserved parts of the country, reawakening aspirations and fostering a culture of hard work and excellence among children.

Tata Trusts believe that the work of their teams and partners can build and nurture young children by working to create an ecosystem that can assist in their development. The Trusts' effort is to collaborate with partners and government to make the most of the country's facilities in shaping an environment that is conducive for development. The Trusts actively seek to engage with professional trainers with significant experience in sport to offer quality learning opportunities for the children.

With a view to help India rediscover its glory in sports; Tata Trusts are incubating programmes for professionalising grass-root level sports and nurturing talent.

Tata Trust will give Rs.300-cr funding to build and run the proposed Indian Institute of Skills (IIS) will be set up in Mumbai in association with the Tata Trust. It is expected to lay the foundation of this project b mid-September and hope that the institute will be fully operational by next year. The institute, which is expected to be ready in 18 months, will have a capacity to train 10,000 students. The institute will be on the same line as those in Singapore and Germany, providing new age skills, including factory automation, digital manufacturing, cybersecurity, additive manufacturing, data analytics, digital design and smart mechatronics.

The government is working on creating a future-ready workforce that can cope with the changing technology and digital environment. Along with the new-age courses, the institute will also continue to provide traditional skill training courses. The institute aims to draw in major private sector companies across sectors to create replicas and work-like environment for imparting practical training. The Skill India Mission was launched by Prime Minister Narendra Modi in 2015 with a vision to make India the "skill capital" of the world.

The aim was to impart skills training to 400 million people by 2022 through flagship schemes such as Pradhan Mantri Rojgar Prohatsan Yojana, the Deen Dayal Upadhyaya Grameen Kaushalya Yojana, and National Apprenticeship Promotion Scheme. However, barely 30 million people have been imparted skill training so far under the schemes.

Tata Water Mission: India, along with the rest of the world, is facing challenges in providing safe drinking water to all citizens, especially those living in rural areas. On the one hand, there is severe scarcity of drinking water, deteriorating water quality, and depleting groundwater resources, and on the other there are floods and surface water logging, aggravating the crisis further.

Tata Water Mission (TWM) is a programme initiated by Tata Trusts to tackle the water crisis with a multi-pronged approach. The three core areas supported by the programme are:

- Technology innovations
- Improved service delivery through sustainable and integrated development through water conservation and water supply
- Behavioural change communication (BCC) models

TWM targets to give better access of pure water to 6 million people in 7,000 villages across 12 states, within the next 3 years. Tata Trusts are not only using the traditional strengths of community mobilisation and capacity building, but the power of innovative approaches and technological solutions to deliver on a scale never attempted before.

One of the key focus areas of TWM is to find alternate, affordable, low-maintenance technologies to tackle heavy metal contamination in water, in order to provide potable drinking water to the community. Tata Trusts are planning community-based interventions to treat arsenic-contaminated ground water in Assam and West Bengal, and fluoride-laced water in Karnataka, Rajasthan and Madhya Pradesh. Further, Tata Trusts are planning to provide Point of Use (PoU) purification systems to address microbial contamination in drinking water.

Current situation: 3,000+ villages have been covered under the mission, which is active in Gujarat, Uttarakhand, Rajasthan, Karnataka, Telangana, Andhra Pradesh, Odisha, Jharkhand, Nagaland, Maharashtra and Assam.

Tata Water Mission also plays a very pivotal role in the sanitation space. In 2016, the Trusts took on the role of development support partner to the Government of India's Swachh Bharat Mission (SBM), which has the target to develop sanitation facilities for over 500 million Indians, who do not have access to toilets, and continue to defecate in the open. Tata Trusts stepped in to make the SBM more effective and sustainable, by looking at all aspects of sanitation and toilets — supply chain, finance, behavior change, toilet design and usage.

Rural upliftment

Central India Initiative: The Central India Initiative is one of the flagship initiatives of Tata Trusts, focusing its work in the central Indian tribal belts of the country. It strives to bring households irreversibly out of poverty with increased life choices. To propel its mission, Collectives for Integrated Livelihood Initiatives (CInI), the nodal agency of the Trusts, is working on the promotion and strengthening of institutions that are the base for the core work being undertaken. Various livelihood prototypes in Agriculture, Livestock and Non-Timber Forest Produce have been promoted along with Water Resource Development. The principles of innovation and being demand-led, instead of a stereotypical approach, are at the core of initiatives.

CInI, in its mission 2020, envisages working with 300,000 households concentrated in 45 blocks across the four states of Jharkhand, Odisha,

Maharashtra and Gujarat. This is the beginning of an ambitious proposal to bring about large-scale irreversible change in the Central Indian Tribal belt. Over 10 years, CInI hopes to reach 1 million households and develop 100 blocks as drivers of regional growth.

Kharash Vistarotthan Yojana: Gujarat has been grappling with an environmental problem for over 30 years. Indiscriminate ground water extraction has led to the ingress of sea water into arable land, in many places reaching 10-15km inland. With underground water aquifers affected, it has left over 1,500 villages with water unfit for consumption. The increased salinity has affected crops, decreased productivity and soil fertility, and resulted in migration and social unrest in many villages.

Sir Ratan Tata Trust & Navajbai Ratan Tata Trust, with its partner organisations, launched the Kharash Vistarotthan Yojana (KVY) in 2002 to mitigate the problem. An umbrella organisation, the Coastal Salinity Prevention Cell (CSPC), was also set up to address the issue in a comprehensive manner.

The focus has been on integrated water resources development and judicious management of the available resources through ground water recharging, aquifer mapping, water use efficiency, and improving water quality through technology interventions.

Farmers were encouraged to switch over to crops that consume less water, and provided technical and advisory services on improved farming practices, vegetable cultivation and horticulture, and diversifying to non-farm-based economic activities.

KVY is also working in the area of education through a project that is being implemented in Devbhoomi Dwarka district, through a joint arrangement between CSPC and Tata Chemicals Society for Rural Development.

Himmothan Pariyojana: The Central Himalayan regions of Uttarakhand have seen severe environmental degradation over the last century. Almost two-thirds of the state is designated as forest area; in reality, it is limited to about 46 percent . The loss of forest cover has resulted in soil erosion and reduced agricultural productivity. Barely 15 percent of the geographical area is cultivated and landholdings on an average are less than one hectare. Consequently, people find it increasingly difficult to gather basic resources such as food, fuel, fodder and water. The problem is compounded by the heavy out-migration of males in search of employment, leaving the burden of labour on women.

The Himmothan Pariyojana, initiated by Trusts in 2001, attempts to target the root causes of under development in the Central Himalayan region of Uttarakhand, mostly related to developing sustainable community institutions working for ecologically and environmentally sustainable livelihoods, in a natural resource-rich state. A MoU with the state government of Uttarakhand was jointly signed in May 2004 for a period of ten years, under the umbrella of which the initiative substantially expanded its rural development programmes in collaboration with partner non-government organisations, community institutions and state bodies. In March 2014, the MoU was extended by a further period of 10 years.

Currently, Himmothan focuses on the following three initiatives: (a) Central Himalayan Livestock Initiative (b) Central Himalayan Microfinance Initiative, and (c) Central Himalayan Education Initiative. The Himmotthan Society (Himmothan) co-ordinates / implements the Himmothan programme.

Reviving the Green Revolution: Punjab was the leading state in North India to harness the benefits of the Green Revolution. But with time technologies such as high-yielding seeds, chemical fertilisers, pesticides and farm mechanisation lead to exploitation of natural resources — particularly ground water, deterioration in soil fertility, and environmental pollution. The Sir Ratan Tata Trust and Navajbai Ratan Tata Trust launched the Reviving the Green Revolution (RGR) programme in Punjab in 2002 to reverse these ill effects. The programme encourages agricultural diversification by shifting to economically viable water saving crops. It focuses on improving soil health, arresting environmental degradation through judicious use of agrochemicals, reducing cost of cultivation and making agriculture sustainable and economically viable. The Trusts partnered with numerous departments at the Punjab Agricultural University (PAU), and established a Reviving the Green Revolution Cell in 2008 housed at PAU, Ludhiana. The initiative covers 1,300 villages in 40 blocks of 9 districts in Punjab.

A regional centre of the RGR Cell was set up in Coimbatore in 2010 at the Tamil Nadu Agricultural University (TNAU) to act as a central coordination point for the initiative in Tamil Nadu. Currently, it covers approximately 10,000 households across Perambalur, Coimbatore, Erode, Salem, Dharmapuri and Thiruvannamalai districts. Its work focusses on agriculture and allied livelihood building activities, specifically in rainfed and drought-prone areas, with a focus to increase profitability and productivity for small and marginal farmers.

Sakh Se Vikas: Rajasthan lags behind other states on many development indicators. Its hostile climatic conditions, arid terrains, weak infrastructural facilities and frequent droughts have impeded efforts for development.

In March 2003, Tata Trusts launched the Sakh Se Vikas programme in Rajasthan to promote self-sustaining community-based microfinance initiatives to strengthen livelihoods and reduce the vulnerability of marginalised people. It helps rural communities avail of financial support at reduced interest rates, setting them free from the tyranny of money lenders. The programme has brought social change by increasing the involvement of women in decision-making processes.

The overarching goal is to usher in a better tomorrow for the rural community. Consequently, the programme now also targets areas such as agriculture and livestock, drinking water and sanitation, health and nutrition, and education in 70,000 tribal households across villages in five blocks of south Rajasthan.

The nodal agency for the implementation of all the Trusts' projects under Sakh Se Vikas is the Centre for micro Finance (CmF).

Sukhi Baliraja Initiative: In 2005, Vidarbha in eastern Maharashtra came into national and international focus due to a series of farmer suicides. This distressing situation in this primarily agrarian-driven economy was caused by many factors – years of drought, low yields, poor market access, dependence on money-lenders and unfair trade practices, among others. An increased input cost aggravated the pressure on the farmers and left them burdened with debt. The worsening situation prompted the Sir Ratan Tata Trust and Allied Trusts, and the Sir Dorabji Tata Trust and its Allied Trusts (the Tata Trusts) to intervene in the area.

In 2008, the Tata Trusts launched the Sukhi Baliraja Initiative (SBI) in Vidarbha to address and alleviate the farmers' distress. Concurrently, the Government of Maharashtra initiated a bilateral project – the Convergence of Agricultural Interventions in Maharashtra Programme (CAIM) with the support of the International Fund for Agricultural Development (IFAD) – and invited the Tata Trusts to participate in the programme.

Today, this joint initiative reaches out to 25,600 households across 320 villages in the six distressed districts of Yavatmal, Amravati, Washim, Akola, Wardha and Buldhana in Vidarbha.

SBI has been developing a holistic livelihood strategy for the region to reduce distress among the farming community and empower them to face production and market risks. Efforts have been made to promote livelihood options through thematic interventions, with focus on the most distressed districts in Vidarbha, especially Yavatmal, Amravati and Akola.

In mid-2015, after years of working in the region and having made an impactful presence on field by gaining enough expertise, the Sukhi Baliraja Initiative supported by the Tata Trusts moved from a partner-based programme implementation to a direct implementation mode. The goal, however, was still to develop resilient production methods and diversified on-farm / off-farm livelihood options for sustainable income generation, thereby enabling farmers to face production and market-related risks without falling back into poverty and distress.

The thrust of the SBI programme is on sustainable agriculture, soil and water conservation, community-based microfinance, community-based marketing, farmer-producer organisations and collective agri-marketing, education, mental health, skills development, poultry, fisheries, and dairy, which together form a livelihood basket to be readily offered to the communities we work with.

While expanding into newer locations in the same geography, a few other themes were also focused on, with a view to holistically impact beneficiary households. This has made it possible for SBI to jointly scale up and intensify efforts in the region. Currently, SBI projects penetrate across Vidarbha with presence in 9 districts.

These interventions are monitored at various levels, by in-house personnel and external agencies, and detailed reports are published based on the studies on their impact and progress.

South Odisha Initiative: According to a 2012 World Bank report, South Odisha is no better than sub-Saharan Africa when it comes to human development indicators. Infant and maternal mortality, female illiteracy, lack of access to education, sanitation, clean water, basic healthcare facilities, etc., are some of the factors that contribute to low quality of life in South Odisha.

Since 2003, the Sir Dorabji Tata Trust and the Allied Trusts have partnered with more than 30 organisations on projects targeting livelihood enhancement, education, health and improving the condition of migrant labourers in South Odisha. Together, they have impacted changes such as crop productivity enhancement, supporting multilingual education, curbing malaria and setting up migration resource centres in the region.

In the coming years, Tata Trusts aim to transform the quality of life of 25,000 households in a cluster of five blocks in South Odisha that score very low in the human development index. The programme will focus on areas such as cultivation of high-value crops, supporting youth entrepreneurship, reducing dropout, ensuring grade appropriate learning level in children, health services in remote locations, providing safe drinking water and improving sanitation facilities.

The North East Initiative: The economy of the northeastern states is mainly based on subsistence agriculture and a system of shifting cultivation called jhum. Rampant and unchecked practice of jhum has put pressure on the fragile ecosystem and resulted in food scarcity; coupled with other problems, this has affected the quality of life in the region.

The Trusts launched the North East Initiative in 2008 to address developmental issues in the region through the provision of enhanced livelihood opportunities, improved agricultural practices and sustainable use of natural resources. It aims to create an effective channel for the dissemination of knowledge and expertise in the region. The North East Initiative Development Agency (NEIDA), the Trusts' associate organisation, plans to reach out to 37,000 households in the states of Mizoram, Nagaland and Arunachal Pradesh in the coming years. The key focus areas of the initiative now are agriculture and horticulture, household-level piggery enterprise, formation and strengthening of community institutions, skill building, education, and water and sanitation.

Eastern Uttar Pradesh initiative: Underdevelopment, poor infrastructure and limited natural resources place Eastern Uttar Pradesh low on the development index. The predominantly rural population depends on agriculture for subsistence, but erratic irrigation due to alternating floods and droughts and exploitative market systems make agriculture a low-profitable venture. Oppressive social systems add to the factors that have stymied development in the region.

Sir Dorabji Tata Trust and the Allied Trusts recognised that civil society engagement and strengthening is the engine which would drive development projects in the region. The Trusts initiated the Eastern Uttar Pradesh Programme with the institutional collectivisation of rural women. The programme now undertakes developmental work in the region in the focus areas of rural livelihoods, natural resource management, and education and health, with active participation from women. Viable partnerships have been formed with NGOs and other stakeholders with proven institutional and programmatic capabilities to undertake systematic development work.

Urban Poverty Alleviation: Urbanisation in India is skewed. Cities and towns in the north, west and south of India are expanding rapidly, while cities in the east and small towns in most parts of the country are decaying. Stagnation in the rural economy leads to seasonal and permanent migration to urban areas. The influx of migrants compounds the problem of unplanned growth, and poor living and working conditions in urban areas. The Urban Poverty and Livelihoods Portfolio of Tata Trusts works within three sub-themes: Migration, Skill Development, and Habitat.

Solar energy: Tata Trusts are implementing and supporting various clean energy projects such as popularisation of solar-based irrigation pumps, facilitating access to energy through community-based off-grid solar systems, facilitating lighting systems for individual homes, installation of rooftop solar systems, popularising clean cooking systems, adoption of biogas, etc. Tata Trusts are also promoting solar-based livelihood generation and supports activities in the sectors of education and health. Programmes supported by Tata Trusts have facilitated the installation of 1,586 kWp (installed and ongoing) of solar energy capacity. Of this, 112 kWp comprises the off-grid system, 480 kWp through solar irrigation systems and 1,004 kWp towards livelihood, education, health, etc.

Major partners

- NABARD - National Bank for Agriculture and Rural Development
- Indian Institute of Technology, Bombay
- Pradan
- Prayas Juvenile Aid Centre
- Livolink Foundation

- Collectives for Integrated Livelihood Initiatives
- Sanjeevani Seva Trust

Clean cooking programme: The clean cooking programme focuses on providing quality clean cooking devices to rural households to address issues pertaining to the health and degradation of the environment. It attempts to popularise the improved cookstoves among rural communities, create market demand and effect a behavioural change for the adoption of the stoves as compared to traditional cookstoves. The programme is presently underway in Gujarat, Rajasthan and Uttar Pradesh, and about 5,000 improved clean cooking devices have been sold to the community through a private entity (which works on promoting socially impactful products in rural areas) and community institutions promoted by Tata Trusts. The community institutions provide loans to households to purchase improved cookstoves and encourage them to use the stoves. Technological solutions that ensure the best low-emission cooking devices for the community, which are aspirational as well as affordable, are being developed through a market-led approach.

Major partners:

- Pradan
- Dharma Life

Arts, Crafts & Culture: India's long tradition of culture over the millennia is now established in highly evolved art forms. However, artistic and cultural practices are at risk of disappearing due to rapid social changes and the inability of artists and artisans to make a living from them. Monuments, museums and archives of historical value in India have also been slowly decaying, due to a lack of interest in conserving them.

Over the years, Tata Trusts have worked towards enhancing livelihoods and quality of life of artistes, artisans and craftsmen, by supporting:

- Initiatives to secure the livelihoods of crafts communities
- Sustainable livelihoods in performing arts
- Preservation and conservation of culture
- Identifying and supporting education in the arts across various disciplines

In addition to supporting projects in the arts across India, Tata Trusts have also initiated their own platform in 2017 — Kalapana. Kalapana is an invitation to people who have chosen to dedicate their lives to practice the arts and to those who participate in that imagination. Conceived as a two way celebration, it showcases organisations and artists supported by the Trusts and how the Trusts make these choices to support them — through discussions, exhibitions, talks, screenings and performances. Kalapana hopes to bring about a deeper understanding of what it takes to survive in the arts, to bring together diverse stakeholders involved in its sustained expression, to address challenges and to celebrate and support the current that will be our heritage of tomorrow.

Innovation: Since its inception, Tata Trusts have been focusing on innovative technologies and approaches to enhance the quality of life of communities. The focus has been on bringing in high-quality talent and technologies to speed and scale up interventions. Tata Trusts have tied up with premier educational and technical institutions such as MIT, IIT, IIM, etc., and like-minded multinationals to design, develop and implement innovative programmes across different sectors such as education, digital literacy, health, livelihoods, etc.

Points for People: Points for People is a unique platform of Tata Trusts that enables an individual to contribute to the development of a healthy society by donating funds towards the growth of communities supported by Tata Trusts. Individuals can opt to convert loyalty points (earned through transactions with the Trusts' partners) into donations or pay online. All donations are eligible for tax exemption.

Initially tribal individuals and tribal women led groups covered under the Central India Initiative — one of the flagship initiatives of Tata Trusts — will be the community that will benefit through Points for People. Thereafter, beneficiaries under other initiatives supported by Tata Trusts will be covered through Points for People.

Internet Saathi: In collaboration with Google India, Tata Trusts launched the Internet Sathi programme to promote awareness of the internet and its uses in the rural geographics where the Trusts operate. The objective is to empower rural women, and through them, create awareness among the larger community on internet and its benefits for their various needs. The 'sathis' would promote awareness of the internet and highlight its utility for seeking information across disparate sectors. The plan is to have 1,000 internet carts in rural villages, covering approximately 3,000 villages and 1 million people of which most will be women. The programme dovetails with the community institutions promoted by Tata Trusts and strengthens them through linkages with larger communities and providing internet as a service.

Project DRUV: Project DRUV is a new community development programme that uses innovative technology to help transform the lives of rural and remote populations in India. DRUV is a part of the 'Digital India' initiative launched by the Government of India. The project has been launched in Rajasthan and will be expanded to other states in the country soon. DRUV will make a difference to the quality of life of the underprivileged and under served populations by bringing digital connectivity to television screens to help gain access to information and benefits that the community is entitled to. Project DRUV is an initiative of Tata Trusts in association with Prodea Systems.

Foundation for Innovation and Social Entrepreneurship (FISE): Foundation for Innovation and Social Entrepreneurship (FISE) is promoted by Tata Trusts and plays a critical role in promoting social businesses with a revenue model that creates social value. The first-of its-kind initiative in India, and perhaps the world, in terms of thought, philosophy and process, is branded Social Alpha and will focus on social enterprises in the areas of livelihoods, education, health, water and shared services.

Institutions: Tata Trusts have pioneered several leading institutions. The centres of excellence have made significant contributions to several fields, particularly medicine, science and education.

As financial aid to organisations is given to enable them to implement a specific project, it has a discernible and concrete impact of limited magnitude and sweep. However, grants made to the institutions have a longer time frame and a wider canvas of impact. Even though the daily administration of most of these institutions has now been handed over to the respective governments, Tata Trusts continue to support and nurture them in myriad ways.

Stories on Trust projects

Card play to make a point on charity: The Points for People initiative makes it possible for individuals to support underprivileged communities simply by using the points accumulated in a credit or debit card.

Balamdina Nag seems at first sight to be an ordinary young tribal woman, except that a 10-day training programme as a learning assistant changed her life. Instead of being tied to her kitchen, Balamdina started working to increase school enrolment by motivating parents in her tribal village of Maliburu in Khunti district of India's Jharkhand state. She and her colleagues have got 250 children from six villages to join school.

Balamdina's new role became possible because she is a beneficiary of the Central India Initiative (CInI) of the Tata Trusts, which works to uplift the lives of tribal populations in the four Indian states of Jharkhand, Odisha, Maharashtra and Gujarat. CInI is unique in many ways — one of which is that it is the only programme of the Tata Trusts that has accepted donations from individuals who have contributed through a unique loyalty points donation scheme called Points for People.

Points for People is a crowd-sourced donation platform launched by the Trusts to open up philanthropic funding to the Indian public. It is based on an unusual strategy — enabling people to contribute by donating loyalty points accumulated on their cards. "Points for People is a concept designed to enable self-sustaining societies by encouraging donations from those who are privileged," says Ganesh Neelam, zonal manager, north and central India, Tata Trusts. The idea is that though people can (and do) donate cash for philanthropic projects, they can also set up a process for steady donation by contributing their loyalty points.

Maximum reach: A website — pointsforpeople.org — enables people to sign up. The donor has the option of selecting how many points to contribute and which project the funds should benefit. The card service provider ensures that one rupee for every loyalty point earned by a customer goes towards funding livelihood, education or water and sanitation projects that are managed by the Trusts.

For this, the Trusts tied up with Strategic Caravan, which manages the website and works on building the partner base. The platform has tied up with a few leading service providers — Loylty Rewardz (which manages loyalty programmes for some of India's biggest debit and credit cards), HDFC Bank, Edenred (which manages the Ticket Restaurant cards), and Xoxoday (which offers cards for dining and travel experiences). The Tata Trusts are also in talks with a few Tata companies to enable their customers to contribute via the company loyalty programmes. Word about the project is being spread through social media and brochures.

Started at the end of 2016, the Points for People project has already connected with 5,000 card holders. The donation target for this year, according to Mr Neelam, is ₹ 30 million. As a crowd-funding idea that makes it easy for individuals to reach out and support underprivileged communities, Points for People deserves several brownie points for its innovative strategy.

Cash in the crop: The Lakhpati Kisan project is transforming the lives of over 100,000 tribal farming households in four Indian states — and it has the potential to deliver more Kantibhai Makwana could barely make ends meet with what he earned by farming his field in Ratanpur village of Gujarat's Sabarkantha district. Three years down the line, his income from agriculture has jumped from 25,000 per annum to about 175,000. The money has been meaty enough for him to do up his home — with a pipeline to boot, he says — buy a motorbike and start a flour-mill business.

Sushila Khanda, who lives in Gaduan village in the mineral-rich Keonjhar district of Odisha, was a subsistence farmer till three years back. A member of the Gond tribal community, she managed to pull in 73,000 last year, modest in comparison with Mr Makwana but good enough to complete the plastering work of her house, send her son to a better school and spend on clothes and trinkets.

Separated by some 1,800km and differences in language and culture, Mr Makwana and Ms Khanda have never met and are unlikely to. They are, nevertheless, part of a single extended family, one that has under its canopy more than 100,000 households in 800 underserved villages spread across the states of Jharkhand, Maharashtra, Gujarat and Odisha. This is the family that populates Mission 2020 — Lakhpati Kisan: Smart Villages, one of the most ambitious and challenging projects supported by the Tata Trusts.

The upside and after: Lakhpati Kisan, loosely translated as '100,000 farmer', is designed to lift those who have been incorporated into the programme irreversibly out of poverty. Operational since April 2015, it has a spectrum of schemes and principles to realise the objective, all of them aligned to agriculture-centred livelihoods. The households are mainly from tribal regions and *the building blocks are women's self-help groups (SHGs).*

We were looking at raising the income of these farmers by three to four times. We had to think outside the box. We had to take ownership and risks and that's what we have done."

Ganesh Neelam, zonal manager, north and central India, Tata Trusts: The aggregation of SHGs into village organisations and, further on, into federations enables the project to gather strength in scale and nurture the women-led institutions spearheading their own development. The manner of the project's execution pours attention on making the communities in its care resilient and cohesive, self-reliant and self-sustaining.

The goal is to get 120,000 into the hands of each participating household every year through farming and allied activities, bit by incremental bit. It's a complicated task, made more difficult by the project's stringent 2020 deadline for completion.

Lakhpati Kisan is a welcome balm amidst the melancholy that envelops Indian agriculture, a pursuit rendered perilous for many by forces natural and induced. With its focus on tribal farmers and their fundamental problems, the programme aims to lift some of this gloom and, it is hoped, provide a template that can be employed by governments and their agencies to similar effect on a wider canvas.

Lakhpati Kisan supplements and often times supplants the ways of traditional farming. That means adding on to conventional crops such as maize, wheat and paddy with high-value vegetables. It means improving irrigation access — drip irrigation is a crucial feature of the project — and water usage efficiency. Also on the menu are year-round farming, developing linkages to markets, aggregation of produce to fetch the right price and backing tribal entrepreneurs.

Alongside high-value agriculture, participating households have been encouraged to take up at least one allied livelihood activity — such as animal husbandry, apiculture, lac cultivation, fisheries and horticulture — to hedge risks as well as accelerate income growth. The focus has been on technology and innovations, among them polyhouse nurseries, trellis farming and solar-based lifting devices.

Initiatives for all-round improvements in the quality of life of tribal communities — with projects in education, water and sanitation, nutrition, digital literacy, sports and life-skills development — have been integrated in community clusters. Lakhpati Kisan emerged following a study done in 2013-14 to understand the dynamics of farming by small landholders in India, the bottlenecks they have to deal with and their successes. Vital in this context was the need to spark the community's aspirations and enterprise, to bring together its talents and efforts to ensure the permanence of change.

Collectives for Integrated Livelihood Initiatives, an associate organisation of the Tata Trusts with more than a decade of experience, became the natural vehicle to seed the project and drive it forward. Nonprofits, many of them already working with the Trusts, were brought in to help with implementation. Once off the ground, the programme also connected with government bodies and schemes to intensify the impact of its various endeavours.

What Lakhpati Kisan is trying to accomplish is distinctive, and that poses challenges by the dozen. "We realised we couldn't do the regular stuff and expect to succeed," says Ganesh Neelam, who heads the initiative. "We were looking at raising the income of these farmers by three to four times. We had to think outside the box on all aspects, including technology, irrigation, getting other stakeholders on board, and building capacities and institutions. We had to take ownership and risks and that's what we have done."

With three years of the programmes completed, not everything has gone according to plans and expectations. "We have covered in excess of 100,000 households in Lakhpati Kisan and the idea was to get at least 50 percent of them to an income level of at least 120,000 a year by now," says Mr Neelam. "Our current achievement stands at 20 percent , so we are behind the target. It has taken longer than we expected to build capacities in the community and to get people to try out new things."

Mr Neelam is confident that progress from here on will be faster. "This is our fourth year and I'm sure that by the end of it we will have about 70 percent of our farming families with an income of 100,000 and more. The community institutions, the technology and the training are broadly in place today and we are working on the market linkages part. When we kicked off we had certain hypotheses; those have evolved and we have adapted."

Mindset change: Hidden from view is the psychology of villagers making the leap from traditional agriculture to high-value crops. The majority of these folks were not full-time farmers to begin with and it has taken a while to bring them up to speed. "It requires substantial energy to understand the mindset of the villagers," explains Mr Neelam. "We spend six to eight months interacting with the community before we get started and there are a lot of challenges in convincing them about the multiple facets of the initiative."

There have been variations in outcomes in the four states covered by Lakhpati Kisan. The positive here is the cross-pollination of ideas and the sharing of knowledge from every success and failure. "Gujarat stands out because the institutions there are strong; the people there had an early start and they are proactive," says Mr Neelam. "In Odisha and Jharkhand the adoption of new technologies has been fast. In Maharashtra, village institutions have come to the fore. It's basically about learning from one another and going up the ladder."

Having the state governments on its side is critical for the programme and this, too, is a demanding job. "You have to stay engaged," says Mr Neelam. "What we have learned is that we need to be close to the official machinery at the district level; they are the ones calling the shots."

The reality on the ground is what occupies the attention of Santanu Dutta, the man in charge of the project in Odisha. "In the tribal regions we work in, it is mostly subsistence agriculture, mono crop and rain-fed," he says. "The villagers are not habituated to the commercial growing of crops, which requires a superior degree of skill and experience. We had to create the momentum and the mahol [atmosphere] to attract them."

There were other issues as well in Odisha: shortage of labour, inadequate access to irrigation, lack of market linkages and communities that found it difficult to get mobilised. What did work was drip irrigation and getting connected to the market. "Drip irrigation is not about saving water as much as it is about saving on labour," says Mr Dutta. "And it's not about isolated irrigation structures; you have to saturate the villages with irrigation access." The tribal community in Tomka, a village in Jajapur district of Odisha, has benefitted in good measure thanks to Lakhpati Kisan.

Community care: Virendra Vaghani, Mr Dutta's counterpart in Gujarat, says the Tata Trusts confronted a different set of challenges in the state. "Initially it was about convincing our field partners on the feasibility of the initiative. Then came setting up the SHGs, the primary institutions in Lakhpati Kisan. We were a bit late on this but we have caught up. We got the community to take charge. Once that happens you can trigger aspirations and it becomes easier."

Change agents from within the community are important cogs in the programme and Mr Vaghani and his team has come to depend heavily on them. "We selected the progressive ones and started with them. They were open to new ways of doing things and we showed them how. Other farmers saw the result, believed in it and the village as a whole adopted the approach."

Mr Vaghani emphasises the need to give the community more space and responsibility. "They may fail but they will learn from it. Having said that, I must add that I've never seen the community contributing as much in any programme. I'm very optimistic that we will achieve our results."

Lakhpati Kisan is still in the first stage of implementation, which is about enhancing livelihoods and getting households to the 120,000 mark and beyond. The second phase, which has been initiated in select clusters, will see greater stress being put on quality of life indices. In the thinking of the Tata Trusts, what lies after that is a surety.

Sustainability equation: "Our involvement will be reduced substantially and the community will take the lead," says Mr Neelam. "What we are also saying is we have a fine opportunity here to scale-up the initiative, through the institutions that have been put in place and by getting the government convinced that this concept can be taken far and wide."

The Tata Trusts have committed significant resources to the Lakhpati Kisan programme, spread over its five-year duration. About as much will come in from other donors and government agencies. More heartening still is the monetary contribution the villagers are making to their own uplift. Where 10 percent or less is the norm, these villagers are putting in 20-30 percent of the money required.

"I don't know what plans God has for me but I believe things will get better," says Mr Makwana, who, unlike scores of farmers across India, does not think agriculture will be anathema to those following in his stead. "I have a grandson now and, with the progress we have achieved, he will do four times as well as me."

The upbeat nature of Mr Makwana and his mates is not an aberration. After all, it is difficult for those who can afford to take the necessities of everyday life for granted to understand the difference a swell in money earned makes to those surviving on the margins. Not so for Shardaben Makwana, once a sharecropper with an income of 40,000 a year, now a rejuvenated farmer who made 150,000 in 2017. Asked what the future holds for her, she says, "Next, I'm headed for the moon."

Sumitraben Patel, a self-assured 60-year-old from the Bhil tribal community, is an example of how Lakhpati Kisan is enabling farmers of modest means to fashion a better life for themselves. A resident of Dhabada village in Gujarat's Dahod district, Ms Patel has hauled herself and her family up from a hardscrabble existence to find a fair measure of security, a voice in her community and her place in the world. This is her story:

Traditional, low-scale farming was what we were doing and we grew maize, wheat and pulses. The work was tough and the money we made barely enough to get by. There were plenty of days when we struggled to put decent food on the table; dal-roti was the staple. Then came the Lakhpati Kisan project and it transformed everything.

The programme opened our eyes. The training and learning, the exposure to better farming practices, the coming together of our women through self-help groups [SHGs], the growing of cash crops, the concept of year-round cultivation, the aggregated marketing and selling of produce — all of these were part of the programme. There was so much to discover and understand.

We had an irrigation scheme in our village but the Lakhpati initiative was the real accelerator. I was making 50,000-60,000 a year before the programme was introduced in 2015. Now, three years later, my family's income has risen to 300,000 a year. We grow vegetables, we produce honey and we have a small business providing decorations, catering and music bands for weddings. None of this would have been possible without the programme.

The money coming in has been a huge help for my family. We have been able to refurbish our house, invest in digging borewells and also fund the education of my grandson, who's studying to be a homeopathic doctor. As for me, I've gained so much confidence from the project. My grandkids may well find employment elsewhere, but there is no question of me giving up on agriculture. Besides the money, we get to eat fresh and wholesome food. No pesticides.

I was the one who took the lead. My husband is the kind who does not like taking advice from outsiders; I wanted to listen to everybody and learn from them. I mobilised other women from my village to form one of the earliest SHGs in the project.

I used to work for daily wages before joining the programme. No matter how sincere my labour, there would always be complaints. I was convinced that if I put in the same effort on my land, and with the knowledge I had gained, at least there would be nobody complaining. This is my field, my produce, my earnings, my business. That makes me feel good.

I can't read and write and that's a disadvantage, but my position in the family is strong. The final word is mine. That definitely is due to what I have achieved. Thanks to the exposure I got, I learned about the world and how it functioned, about leadership and organising people. There was a time when I wasn't comfortable sitting on a chair. That's long gone.

I'm certain we can sustain this success even after the project winds up here. We have moved from growing crops to marketing them. We have become entrepreneurs. We have created vibrant village communities that can speak — and do good — for themselves.

All these examples seem to suggest that the idea of trebling of farm income being mooted by the Modi Government is not a utopian idea but a practical proposition with hard work and committed officials concerned with the programme. They can take a leaf or two from the experience of Lakhpati programme being implemented by the Tata Trusts in different parts of the country. The example of Kudumbashree operating in Kerala for many years is also a worthwhile project to look at and learn.

Kudumbashree is the poverty eradication and women empowerment programme implemented by the State Poverty Eradication Mission (SPEM) of the Government of Kerala. It consists of a three tier structure with Neighbourhood Groups (NHGs) as primary level units, Area Development Societies (ADS) at the ward level, and Community Development Societies (CDS) at the local government level. It is arguably one of the largest women's networks in the world. While the community network is formed around the central themes of poverty eradication and women empowerment, its main features include democratic leadership, and support structures formed from the 'Kudumbashree family'.

Reliance Foundation

Reliance Foundation's flagship programme, Bharat-India-Jodo (RF BIJ), works to bridge the development gap between rural and urban India. Committed to rural transformation, the programme works with small and marginal farmers and helps farming households that have limited livelihood options. These farmers, who mostly own rain-fed lands, often lack irrigation sources and are typically dependent on single crops. They are often unable to cultivate their entire landholdings, either because the quality of land is poor or because they lack the necessary resources. With these factors severely limiting their earning potential, most of them are forced to migrate and seek work as unskilled labourers.

In this socio-economic landscape, RF BIJ empowers marginal farmers with sustainable livelihood practices. It strives to de-risk farming, minimise external dependencies and improve rural lives and livelihoods. It supports low cost and high output in sustainable agriculture, helping farmers increase their productivity and leverage the market to increase their income. The programme also organises farmers in collectives, to leverage the power of unity. These models of social and economic development are owned, controlled and managed by communities themselves, for the larger development of their members, the village, and the region.

Vision of RF BIJ

RF BIJ aspires to establish a holistic, self-reliant and sustainable model of rural transformation based on the principles of:

- Direct Action
- Sustainable Development, and
- Participatory Approach

Objectives

Institution Building: At the heart of all RF BIJ efforts lies the desire to build strong and vibrant community-owned and managed institutions. Today, the programme supports more than 52,000 families across India through more than 500 vibrant village associations (VAs). RF BIJ mobilises and organises communities into these associations to promote collective ownership, decision making and common welfare. The VA members work together to meet collective aspirational goals.

Nutrition Security: In its endeavour to improve nutrition security, Reliance Foundation has supplemented the nutritional intake of rural households through promotion of small kitchen or backyard gardens, known as Reliance Nutrition Gardens (RNGs). These RNGs help improve the nutrition status of small and marginal farmers and their families, providing them with a diverse mix of vegetables, fruits and medicinal plants throughout the year.

Food Security: Reliance Foundation works with small and marginal farmers to ensure food security in rural households. To increase the availability, affordability and accessibility of food, the programme is directly engaged in transforming more than 56,000 hectares of land with little or no productivity into fertile and productive lands (dharti farms), through sustainable agricultural practices.

Water Security: RF BIJ follows a watershed approach, conserving every drop of water in-situ, through the adoption of local conservation methods. De-risking farmers and their farms from the extreme vagaries of the monsoons forms the basis of this engagement with communities. Depending on the geographical location, type of soil, agricultural practices and needs of the community, the Foundation has undertaken appropriate initiatives across 12 states. Many such RF BIJ initiatives have been appreciated by external agencies, including state governments.

Ecological Security: RF BIJ helps communities secure their local ecosystems, with the larger aim of achieving sustainable development through biodiversity and natural resource management. The Foundation has put in significant effort to encourage ecological sustainability through resource conservation, use of cleaner resources and promotion of biodiversity.

RF BIJ has engaged directly with more than 52,000 families in more than 500 villages across 12 Indian states. The model has been replicated from Radhanpur in Gujarat to Balangir in Odisha and from Rudraprayag in Uttarakhand to Karaikudi in Tamil Nadu. Furthermore, to facilitate research and development, RF BIJ has established the Centre of Excellence in Sustainable Agriculture in Mouda, Nagpur.

Reliance Foundation was instituted with a vision to build an inclusive India. Most CSR activities of RIL are carried out under the umbrella of Reliance Foundation. Led by Smt. Nita M. Ambani, Reliance Foundation has a comprehensive approach towards the nation's development. The Foundation addresses some of India's most pressing development challenges, with the aim of building better lives and improving the livelihood of the people for a stronger and inclusive India.

Collaboration and Digital Technology: Reliance Industries Limited strongly believes in inclusive economic growth. The Company's CSR initiatives are based on this principle, and resonate with India's National Development Goals as well as the Sustainable Development Goals (SDGs) outlined in the United Nations 2030 Agenda for Sustainable Development.

Most of the CSR activities of the Company are carried out under the aegis of Reliance Foundation (RF), it has emerged as a leading corporate foundation addressing nation's multiple development challenges. The Foundation was established in 2010 under the leadership of Smt. Nita M. Ambani.

Schedule VII of Section 135 of the Companies Act, 2013 lists out various areas in which corporate entities are expected to deploy their CSR funds and implement programmes for social development. Reliance has strategically chosen the company's CSR initiatives with a focus on improving the quality of life. The initiatives focus on seven areas: Rural Transformation, Health, Education, Sports for Development, Disaster Response, Arts, Culture and Heritage and Urban Renewal.

The key philosophy of all the social development initiatives of RIL is based on three core commitments of Scale, Impact and Sustainability. Reliance's development initiatives have touched more than 20 million people across India. The Company's initiatives registered an impressive reach across India.

Reliance Foundation directly engages with the communities through a team of trained professionals. It collaborates with the communities right from understanding their needs, planning and implementing the programmes, and measuring the values and impact it has created. In the process, Reliance engages the community members in planning and implementation empowers them through trainings and works towards scalability and sustainability of the initiatives.

Reliance Foundation forms strategic partnerships with organisations to bring in synergy to its development initiatives. These partnerships include state and local governments and non-government organisations working at the grassroots level. Reliance collaborates with the organisations for sharing technical know-how, human resources and infrastructure. These partnerships support in delivering Reliance's commitment by intensively engaging with the communities and penetrate into the critical issues that are physically untouched through direct interventions.

Reliance leverages technologies to provide sustainable solutions. These technological interventions connect communities on multiple digital platforms for optimum use of resources, informed decision making and capacity building. This has been greatly aided by the emergence of Jio Infocomm as a major player in digital services in recent years. Through the use of technology, Reliance has made significant progress in reaching out to the people with various products and services such as information advisories, digital classrooms, virtual sports clinics, record keeping of patients among others.

In addition to Reliance Foundation's interventions, the Company also encourages its employees to voluntarily contribute to social causes. Periodic inputs are obtained from employees on their interest to contribute to a particular cause. Additionally, depending upon the needs of communities, the Company leverages specific skill sets of employees and allocates resources for effective delivery. Given below is an overview of various CSR initiatives taken up by the Company.

Rural Transformation: Reliance has been addressing the challenges of rural communities through its rural transformation programme. Key initiatives in this programme include building rural institutions, making villages water secure, mentoring producer companies and enabling alternative livelihood options on and off the farm. The programme also uses technology based solutions for securing livelihoods of farmers, fisher folk and livestock owners across the country.

In addition to direct engagement, Reliance supported several organisations working in the field of rural development with an aim to benefit the rural community. The initiatives supported are aimed at building drought-resilient villages by ensuring water sufficiency, income enhancement through women-led cooperative societies and fishermen producer companies, and capacity building of farmers for better price realisation. Together, these initiatives help achieve the SDGs 1 (No Poverty), 2 (No Hunger), 6 (Clean Water and Sanitation) and 10 (Reduced Inequalities).

Institution Building: The programme empowers rural communities to organise themselves into Village Associations, Producer Companies and Women Thrift Groups. These community level institutions have facilitated the development of village level leadership for addressing local social development issues. Many of these institutions have taken up advocacy roles at different levels.

For long-term sustainability of these institutions, the members have come together to contribute towards creating a community owned fund, infuse equity into producer companies, savings and thrift activities. They have also been instrumental in mobilising physical and financial resources in times of crisis. Some of these leaders are also elected by people as representatives of Gram Panchayats, given their active participation in community development initiatives. Over 86,000 rural households in 1,100 villages from 32 districts across 12 states in India are reportedly with the programme.

Water Security: The programme aims to provide water security to villages for irrigation and domestic use. Reliance works for conserving every drop of rain within the village. More than 73 billion litres of water harvesting capacity has been created since inception by constructing or renovating water harvesting structures, including earthen/masonry dams and check dams, farm ponds, open wells, etc. Owing to this effort, over 32,000 hectares received assured irrigation for two cropping seasons. These efforts resulted in water security of 307 villages. Moreover, several villages have reported an increase in ground water level by over 2 metres, even at the peak of summer seasons.

For efficient water management, user groups were formed across 260 villages that manage and regulate sustainable water use. Assessments show that the intervention has positively impacted farmer livelihood in terms of land use pattern, cropping intensity and income levels.

Reliance supported Paani Foundation's Water Cup initiative to ensure water security in rural Maharashtra. Through this initiative, over 96 billion litres of water storage capacity has been created across 1,300+ villages.

Water Conservation in Sendhwa: In Bijapuri village of Sendhwa block (Barwani, Madhya Pradesh), people tend to migrate annually to neighbouring states including Maharashtra and Gujarat. With predominant rain-fed agriculture and lack of irrigation, the farmers were unable to cultivate more than a single crop that resulted in dependency on non-farm livelihood options during Rabi and Zaid seasons.

A water-budgeting exercise carried out revealed that the village could be made water secure by harvesting rainwater at strategic spots. After technical assessment, Reliance constructed a check dam that helped assure irrigation of 80 hectares. With this support, the farmers can now cultivate in at least two cropping seasons annually. This has resulted in year-round availability of livelihood options within the villages.

Farmer Producer Companies: Perennially, India's farmers have faced the challenge of establishing market linkages. To help the farmers overcome this challenge, Reliance empowers them to set up Farmer Producer Companies (FPCs). These farmer-owned and farmer-driven companies sensitise rural producers on the need to come together as collectives, aggregate farm produce to bring in economies of scale for fetching better prices, have sustainable access to markets, etc.

This aggregation also enhances the bargaining power of farmers. Reliance has mentored 19 FPCs, spanning 10 states. As on 31st March 2018, the RF-mentored FPCs had 21,500 farmers associated with them. During FY 2017-18, the annual turnover of FPCs was Rs. 67.5 crore. Each farmer who transacted through FPCs, on an average had an additional income of Rs.5,000 to Rs. 6,000.

- RF received Krishi Pragati Award 2017 from NCDEX for outstanding contribution in improving income of small and marginal farmers through FPCs.
- Bhimpahad Krushak Producer Company in Balangir, Odisha was licensed as a supplier of seeds and fertilizers by the Govt. of Odisha. This would benefit the farmer members in getting quality seeds at nominal subsidized government prices. The FPC has been ranked as Grade "A" organisation by NABARD.
- Jamwa Ramgarh FPC was recognized as the Most Promising Producer Company.
- In collaboration with Gujarat State Co-Operative Cotton Federation Limited, Jasdan Producer Company transacted 54,000+ quintals of groundnut that benefited 5,700 farmers.

Nutrition Security: To improve nutritional outcomes among rural population, Reliance has been promoting its unique kitchen garden model across its programme locations as well as providing technical support to government. Reliance Foundation has extended the scope of its partnership under Rajmata Jijau Nutrition Mission of Government of Maharashtra. Under this, RF would provide technical support to anganwadis across 16 districts in setting up Reliance Nutrition Gardens. This initiative is aimed at improving nutritional outcomes of 20 lakh mothers and children in these districts thus reducing the burden of malnutrition in the state.

Rural Livelihoods and Entrepreneurship: Reliance promotes alternative livelihood options to provide protection against uncertainties and catastrophes that affect farm-based livelihoods. The Company encourages small farmers to initiate goat-rearing, poultry, nursery raising and vermi-composting, among others.

Ecological Security: Reliance promotes ecological security in three ways: increasing the supply of cultivable land; enhancing the green cover through large-scale plantation activity; and improving soil health.

The Company adopts eco-consistent soil conservation methods that resulted in bringing an additional 7,000 hectares (64,000 hectares since inception) under sustainable agricultural practices. This has led to an improvement in soil texture, structure, microbial activity and aeration, and almost 80 percent of this land has been used for food production.

To promote biodiversity, over 7 million saplings were planted during FY 2017-18 (over 20 million saplings planted since inception). Reliance observed the World Environment Day and motivated rural communities and employees to plant saplings. The event saw an enthusiastic participation of 20,000+ people from over 150 villages across 12 states.

Reliance endorses the protection of the soil ecosystem. It conducted over 11,000 soil health tests and accordingly disseminated relevant advisories.

Informed decision-making: Reliance Foundation has been using multiple digital solutions tailored to the needs of its beneficiaries. RF leveraged Jio Infocomm's "JioChat" application and added essential features in it to provide solutions to a range of rural users seeking customised information and advice on improving their lives and livelihood. The app allows users to send and receive information in the form of text, images, voice and video.

In addition, the users can also seek information with the help of key words through chat. So far, 15,000 different advisories have been uploaded in 9 different languages. The content disseminated through the app is benefitting a large population which seeks information to make the best decisions about their livelihoods.

Information Services: Reliance, through its information services programme, empowers communities by providing reliable information, tailored to the needs of farmers, fisher folk, livestock owners, etc. in more than 13,000 villages across 12 states. This is disseminated both digitally and through community level interventions that include information on crop management, livestock care, schemes and subsidies, healthcare, civic services etc. The mobile based advisories have reached an additional 1.2 million individuals this year. Overall, these advisories have reached out to 4.8 million individuals since inception; thus emerging as a powerful tool of knowledge dissemination.

As part of the programme, Reliance has created an ecosystem that comprises of more than 1,000 knowledge and infrastructure partners, thematic experts, including research institutions, government departments, NGOs, etc.

Access to Social Infrastructure: Reliance improved access to social infrastructure through development of concrete roads connecting 32 villages in Uttar Pradesh. The development of roads is a turning point for many of these villages as it has improved access to local markets, schools and healthcare facilities.

Social Transformation Mission: In 2017, Reliance joined hands with Govt of Maharashtra in its holistic mission of transforming 1,000 villages. As part of this, Reliance is demonstrating a comprehensive model of rural transformation. The model empowers communities to establish transparent and accountable governance systems, achieve food, water, nutrition and energy security contribute to sustainable livelihoods. The model also emphasises on education, and awareness on rights and entitlements. It works towards strengthening physical and digital infrastructure, and making villages resilient to disasters.

Early results from the direct engagement by Reliance in 51 villages indicate:

- 252 community leaders have emerged as change agents driving the transformation in 33 villages
- Increased water harvesting capacity has been assured irrigation for 2,600 hectares
- 3,500 families earning an income of more than Rs.1 lakh per annum.

The health programme of Reliance addresses primary healthcare issues around affordability and accessibility of quality healthcare. It strives to improve awareness and healthy living practices, and provides a range of healthcare services, spanning the entire life cycle. The Company also provides specialised services through tertiary healthcare facilities such as multi-specialty hospitals, at subsidised prices to the communities. The objectives of this programme are aligned to the SDG 3 (Good Health and Well-being).

Collectively, the health programmes have reached out to 2.5 million people and provided over 4.5 million patient consultations since inception. Through partnerships, Reliance supported several organisations working in the field of healthcare in providing a range of services, both at primary and tertiary level. These services include preventive care, maternal and child health, specialised care for patients with cardiac and kidney problems, palliative care for terminally ill cancer patients, etc.

Sir H N Reliance Foundation Hospital and Research Centre: Since its inauguration in 2014, Sir H N Reliance Foundation Hospital and Research Centre has emerged as a centre of quality care in Mumbai. By keeping abreast of medical innovations and adopting the best practices in clinical care, the hospital is poised to offer world class medical care. It has won India's foremost quality accreditation from National Accreditation Board for Hospitals and Healthcare Providers (NABH). A large number of patients with complex medical issues have been treated here. Its state-of-the-art operation theatre complex, including robotics, cutting-edge diagnostics and imaging facilities, enable the hospital to offer excellent care.

The hospital has successfully performed 6,500 procedures with excellent outcomes within a strong ethical framework. These include some of the most complex surgeries across different specialties such as cancer, paediatric cardiac surgeries, spine surgeries, joint replacement surgeries and vascular interventions. The hospital conducted the first Robotic kidney transplant in Maharashtra. The hospital has successfully undertaken advanced Child Haplo-identical Transplant by TCR Alphabeta and CD45RA Depletion Method, the first such transplant in India.

The Hospital organises health awareness programmes to empower people to take informed decisions on health issues. Over 9,000 people have been covered so far, through ~100 programmes. The Hospital also organized corporate health awareness talks and school screening camps covering over 5,000 people. Through subsidised and free services, the hospital benefitted ~ 10,000 out-patients. True to the hospital's motto, 'Respect for Life', it provided over 200 charity patients with varied medical services including paediatric cardiac surgeries, cochlear implants and cancer therapies.

The Hospital's Emergency Care Department caters to a large number of patients every year, and saved many from death and permanent disability. Its emergency teams meticulously follow international best practices to offer lifesaving services in the 'golden hour' to treat stroke, heart attack, other ailments and accidents. Over 9,000 patients benefitted from the services. The Hospital has initiated "Digital Push" mobile application using which individuals can digitise and manage their medical records.

The Hospital's ethos of 'patient first' is exemplified in the numerous steps it has taken to improve patient care and give patient's family members a reassuring experience. The Hospital has leveraged technology not only to improve medical care but also to ensure service excellence. Its online reports reduce visits to the Hospital and the online registration and mobile applications help find suitable doctors and expedite online appointments. Efforts have been taken to reduce waiting time and discharge time of out-patients. All these make the Hospital truly a place where people, processes, technology and infrastructure converge to provide the best experience and care.

Dhirubhai Ambani Hospital: The Dhirubhai Ambani Hospital at Lodhivali near Patalganga (Maharashtra), has provided free and subsidised healthcare to over 18,600 since inception. A majority of these patients include the underprivileged, senior citizens, and trauma victims from the economically weaker sections of the society.

The Hospital's Anti-Retroviral Therapy centre is the largest in Raigad district. It has registered over 4,000 persons with HIV/AIDS (PLHIV) since inception, of which 210 were registered during FY 2017-18. The patients receive free consultation, counselling, investigation and treatment. In FY 2017-18, specialised health consultations were provided to over 17,500 PLHIV taking the total number of consultations to 0.14 million.

Through Reliance managed hospitals and community level interventions, care and treatment services were provided to over 1,200 HIV infected and affected people, including children. The Company also provided nutrition and education support to 112 children affected with HIV. Moreover, 190 tuberculosis screenings were completed. Specialised events were conducted to sensitise migrant workers, truck drivers and sex workers on HIV infection. Awareness was further created to reduce the stigma and discrimination associated with it by distributing IEC materials to them.

A Regional Level Marriage Bureau function was organised at HIV DOTS Centre in collaboration with Gujarat State Network of People Living with HIV/AIDS (GSNP+). The programme saw large participation of over 1,300 PLHIV from 4 states, where 25 couples tied the knot.

Alliance for Saving Mothers and Newborns (ASMAN): Through Project ASMAN, Reliance, along with four other organisations, is working in Rajasthan and Madhya Pradesh to strengthen the health systems by enhancing quality of services in public health facilities for improved maternal and newborn outcomes.

The intervention provides technology-based solutions to healthcare providers, backed by on-site mentoring and supportive supervision visits during critical phases of intra-partum and postpartum care. Covering 81 multi-level health facilities, the programme has trained 80 Medical Officers and 338 staff nurses on obstetric and newborn care. During the project cycle, the programme will benefit at least 0.5 million mothers and newborns.

Eye Care Services: For more than a decade, through RF Drishti progr-amme, Reliance has been supporting visually impaired underprivileged people to undergo corneal transplants by partnering with the National Association for the Blind, Arvind Eye Hospital and Sankara Eye Foundation, 1,207 visually impaired individuals were supported under the programme (17,031 corneal transplants since inception). To increase the awareness about importance of eye donation, the programme organises a week-long Drishti Art and Essay Competition every year. This year, about 10,000 children participated in it.

At the community level, vision screening camps and mobile eye clinics are regularly conducted across the plant locations including Jamnagar, Nagothane, Vadodara and Patalganga. Over 16,500 individuals were screened for vision related issues, of which 1,185 cataract surgeries were done. Over 1,050 individuals with refractive error were further linked to specialised facilities for optical correction and using spectacles.

Menstrual Hygiene: Reliance engaged in the promotion of menstrual hygiene across the rural areas of Nagothane (Maharashtra) and Dahej (Gujarat) through several community level interventions. These sessions are aimed at addressing myths and misconceptions, increasing the awareness levels on menstrual hygiene and use of sanitary napkins. These initiatives benefited over 1,400 adolescent girls and women.

Pad Woman from Sawai Madhopur: Chandra Kanwar, a leader of women's thrift group in Sawai Madhopur, is now leading the menstrual hygiene initiative, and emerging as a change agent in her community. She hails from a conservative family where women do not have the freedom to make choices, yet she is breaking the socio-cultural taboo on this stigmatised issue. Due to her awareness efforts, 300 women and girls have started using hygienic and quality sanitary napkins. Not stopping at this, she has founded an emerging enterprise trading in quality sanitary napkins, making them available at an extremely affordable price to women in eight surrounding villages.

Strengthening of Health System: Reliance is working towards improving the quality of healthcare in Warangal (Telangana) by strengthening the public healthcare ecosystem through technical support to the Government. The objective is to achieve the process quality standards according to benchmarks of the National Accreditation Board for Hospitals and Healthcare Providers and National Quality Assurance Standards.

The project works towards improving the quality of care through the adoption of quality management health systems, process standardisation, capacity building and technology integration. The programme positively impacted 8 primary and secondary healthcare facilities and a tertiary care teaching hospital (MGM Hospital).

The project has shown improvement in quality parameters such as safe disposal of biomedical waste, improvement in management of deliveries and informed decision-making of district health administration. It also assisted in improvement in counseling and implementation of digital record keeping, among others.

Health Outreach Programme: Reliance's health outreach programme provides primary health services including screenings and consultations. It employs 10 Mobile Medical Units (MMUs) and 3 Static Medical Units (SMUs) across Madhya Pradesh, Maharashtra and Uttarakhand to offer medical help to the underprivileged communities. In Mumbai, the high-risk cases are further referred to tertiary level facilities. The Company reaches out to the underprivileged segments with information, education and communication messages through camps and technology-enabled information services to emphasise preventive care and correct health behaviours.

The medical units are equipped with state-of-the-art technology to store patient information, which helps healthcare providers in decision-making, based on the case history. Through MMUs, SMUs and camps, over 0.2 million consultations were provided during the year under review. Further, 35,000 individuals were provided health related advisories through digital platform. The health outreach programme also empowers community volunteers to help prevent seasonal outbreaks.

Education: Initiatives of Reliance in the education space are aimed at promoting primary and secondary education and enabling higher education through merit-cum-means scholarships across the country. Reliance has been leveraging appropriate technologies and learning resources for improving the quality of teaching and, in turn, student performance.

To diversify its initiatives in education space, Reliance supported various organisations in providing quality education to children from underprivileged communities. The initiatives of these organizations focus on improving enrolment rate, improving skill sets of teachers, improving English language skills of children, education on child sexual abuse and positive communication, mainstreaming of children with special needs and improving educational infrastructure. Through these partnerships, Reliance is improving the learning outcomes of over lakh children across the country. The Company's work in education sector corresponds to SDG 4 (Quality Education).

Scholarships for Higher Education: In order to nurture talented young leaders, the Dhirubhai Ambani Scholarship (DAS) programme has so far provided financial support to 11,781 meritorious students to pursue graduation in any stream and institution of their choice. Nearly half of the DAS scholars are girls, while one-fifth are specially-abled students. DAS the programme supported 423 students across the country. Under Protsahan Scheme in East Godavari (Andhra Pradesh), scholarships are provided to meritorious students from the villages around plant location. 290 students were provided scholarships under the scheme for pursuing higher studies.

Together, Reliance has supported 13,644 students through various educational scholarship programmes.

Reliance Foundation Schools: Thirteen Reliance Foundation Schools located in Jamnagar, Surat, Vadodara, Dahej, Lodhivali, Nagothane, Nagpur and Navi Mumbai; provide education to over 15,000 children annually. The schools offer education from kindergarten to class 12 and are affiliated to the Central Board of Secondary Education and State Education Boards of Gujarat and Maharashtra. Reliance Foundation School, Koparkhairane was ranked among the Top-10 schools in Navi Mumbai by Hindustan Times.

The RF Schools have constantly maintained excellent standards of academic performance. In 2017, 22 percent students secured the maximum achievable score of CGPA 10 in the CBSE Class 10 Board examination, 30 percent students of Science stream scored above 90 percent in CBSE Class 12 Board examination, and 27 percent students of Commerce course scored above 80 percent . Schools affiliated to the Maharashtra State Board reported 100 percent pass percent age, both in Class 10 and Class 12 Science stream, whereas the schools affiliated with Gujarat State Board reported 93 percent pass rate in Class 10 Board examination, and 97 percent and 88 percent pass rate, respectively in Class 12 Board exam for Science and Commerce streams.

Besides academics, the students of RF Schools continue to excel in co-scholastic, sporting and co-curricular pursuits, while winning awards and recognition at the district, state and national levels. RF School, Koparkhairane won the 'Best School' award for the third consecutive year at the Inter- School Elocution Competition. Other achievements included gold medals in International Skating Competition, Senior National Aquatic Championship and CBSE National Level Athletics Meet 2017; bronze medal in athletics at the inaugural Khelo India School Games, football team representing the School at the national level; and Swami Vivekananda Award and Scholarship for state and national level sports achievement. Three RF Schools were selected for presenting their Science Projects at the National Level CBSE Science Exhibition.

Dhirubhai Ambani International School: DAIS prepares students for the ICSE, the IGCSE and the IB Diploma examinations. The school is a member of the Cambridge International Primary Programme. DAIS provides world-class education to 1,000+ children annually; and has about 150 teachers with rich experience in national and international curricula. Students have consistently achieved outstanding results across all three curricula.

In 2017, two students of IGCSE Class 10 topped the world in Mathematics and five students topped in India in various subjects. The school's ICSE average score was 96 percent and the highest score was 98.4 percent . In the IB Diploma Examinations, eight students earned the perfect score of 45, average score of the class being 39.2. The IB Diploma graduates of 2017 earned admissions and scholarships to 22 of the top-30 universities worldwide. During the academic year, students won over 500 awards in various sporting, scholastic and co-curricular events at the state, national and international levels.

Over the years, the School has achieved highest standards of excellence on all performance parameters. DAIS is among the very few schools in India to be jointly accredited by the Council of International Schools and the New England Association of Schools & Colleges. In 2017, Education World ranked DAIS as the No. 1 International School in India for the fifth consecutive year. Hindustan Times ranked DAIS as No. 1 School in Mumbai for the fifth time. Times of India ranked DAIS as the No. 1 'National and International Curriculum' School in Mumbai for the third consecutive year. DAIS is also one of India's few schools to be certified by the Indian Green Building Council with the highest-level 'platinum' rating.

Reliance University: Reliance is working towards establishing a globally benchmarked, multi-disciplinary university in Maharashtra. It will provide an enabling environment and cutting-edge research facilities to students.

Infrastructure Support to Schools: Reliance constructed two schools for the Government of Uttarakhand as part of its relief and rehabilitation support in the aftermath of devastating floods in 2013. The two schools, which are now operational, stand testimony to the Company's commitment towards rebuilding Uttarakhand. These schools cater to nearly 1,000 students, coming from around 30 villages in the vicinity.

The Government schools across several locations were supported in enhancing their infrastructure including furniture, computers, RO plants, school uniform kits, etc. The spouses of Reliance employees held English language classes for students of Moti Khavdi Kanyashala and helped deprived and school dropout girls to compete through the National Institute of Open Schooling.

Digital Classroom: Reliance has worked with local governments to establish model digital classrooms in 129 government schools across Andhra Pradesh, Gujarat, Madhya Pradesh, Maharashtra and Telangana benefitting about 30,000 students.

A central relay station connects teachers to all schools for teaching live virtual classes and facilitates interaction between teachers and students. Offline classes on specific subjects are also conducted. The virtual classroom has bolstered the confidence of students and has resulted in higher pass percent ages. Additionally, the platform is being used for conducting classes on development of life-skills, career guidance, etc.

Dhirubhai Ambani Institute of Information and Communication Technology (DA-IICT): DA-IICT, Gandhinagar represents *Wave-4* of educational innovation in Gujarat. The first wave was the nationalist wave and led to Gandhian experiments in education including Nai Talim. The Gujarat Vidyapith established in 1920 was a hybrid model of a University based on Gandhian principles.

The second wave led to the establishment of a whole range of educational institutions in Gujarat, mainly private colleges. The third wave, an inspired one, was spearheaded by the Industrialist Kasturbhai Lalbhai and the Scientist Vikram Sarabhai and led to the establishment of a network of national institutes of international renown. A whole array of remarkable intellectuals provided the leadership of these Institutes.

It was in *Wave 4* when the focus shifted to higher education and private participation. One of the Institutes created during this period is DA-IICT in 2001. It is the only advanced research and teaching Institute named after the Late Dhirubhai Ambani, the founder of Reliance Group.

Environment: DA-IICT is spread over 50 acres of land in Gandhinagar, Capital City of Gujarat. The DA-IICT campus is caringly planned and designed as an environmentally conscious campus in the country. The architecture of DA-IICT is functional, but what surrounds it is a fascinating garden. The entire design is oriented towards preserving the environment. The campus with trees, lawns and bushes bearing green leaves and exotic flowers surrounding the buildings and pathways instils environment consciousness among students and enrich their learning. The campus also has a herb garden with species of rare medicinal plants. The landscape was planned and developed in a manner that no rainwater is lost. The irrigation for campus garden and lawns is carried out with recycled water. Its solid waste management system churns out organic fertilizer out of dry leaves, vegetable and food waste generated from food courts.

The campus is a haven for bird-watchers, with a variety of species of birds being spotted.

DA-IICT can be reached in about 30 minutes from Sardar Vallabhai Patel International Airport and the Central Railway Station located in Ahmedabad.

Courses offered

B. Tech. (ICT): DA-IICT offers two unique four-year undergraduate programs leading to the degrees of:

- Bachelor of Technology in Information and Communication Technology – B.Tech. (ICT)
- Bachelor of Technology (Honours) in ICT with minor in Computational Science – B.Tech. (Honours) in ICT with minor in CS.

M. Tech. (ICT): The program has been specially designed to meet the increasing needs of professionals who would be able to respond to the convergence between computers and communication systems. The program aims to provide exposure to students who wish to build a professional career in ICT. On successful completion of the program, the students will be able to acquire essential technical and practical knowledge for solving real-world problems in the ICT domain using modern technologies and tools, and will have the necessary ability to demonstrate excellent analytical, logical and problem solving skills. Apart from receiving rigorous exposure to various areas of scholastic study and research, students are at the same time groomed to cultivate an astute moral sense and a sound professional ethic.

The curriculum is organized with core courses, elective courses and thesis/ project work. Program Core courses are foundational and compulsory, which will build core competencies necessary for ICT domain knowledge areas. Once the student acquires knowledge in foundational courses, he/she will have the choice of selecting group core courses which are interdisciplinary in nature and will provide a broad based exposure to ICT research. Subsequently, the student will have adequate choice of electives in order to penetrate deeper into areas of his/her interest. Finally, the student will have an option to pursue one full year (two semesters) of research work in the form of thesis or a semester long internship/project work, depending on his/her category (Thesis or Project mode) in the program.

The structure of the curriculum is broadly classified into 4 categories. The first category, referred to as Foundation (Program Core), is a set of compulsory courses mandatory for every student in the program. The next one is domain knowledge in ICT, termed as Group Core. The third category is Electives in ICT. The fourth one is either a Thesis spread over the third and fourth semesters or a Project in fourth semester.

M.Sc. (IT): The Master of Science (Information Technology) is an intensive two year post-graduate program (4 semesters) designed for students who wish to pursue a professional career in Information Technology. The courses are carefully designed to guide the students through basic concepts to the current practices in industry. Hands-on Laboratory experience is emphasized at every stage of the Program. In the last semester, the students are required to carry out an industry internship. At the end of the program, it is expected that the students attain a sound theoretical foundation; an ability to analyze, conceptualize and design systems; and competence in modern software design and development tools. A typical graduate in IT at DA-IICT can expect to build a career as a software engineer, an analyst or a system designer.

M.Des. (Communication Design): The Master of Design (Communication Design) is a two-year post-graduate program (4 semesters). The program offers the students opportunity to specialize in Visual Communication Design and Interaction Design. Its distinctive pedagogic format encourages learning of basic design skills, the use of digital technologies and an understanding of the cultural and aesthetic aspects of communication practices. The objective of the program is to prepare young professionals for careers in the publishing, creative media and infotainment industries and the academia. Unlike other Design programmes offered in various institutions, the MDes programme in DAIICT blends Design concepts, skills and practices with Liberal Arts inputs from the domains of sociology and anthropology that help the student to understand and engage with diverse real-life contexts within which they have to evolve specific communication strategies.

The overall objective of the programme is to prepare students towards employability in the creative media industry (as a conceptualizer, visualizers, app developers, advertising creatives etc) to develop their own independent studios and start-ups and also pursue further studies in Design Research and Teaching.

- To create a uniquely creative individual who would be capable of using digital technology, (among others) to integrate various channels, forms and media of communication in a culturally sensitive manner that is crucial for meeting the challenges of the modern world.
- To train individuals who are thoughtful, creative and have an understanding of techno-aesthetic. The aim is to produce individuals capable of carving a unique position for themselves in the world of ICT by equipping them with the knowledge of multi-disciplinary approaches to issues of communication.
- To situate ICT in a domain of intellectual engagement that arrives at a more effective understanding of the multiple cultures of communication that hold societies together.
- The training provided at this Institute is aimed not at just providing students with skills required in the market but to make them learn and apply the ever-increasing tools of communication in culturally sensitive ways.

Given the growing and ever-changing demands of the market, the program wishes to direct the creative potential of its students to two major areas of specialization viz. 'Visual Communication Design' and 'Interactive Communication Design'. Both areas of specialization would be built upon a strong foundation that will impart training in basic design sensibility, the uses of digital technologies and the cultural and aesthetic components of communication practices.

Ph.D.: The Doctoral Program leading towards the award of the Degree of Doctor of Philosophy (Ph.D.) provides the students an opportunity for a career in academia or in Research & Development Establishments. A strong foundation and original contribution to knowledge in a chosen area of interest is expected from Ph.D. graduates of DA-IICT.

Broadly, faculty members at DA-IICT are engaged in research activities in Information and Communication Technology (ICT) and related areas, selected areas of Basic and Computational Sciences, and selected areas in the Humanities and Social Sciences.

Education and Sports for All (ESA): Using sports as a vehicle, Reliance promotes health, fitness and active lifestyle to bring about a positive change among youth and children in both urban and rural landscapes. Popular sports such as football, basketball and athletics are used to cultivate strategic thinking, competitive spirit and leadership abilities among children and youth. Reliance partners with various national and state sports bodies in improving the quality of sporting ecosystem through better facilities, training, infrastructure and equipment.

Quality Education to Underprivileged: Under ESA, Reliance supports education of underprivileged children by partnering with NGOs and works at grassroots level. As an extension under this initiative, an innovation in the form of Digital Learning Van was launched in 2017. The van has reached out to more than 4,000 children from 10 government schools in Mumbai and Thane districts. This initiative has positively impacted 0.2 million children.

Reliance Foundation Jr. NBA programme: RF Jr. NBA programme, a comprehensive school based basketball initiative, completed its fifth consecutive year. The programme has successfully integrated basketball into the physical education curriculum in 10,000+ participating schools nationwide. The programme has reached out to 9 million students across 34 cities in India since inception and 5.6 million students.

Reliance Foundation Youth Sports (RFYS): RFYS provides a nation-wide unique platform for promoting grassroots sports. In 2007, the programme continued with football and introduced athletics to further identify and encourage sporting talent across the country.

During FY 2017-18, football tournaments of RFYS expanded to 34 cities, including the cities of Northeast India, entire Kerala and key cities like Bangalore, Hyderabad and Chandigarh. Overall, 4,900 teams (including 450 girls' teams) from 3,400 institutes participated in the tournaments. All India Football Federation has backed the RFYS grassroots development programme, counting these players among 'the finest young players in the country'. The programme also sponsored 400 best physical education teachers for 'D-License Coaching Certification'.

Under athletics, different categories have been promoted, including sprints, relays, long- distance run, high jump and long jump. Competitions were held across 8 centres, including sports hubs such as Punjab, Haryana and Kerala. An inaugural National Athletic Championship was held in Mumbai, which saw participation from 2,900 institutes with over 9,000 athletes competing in over 3,000 events.

Rashtriya Khel Protsahan Puraskar: Reliance Foundation was conferred with Rashtriya Khel Protsahan Puraskar in 2017. On behalf of Reliance Foundation, Smt. Nita M. Ambani received the prestigious award from Honourable President of India Shri Ram Nath Kovind, for her influential role in transforming India into a sporting nation.

The programme strategically partnered with 20 institutes across the country for effective implementation. On the ground, the tournaments were conducted by officials from Athletics Federation of India and All India Football Federation. Reliance further donated equipment to the participating institutes to promote sports. For motivating young talent and expanding the reach of RFYS, all final matches at city level, zonal level and national level were live-streamed on the RFYS website.

RF Jr. NBA enters Guinness Book of World Records: In 2017, the RF Jr. NBA programme entered the Guinness Book of World Records. The programme witnessed over 3400 Jr. NBA students at Delhi, Bengaluru, Chennai, Hyderabad and Kolkata receiving basketball lessons from the legendary Kevin Durant in the world's largest ever tech-enabled NBA clinic held for the future basketball talent on July 28.

Reliance Foundation Young Champs (RFYC): RFYC is a unique, scholarship-based, full-time residential football and education programme. It aims to provide India's aspiring football talents the opportunity to hone their skills with world-class facilities and best-in-class training.

During FY 2017-18, eight young football talents were awarded scholarships to develop their football skills, taking the total to 48 scholarships. Under the programme, 30 Young Champs were sent for international exposure trip to Spain where they got an opportunity to play friendly matches, with teams including Real Madrid, Atletico de Madrid, Valencia, Villarreal, Rayo Vallecano and Leganes.

The Young Champs Sports Academy has been accredited as one of the best in India by the All India Football Federation. Reliance's objective is to maintain this position; and also strive towards the cherished milestone of achieving 5/5 grade.

Improving Access to Sports Infrastructure Reliance installed a multi-sports complex in two stadiums under Thane Municipal Corporation. This facility has a specially designed net cage to suit all playing fields with LED illuminated line markings to facilitate the sports being played. The sports facility can accommodate six different games: soccer, ring hockey, volleyball, handball, cricket and tennis. With the space for sportspersons and fitness enthusiasts shrinking in urban areas, these multi-sports stadiums in the centre of densely populated cities address an acutely felt need.

Disaster Response: Reliance aspires to respond swiftly and effectively to disasters that endanger human lives and livelihoods, by directly engaging with affected communities. It leverages all its strengths – including human resources and information technology – to provide relief and rehabilitation support. During FY 2017-18, the Company promptly helped communities affected by floods and cyclone in Assam, Gujarat and Southern India.

Flood Response in Assam: The Assam floods in August 2017 affected several people across the state, leaving them stranded and dispossessed. Responding to the need, Reliance identified the 22 villages that did not receive adequate relief support, and supplied ration-kits to more than 10,000 people, enough to sustain them for duration of 15 days.

Flood Response in Gujarat: With heavy rains battering Gujarat, floods wreaked havoc in the state, bringing life to a standstill and causing widespread damage. Taking note of the grim situation, Reliance worked relentlessly to support the afflicted communities. For immediate sustenance of the victims, teams of Reliance with support from community volunteers distributed relief kits to 0.15 million people across 87 villages. Besides, health camps were conducted to secure 6,000+ people against immediate and medium-term health risks emanating from floods.

To maximise the benefits to affected communities, Reliance used technology to reach out to them with useful information. Advisories were sent across to over 0.3 million flood victims to guide on the correct use of chlorine tablets in water, health precautions, livestock care, and government schemes. In addition, over 0.1 million people contacted toll-free helpline numbers for specific relief requirements.

Support during Ockhi Cyclone using Technology: Reliance played a key role in saving many lives when Cyclone Ockhi hit the southern parts of India. The Company disseminated advisories related to warnings on cyclone to coastal areas in Tamil Nadu and Kerala through its different communication channels. Due to high windspeed and waves, along with heavy rainfall, fishermen in these areas were urged not to venture out into the sea. The timely information provided by Reliance saved lives of over 27,000 fishermen.

Besides, the farmers were reached through various communication modes such as 'Flag Method', 'Knowledge on Wheels', help line and multi-location audio conferences that saved over 4,600 hectares of paddy fields.

Leveraging technology, Reliance acted as a bridge between government functionaries and fishermen. Reliance Foundation's toll free helpline received several calls asking for help to locate missing boats and fishermen. The information was immediately shared with the Coastguard and Indian Navy to facilitate the rescue work and the information on rescued fishermen was shared with their anxious families. Over 300 fishermen and 35 boats were rescued from the deep sea. An assessment shows that almost 91 percent of cyclone-affected fishermen reported having benefited from the advisories.

Arts, Culture and Heritage and Urban Renewal: Reliance works to preserve the rich heritage, art and culture of India for its future generations and makes conscious efforts to improve the livelihood opportunities for traditional artisans and craftsmen. This is done primarily by undertaking various promotional projects and documenting India's heritage for the benefit of future generations.

Abbaji Annual Concert: Reliance supports the annual concert "Abbaji" organised by Ustad Zakir Hussain. The concert featured several renowned musicians who came together to pay tribute to the legendary Guru, Ustad Allah Rakha Khan.

Concert on Indian Classical Music Reliance supported '8 Prahar', an event dedicated to Indian classical music. This unique event, jointly initiated by Art and Artistes and Pancham Nishad, brought together leading exponents of classical music, including Padma Vibhushan Sangeet Martand Pandit Jasraj to delight Mumbai's music lovers. The event featured performances from 6.30 a.m. to 3 a.m. of the next day with artistes performing the Ragas of the respective 'Prahar' (time of the day).

Beautification of Public Places Reliance works on city modernisation initiatives through its urban renewal programme in order to improve the quality of life and infrastructure in cities. The initiatives strive to improve public spaces to revitalise the ageing infrastructure and provide newer facilities. Reliance supported beautification of public places during FY 2017-18 to improve the available infrastructure for ease of people. As part of this project, protective grills on Magdalla Bridge, Hazira were installed to prevent mishaps. Three parks in the crowded urban spaces of Mumbai were revitalised with fencing and periodic maintenance services.

Contribution to Swachh Bharat: Reliance has been motivating its programme beneficiaries across rural and urban areas on the importance of cleanliness, hygiene and sanitation. As part of this, awareness campaigns are carried out to sensitise people about the advantages of cleanliness. Reliance has been an active participant in the ambitious Swachh Bharat Mission of Government of India.

Campaign on Swachhata Hi Seva: Reliance Foundation launched a massive awareness and cleanliness campaign titled Swachhata Hi Seva across the country. The week-long campaign organised during September-October, 2017 aimed at supporting the Government of India's Swachh Bharat Mission. The campaign mobilised communities and enabled them to actively participate in the Swachh Bharat Mission by 'shramdaan', that is, donating labour. The campaign covered 15 States and Union Territories and engaged around 1,00,000 people.

These campaigns actively engage community members to drive change. Sensitised villagers are leveraging government schemes and constructing toilets. Almost 15,000 toilets have been constructed so far and 87 villages declared as Open Defecation Free by the government. Through digital platforms, people were informed about the application procedure for availing the benefits of government schemes such as Sardar Awas Yojana, Pradhan Mantri Gramin Awas Yojana, and so on.

Empowering Women through Collectivisation and Financial Literacy: For various socio-cultural reasons, women have been a disadvantaged group in India. Driven by its belief in inclusive growth, Reliance with its experience of working with marginalised communities, undertook systematic efforts for accelerating financial inclusion by promoting financial literacy among them. Under this programme, participants would learn the nuances of personal finance, importance of savings and would get formally linked to at least one formal financial institution. Besides, rural women have been supported to form

Women Thrift Groups providing them a platform to participate, drive and manage the socio-economic change while being financially self-reliant. Reliance's initiatives for women take intervention areas closer to achieving SDG 5 (Gender Equality).

The model has not only helped in wealth creation but also enabled women in making their presence felt in male-dominated spaces. Besides starting their own enterprises, women have taken the lead in addressing the pressing issues related to health, hygiene and sanitation that affect them and their families. Till date, over 12,000 women have been provided financial literacy trainings and 3,000+ rural women have formed 110 thrift groups across 14 districts in 7 states, having collected over '4.5 million

Skilling and Employment: Skilling the youth and creating right employment opportunities for them is Government's key priority. Through its skilling and employment programme, Reliance is working to make the youth employable by equipping them with marketable skillsets and providing placement support. This year, nearly 11,000 youth were provided skill training, of which 70 percent were assisted with placements across retail and other sector.

Across rural areas, skill enhancement trainings were provided to around 3,000 women and girls. These trainings include paper quilling, jewellery, LED bulb and lamp making, tailoring and embroidery. Through another initiative, in addition to traditional medium of sales, 700+women were taught to create Facebook page and WhatsApp groups to sell their products. Together, the various skilling initiatives have benefited over 13,800 individuals across India.

Wildlife Conservation and Animal Welfare: Reliance supports several organisations that are working for wildlife conservation and animal welfare. These organisations protect wildlife against poachers, reducing the incidence of wild animals straying into human settlements, provide relief and rehabilitation support to the injured wild and domestic animals including rescue, treatment and surgical care, providing shelter, etc. These organisations also sensitise communities about the importance of protecting wildlife, and avoiding human-animal conflict.

Shiv Nadar Foundation

Established in 1994, the Shiv Nadar Foundation has focused primarily on creating iconic institutions of excellence in learning across the education spectrum. The Foundation was conceived and created by Shiv Nadar, founder and chairman of HCL - a $6.3 billion global technology and IT enterprise. Mr. Nadar being a product of education himself strongly supports the vision that education empowers individuals and is vital to reap India's demographic dividend.

Since its inception, SNF has striven to promote inclusive education, make higher education more effective and quality-oriented catering to the specific needs of the job market, enhance the focus on research and contribute to areas of global and national relevance.

The quality of education in India has sadly been losing ground in the past decade although the enrollment numbers have seen considerable increase. The Foundation has focused on "quality" and not on "quantity". The aim has been to create leaders in every field from the most underprivileged sections of the society.

Today the Foundation is reaching out to students at both the school and university level across urban and rural India. The objective is to leverage the power of inclusive education and make measurable high impact difference in the lives of the children and the youth. The Foundation aims to achieve this through the route of Creative Philanthropy. The potential impact of Creative philanthropy is that if it impacts 10,000 students in the next 10 years, each one of them has the power to touch several other lives. The concept is that of a force multiplier impact on millions of lives – individuals, communities and the nation at large. The aim is to create "spirals of inspiration" that can drive real inclusive growth for the future. The Foundation is unique in its creative rather than corrective approach and has a more focused outreach rather than the mass-based approach. This is a conscious decision bearing in mind that we are committed to creating leaders, who in turn will become the change agents of tomorrow.

The Shiv Nadar Foundation pursues philosophy of 'Creative Philanthropy'. It is a powerful model which envisages creation of institutions that go beyond the lifetime of its founders and continue to impact future generations for many centuries to come. It is an approach that allows sustained institutionalized philanthropy for long-term, high impact, socio-economic transformation.

Nation building through transformational leadership.

Creating equitable opportunities for leadership, through focused philanthropy

The key pillars of Shiv Nadar Foundation

Leadership Building: Shiv Nadar Foundation aspires to build leaders of tomorrow, by empowering the youth with a future driven by knowledge, acumen, skills, values, and principles through quality education.

Creative vs. Corrective: Looking beyond the 'corrective philanthropy' approach, where issues are identified and addressed through time-bound, project-based initiatives, Shiv Nadar Foundation is driven by 'creative philanthropy' as its guiding philosophy to achieve sustainable high-impact socio-economic transformation. This model affords sustained institutionalised philanthropy as a lasting force multiplier that impacts associated individuals and the society en masse.

Transparency and Governance: As an organisation, the board of trustees and the management at Shiv Nadar Foundation work towards ensuring that the Foundation functions with optimal responsibility and highest standards of functional transparency and governance. With transparency at the core of its operations, Shiv Nadar Foundation is one of the few private Foundations in India that publish an Annual Report with audited financial figures. The working practices align with a set of stringent policies, including committee charters, standards of independence and code of ethics that ensure the philanthropic objectives are met unwaveringly.

Longevity: With its focused vision and unflinching commitment, Shiv Nadar Foundation aims to create institutions that continue on beyond the lifespan of its founders for centuries to come.

Sustainability: With a heritage of conceptualising and building global institutions in education and technology, Shiv Nadar Foundation seeks models of education that are sustainable, scalable and replicable across geographics and societies. With sustainability at the foundation of all ventures, the Foundation seeks to establish institutions of lasting impact that have the power to transform generations.

Partnerships: Shiv Nadar Foundation is committed to pioneering creative partnerships for fortifying its founding pillars with trusted partners who work together as allies in achieving the common goal of fostering avenues for inclusive, transformational education.

A favourable mix of demographic, economic and other factors are propelling India as an emerging world power. With a population as huge and as young as ours, India possesses unlimited potential, which if tapped into efficaciously, has the power to steer the nation towards limitless growth, prosperity, and happiness. However, India too has its own unique set of challenges which must be overcome in order to unleash the vast potential it holds. It is the need of the hour to ensure the youth of today are the catalysts of change tomorrow and leadership building becomes an integral human development paradigm.

The importance of education towards this end cannot be overemphasized SNF beliefs education is fundamental to stimulating growth and empowerment. However, it must not be limited to a matter of eradicating illiteracy and creating employment, but creating leaders in all walks of life who will be the building blocks of tomorrow. Transformational education in that sense is a powerful tool that goes beyond traditional boundaries to transform lives and empower nations. And by adopting creative philanthropy as an enabler, the Foundation seeks to touch lives of students who will go on to impact several other lives, thereby creating a ripple effect impacting millions of people.

From its inception in 1994, the Foundation has ceaselessly been the metamorphosis of an education ideology that enables impactful addition to the lives, futures, and aspirations of the young across the country. Committed towards creation of a more egalitarian society, it seeks youth empowerment through an education system which is radically inclusive and fundamentally exhaustive.

To this cause, SNF have dedicated itself through building institutions of learning and value creation. SNF envision a society guided by the pillars of leadership building, creative philanthropy, transparency, and longevity. SNF believe that transformational and inclusive learning can empower our nation with a future driven by knowledge, acumen, skills, values, and principles. And that's why the Shiv Nadar Foundation works towards creating institutions of lasting impact that have the power to transform future generations. Education is, and will be the most powerful tool for individual and social change and we must do all it takes to facilitate it.

Creative Philanthropy: By creating educational institutions of excellence that seek to prosper as an established culture, foster and catalyse change, and continue to transform lives perpetually, the concept of creative philanthropy is rooted deeply in the guiding philosophies of Shiv Nadar Foundation.

Looking beyond the conventional 'corrective philanthropy' approach, where gaps are identified and addressed through time-bound, project-based, large-scale initiatives, Shiv Nadar envisages 'creative philanthropy' as a means towards sustainable high-impact socio-economic transformation. This model affords sustained institutionalised philanthropy as a lasting force multiplier that impacts associated individuals and the society en masse.

Transformational Education: The initiatives of the Shiv Nadar Foundation are grounded in the realms of transformational education. With the belief that holistic learning is one of the most potent transformation tools, the Foundation works towards mass outreach of high impact education with the potential to change lives forever. Shiv Nadar chose education as a field to channelise his philanthropy endeavours because he believes himself to be a product of education, which played a pivotal role in his life. It is his personal conviction in this belief that drives the Foundation towards transformational education for proactively reaping large demographic dividend. By providing state-of-the-art environments to students irrespective of their socio-economic background, the Foundation forges inclusive learning as the single largest tool for mass transformation.

Transparency and Governance: As an organisation, Shiv Nadar Foundation focuses on transparency and governance as an embedded work flow paradigm. Together, the board of trustees and the management work towards ensuring that the Foundation functions with optimal responsibility, with the highest standards of functional transparency and governance.

The working practices align with a set of stringent policies, including committee charters, standards of independence and code of ethics that ensure the philanthropic objectives are met unwaveringly. The board works autonomously as an authority that oversees, develops and approves the core strategies, objectives, funding policies, budget allocation, and monitoring and reviewing of regulatory standards with keen focus on statutory and operational transparency.

Power of Education: "Education is the most powerful weapon which you can use to change the world"- Nelson Mandela

Education is every child's right and a global issue. The need to educate every boy and girl is gradually seeping into every corner of the world, but the real purpose of education is still widely misconstrued to be just a means to financial independence. In its wider ambit, education is a platform to transform lives at the most fundamental level.

In fact, the solution to most of the deep-rooted problems prevalent in society such as unemployment, poverty, inequality, corruption, etc. lies in extending the reach of education to every corner of the world. It is no wonder that education is one of three parameters that make up the Human Development Index (HDI), a statistical tool used to assess the development of the people of a country. Countries with high Education Index- Norway (0.910), Australia (0.927), Switzerland (0.844), Netherlands (0.894), and United States (0.890) – therefore also naturally rank the highest in the HDI list. While there are other factors involved, the strong correlation between education and economic development too cannot be ignored. Education and economic growth go hand in hand, and hence countries consisting of a more educated population have the highest per capita incomes, and vice versa. One can clearly see the difference education has made even within different parts of India. The difference in reach and standard of education is one of the many factors contributing to the huge disparity between states in terms of the Net State Domestic Product.

Education is the bedrock of transformation for many illustrious personalities across the world, most notable of whom perhaps is Dr. A.P.J Abdul Kalam. His life's journey from a student who sold newspapers to support his family to the 11th President of India, the largest democracy in the world, has inspired countless people. He attributed his achievements to his years as a student supported by virtues like unwavering commitment, a strong desire to learn, and dedication.

There are many such success stories that clearly testify the power of education and how education, as beautifully stated by Nelson Mandela, is a weapon that can be used to change the world.

Shiv Nadar University: The University is a comprehensive, multidisciplinary, research-focused and student-centric institution that seeks to bring a paradigm shift in higher education in India through its innovative curriculum, interdisciplinary focus, and cross-disciplinary thinking across a wide range of disciplines. The University is building an eco-system of knowledge to promote recognition of the inter-connectedness of ideas, systems, and environments in the world inside the campus, and those outside it.

The University has 5 Schools, 16 Departments and 6 Research Centers engaged in teaching, practice, and research in disciplines as diverse as Engineering, Humanities & Social Sciences, Management, Natural Sciences, Art, Design, Performing Arts, Communication, and Extended Education & Professional Development. The schools offer Bachelor, Masters, and Doctoral degrees along with multidisciplinary curriculum to enable students to explore subjects and disciplines that may be widely different from their chosen Majors. In the near future, an estimated 8000 students will be enrolled at Shiv Nadar University.

Shiv Nadar University is built on a sprawling campus spread over 286 acres of land with state-of-the-art infrastructure, sophisticated laboratories, international standard sports facilities, amphitheaters, auditoriums, conference rooms, and smart classrooms. A natural water body in the campus is home to vivid flora and fauna such as migratory birds, wooded groves, palm tree clusters, and more.

Shiv Nadar University was established by the Act no 12 of 2011 of State Legislature of Uttar Pradesh as a State Private University, and was empowered by the UGC to award degrees under Section 22 of the UGC Act, 1956. The University is currently registered with DSIR, Government of India as a Research Institution.

School of Engineering Launched in August 2011, the School of Engineering (SoE) is a pioneering effort in the field of engineering under the aegis of Shiv Nadar University. The School of Engineering aims to provide an international ambience in a local setting with innovative and engaging teaching methods, international guest speakers and key partnerships in research. The institute encourages group learning and provides value-added hard and soft skills workshops along with key internships each summer.

School of Engineering aims to combine research and education at the undergraduate level itself. Drawing upon the rich experience of the SNF in setting up the SSN College of Engineering, the SSN School of Management and Computer Applications and the SSN School of Advanced Software Engineering (in a tie-up with Carnegie Mellon University, Pittsburgh, USA) near Chennai, the School of Engineering has been designed to help students get a well-rounded academic and co-curricular experience.

The School of Engineering currently offers Undergraduate and Doctoral programs in Chemical Engineering, Civil Engineering, Computer Science and Engineering, Electrical Engineering, Electronics and Communication Engineering and Mechanical Engineering. The School of Engineering also provides meritorious applicants with scholarships, internships and other opportunities to enable them to get the finest education.

School of Natural Sciences: Launched in August 2011, the School of Natural Sciences (SoNS) is a pioneering effort for the creation and dissemination of knowledge in the field of natural sciences under the aegis of the Shiv Nadar University.

The School of Natural Sciences aims to provide an international ambience in a local setting with innovative and engaging teaching methods, globally benchmarked curricula, world class faculty, and key partnerships in research. The institute encourages group learning and provides value-added hard and soft skills workshops along with key internships each summer. Undergraduate and Postgraduate programs have been designed on the basis of SNU's underlying philosophy of interdisciplinary and research-led learning.

Located in Greater Noida, Uttar Pradesh and set amidst an integrated, self-sustaining, fully residential green campus, the School of Natural Sciences combines research and education at the undergraduate level itself. The School of Natural Sciences will provide meritorious applicants with scholarships, internships and other opportunities to enable them to get the finest education.

School of Humanities and Social Sciences: In keeping with the overall objective of the Shiv Nadar University, the School of Humanities and Social Sciences (SoHSS) will not only help students distil and assimilate the knowledge that already exists, but also develop new and deeper insights to add to the stock of existing knowledge.

This will be made possible by rigorous classroom teaching, round-the-clock interaction among students from different disciplines housed in the same campus and faculty that follows a single dictum "Good researchers make good teachers." Students will be taught both the abstractions necessary for scientific enquiry and the skills needed to solve immediate and local problems. SNU students will therefore, be adept at whatever career they choose, be it in business, government, or research.

School of Management and Entrepreneurship: The School of Management and Entrepreneurship (SME) has been created to usher in a paradigm shift in business education in India. At a time of global uncertainty, volatility and rapid technological disruption, SME aims to develop leaders who are ready to be successful globally in India; for India and the world.

In addition to a focus on global career readiness and cross-cultural management skills, the SME programs at both the MBA and undergraduate level are distinct because of their focus on the Digital Economy and on providing opportunities for multiple high demand specializations such as Financial Engineering - Quantitative Finance & Trading; E-commerce and Digital Marketing; Data Science and Predictive Analytics; Sustainability & Environmental leadership etc.

SME also strongly believes in a balance between knowledge and career skills at one end and self-awareness, values driven leadership development at the other. Accordingly, there is an important emphasis on experiential learning, strategic thinking and creativity, overseas exposure and personalized coaching. The program encourages diversity of ideas, people and exposure leads to enable innovative thinking and breakthrough solutions to transform society.

School of Extended Education and Professional Development (SEEPD): The School of Extended Education and Professional Development (SEEPD) is being launched with a single overarching mission: to present best-in-class knowledge, practices and skill development offerings to the rapidly expanding Shiv Nadar University ecosystem of learners and leaders, both within and outside the university.

The school will focus on three large segments of learning: Executive Education & Leadership Development programs aimed at business, government and social sector organizations; Continuing Education, Professional Certification and Skill Building courses for individuals and organizations interested in enhancing employability and job performance; and novel University Extension offerings on topics of interest to a broader community of adult learners. This substantial last group may not be eligible or even seeking degrees/diplomas but will be driven by a desire to learn from the best faculty in each field of study - at both Shiv Nadar University and from around the world. For them, SEEPD will act as the gateway to enhanced learning on topics that excite them.

The term "Extended Education" was chosen for the school after much reflection and is intended to accurately reflect a core premise that the learning journey is never over for anyone. It underscores twin commitments made by our founder, the Chancellor and Vice Chancellor that Shiv Nadar University is fundamentally student centric in its design and evolution and is on its way to becoming a world class multidisciplinary institution known for its cutting edge research and innovative teaching.

The first commitment suggests that SEEPD will specifically cater to Shiv Nadar University students, alumni, faculty and staff with a slate of high value "lifetime learning" offerings. Once with Shiv Nadar University, this community and its natural extensions will always remain a key part of our learning family. SEEPD will aggressively market its portfolio of knowledge resources to the world at large but serving its immediate family, par excellence, will remain one of its important anchors.

The second commitment is also central to SEEPD. It is driven to identify, expertly curate and present the very best of Shiv Nadar University's rich intellectual resources to the world of learners at all levels. The goal is to create a 'necklace of pearls' from the Shiv Nadar University community to supplement the distinguished external faculty, programs and resources who may be enlisted by SEEPD to deliver its courses.

Big Data Analytics Center: The Big Data Analytics Center (BDAC) is an interdisciplinary center set up under the aegis of the School of Natural

Sciences (SoNS), Shiv Nadar University in 2014. 'Big Data' refers to the collection of data sets whose scale, diversity and complexity require new architecture, techniques, algorithms and analysis to manage it, and extract value and hidden knowledge from it. Use of information has become central for the survival and development of the human race. Today we experience a true deluge of data which record and shape our lives, ranging from large global issues such as climate change to the smallest local problem such as controlling a thermostat. The critical screening and processing of Big Data has become a worldwide effort, requiring academic attention from diverse disciplines. The challenge is to develop theoretical and innovative scientific and technological solutions to cater to the needs of the industry, the society and the environment.

Given the wide gap between demand and supply of scientists, technologists and key experts in the domain of Data Analytics today, BDAC has initiated graduate (post-graduate diploma and Masters degree) programs to prepare the interested young minds for the academic analysis of such Big Data and its applications in the society today, from business concerns to social practices and cultural change.

The integrated model of BDAC provides a unique opportunity to young aspirants from different academic disciplines and executives from the corporate world to explore the possibilities of next generation solutions in the emerging discipline of Big Data Analytics.

In the view of ever more rapid technological developments in the digitalized world, with new solutions becoming obsolete every few years, the emphasis in our programs is to hone the ability to recognize, define and find solutions to such fundamental problems in an analytical way, to take a leading role in shaping the future society

Center for Emerging Societies: The Center for Emerging Societies (CES) is a center for research under the aegis of the School of Humanities and Social Sciences, Shiv Nadar University. CES aims to produce and disseminate cutting edge research in issues relating to emerging societies and, to that end, create an eco-system of high quality research in India and Asia. The activities of the center are interdisciplinary and the scope of the activities encompasses academic and policy research in subject matters in three areas: emerging market finance, development economics, and law and regulation of capital markets and institutions.

A special focus of the center is to explore mechanisms to expand access to capital markets and institutions for the underserved sectors, especially (but not exclusively) small and medium enterprises and rural households. In addition to knowledge creation and knowledge maintenance, an important objective of the center will be to disseminate the knowledge to the stakeholders through conferences, workshops, and lectures organized by the center as well as through participation in similar forums organized by others. The relevant stakeholders of the center are academicians interested in emerging economies and societies, policy-makers and regulators, and practitioners engaged in emerging markets and institutions.

Center for Environmental Sciences & Engineering: Taking cognizance of increasing environmental problems and to tackle these challenges scientifically and proactively for problem solving, the Center for Environmental Sciences & Engineering (CESE) is conceived in the School of Natural Sciences (SoNS), SNU with the specific objective of creating an interdisciplinary research facility integrating the fields of Science, Natural Resources, Engineering, Social Sciences, Public Policy and Law. The problems will be addressed keeping in view of depleting scarce natural resources and much needed sustainable development of the country. The Center will maintain close liaison with other Schools (SoE, SoHSS, SME) in SNU, and other Departments within SoNS (Life Sciences, Chemistry, Physics) to bring inter- and multi-disciplinarity in research.

The Vision of the Center for Environmental Sciences & Engineering (CESE) is to become a leader in environmental science research in the country by conducting problem solving inter/multidisciplinary research in niche areas and meeting the needs of the society, industry and National and International agencies/ organizations. The Center will provide advance training to students in Environmental Science, Natural Resource Management, Socio-economics, Public Policy and Engineering from the environment perspective for sustainable development.

The Mission of the Center is to undertake focused high quality interdisciplinary basic and applied research on key areas of environmental issues crossing the boundaries of traditional disciplines to look at the relationship between humans and their environment, natural as well as built, and the sets of relationships between them from a variety of perspective leading to technology development and competency building in various areas related to environmental problems, thereby providing solutions to Indian industry and policy makers. The programs and activities of the CESE are designed to address the needs and challenges to meet the current environmental issues/problems of major industrial sectors, governmental sectors, international agencies and various funding institutions.

The Center will carry out research in different aspects of Environmental Sciences, Natural Resources, Social Sciences, Engineering, including research in the fields of Ecology, Biodiversity, Energy, Biofuel, Aerosols and Air Quality, Water and Wastewater Treatment; Environmental Biotechnology, Clean Technology, Environmental Remediation Technology-filters, membranes and catalysts and adsorbents for effective remediation of contaminants in air, soil and water environments, Environmental Systems Modeling and Optimization; Environmental Impact Assessment, GIS and Remote Sensing, Climate Change Impact Assessment, Municipal/Industrial/ Hazardous Waste Management, Engineering and policy solutions to environmental risks; Environmental and Resource Policy; Environment and Developmental Economics; Environmental Management, Environmental Management and Social Ecology; Environmental Ethics; Environmental Governance; Environmental Health and Risk Assessment; Environmental Laws and Policies; Policy Studies, etc.

Through sustainability approach the CESE will strive to find solutions to the stress caused due to pressing global environmental issues such as global climate change, the food production and distribution system, conserving and recovering biodiversity, restoring ecosystem function, etc. The Center will also focus in creating conditions for sustainable businesses and society with environmental approach.

The Center will establish a tripartite relationship between academia, industry and the government agencies to nurture and support growth of environmental science and technology. The Center will also be actively engaged in a variety of outreach programmes, including organizing workshops, conferences, trainings and extension activities, which will attract participants from academia, industries and governmental and nongovernmental sectors.

Center of Informatics: Informatics is the science of information, information processing, and the study of structures, algorithms, behavior, and interactions of natural and artificial systems that store, process, access and communicate information. The science of informatics thus overlaps a wide range of disciplines.

Specific research programs and areas in the Center for Informatics at SNU are set by the individual faculty, who nucleate inter-disciplinary research in select areas, exploiting synergies between overlapping programs in one or more schools at SNU. Currently active areas of interest include:

- Bioinformatics and Cheminformatics
- Computational Nanoscience
- Design of Organic Dyes and Organic/Polymer Semiconductors
- Computational Facilities

Computational facilities at the SNU Informatics Center include Magus, a 32-node, 512-core IBM HPC cluster, delivering a theoretical peak performance of 10.649 TF. Each compute node is powered with dual Intel Xeon E5-2670 8C 2.6 GHz 20 MB cache 1600 MHz processors. A high-speed Infiniband switch provides the primary interconnect. Two Master nodes are loaded with 24 TB of Raw Storage. Two GPU nodes are also networked to the HPC cluster. Additionally several stand-alone Linux computers are used for teaching and research purposes, and as license servers.

Center for Public Affairs & Critical Theory: Center for Public Affairs and Critical Theory (C-PACT) has been established under the aegis of the School of Humanities and Social Sciences, Shiv Nadar University (SNU) to pursue inter-disciplinary research on social policies. It is important to examine social reality from diverse perspectives so that the outcomes of such exercises are accessible across academic specialties and to the members of the general public as well.

C-PACT's research on social policy will meet the highest academic standards such that they contribute to scholarship as well as to actual policy formulations on the ground. By converting research into viable solutions C-PACT aims to address the pressing problems of the day without being partisan or biased towards any political or academic persuasion. In the ultimate analysis, scholars and fellows of C-PACT hope to advance citizenship in practice through their research activities.

Institute for Innovations & Inventions with Mathematics and Information Technology: The Institute for Innovation and Inventions with Mathematics and IT (IIIMIT) has been established in collaboration with the Mathematical Sciences Foundation (MSF). Its emphasis on an integrated research and education program that brings together academia, industry and society makes IIIMIT unique among mathematics institutes in India.

IIIMIT has been envisioned as an expansion of the decade-long activities of the MSF. MSF has created numerous high-value activities in training and research that have involved teachers, students, scientists, government and private institutions and other segments of society.

IIIMIT primarily focuses on the following activities:

Applications of mathematics and information technology to real-world problems

Creation of a training and research platform for teachers and students

Involve and train - in innovation - people drawn from various sectors of academia and industry, including college teachers and undergraduate students.

At present, IIIMIT faculty members are carrying out research in the fields of geology, optimisation, dynamical systems, computational finance and mathematics education. IIIMIT conducts a teaching program Excel in Business for students in Kashmir, and hosts a month-long summer internship program called Inviting All Young Minds (IAYM) every June.

Focus group has been initiated:

- Computational Finance
- Mathematics Education

In future, we expect to create further focus groups in areas such as Cryptography, Signal Processing and Mathematical Biology.

Global Collaborations

E-QUAL: The University is part of the international collaborative project titled Enhancing Quality, Access and Governance of Undergraduate Education in India (E-QUAL), 2013. Funded by the European Union and British Council, the €1.17 million project is implemented by a consortium of partners including Ambedkar University, Jadavpur University, King's College, Shiv Nadar University, the University of Bologna, and the University of Hyderabad. The project activities are being implemented in four key disciplines - Critical Thinking, Cultural Studies, Human Ecology, Natural Resource Management & Sustainable Development.

Shiv Nadar School: A child learns in many ways - questioning adults, collaborating with peers, and experiencing the world through his or her unique perspective. Shiv Nadar School transforms these ways of learning into a methodology of relevance. This means that every child at our schools is equipped with a toolkit of concepts, skills and knowledge, which he or she can shape into endless possibilities and solutions. In a dynamic and shifting world, this kind of learning impacts individual growth as well as global consciousness.

The Seeds of Learning: A joyful and secure environment gives the children in SNS pre-primary classes the freedom to be curious, to wonder, to find their own trajectory of exploration while making sense of their new world. Learning in this way transforms them into lifelong learners. They associate learning with magical, exciting discoveries that they make independently through our hallmark experiential programme, inside and outside the classroom. If you enter a pre-primary classroom at Shiv Nadar School, you might see a child playing with blocks, or dancing, or going for a walk, or drawing. This is actually curriculum in action, provoking the youngest of the students to explore, experience, investigate and comprehend through play. SNS design joyous activities for each domain of learning with care and research-based precision. Even the physical spaces and structures the children interact with everyday are deliberately designed to reflect SNS thinking.

The Happiness Curriculum: Theme-based lessons let the children engage with diverse concepts, from junior math to learning about themselves and their world, to literacy and the arts. The whole spectrum of development from cognitive to emotional to physical is encompassed in these lessons. They imbibe vital skills like decision-making, taking turns, sharing, persistence, creativity and problem solving. They learn to recycle. They participate in events and celebrations, and go on short field trips. During Circle Time, they learn the all-important abilities of communicating and listening, to both peers and teachers.

The Personal, Social and Emotional Development of the children in SNS care, or the 'happiness curriculum' is the centre of SNS world-view. Children love to come to school! Based on international best practices, yet rooted in Indian contexts and values, progressive pre-primary programme births holistic and positive personalities.

I get it. I love it. I want it. Where is it?

These are the components of what is called 'the element'. Translated into the language of educators, it simply means that if a child has an aptitude for something and a passion for it; if he has the right attitude and the opportunity to experience it, he will be in his 'element'

When people are in their element, they connect with something fundamental to their sense of identity, purpose and well-being. Being there provides a sense of self-revelation, of defining who they really are and what they are meant to be doing with their lives. Hence, finding one's element is essential to one's well-being and ultimate success - **Ken Robinson**

Corporate Volunteer programs: Contributing as a volunteer is an integral extension of both organisational and personal development. Many organizations regularly encourage their employees to volunteer for causes they relate to as it offers numerous potential gains such as improving employee involvement, development of soft skills such as leadership capabilities, etc. The Shiv Nadar Foundation envisions innovative corporate volunteering opportunities at its leadership institutions.

Corporate Volunteering—where we step in!

Engagement facilitator with rural students

- Through well-planned entrepreneurial projects
- Tutoring students
- Culturally driven programmes for students involving dramatics, dance, etc.
- Art & craft projects with students.
- Drive collaboration among students with activities such as debating/ public speaking.
- Educational seminars, programmes, etc.
- Soft-skill development
- Book drives

Sports volunteering opportunities

- Sports coaching
- Equipment collection and inventory management
- Conducting matches between corporates and students

Cultural volunteer opportunities

- Organize cultural shows
- Equipment collection and inventory management

- Conducting matches between corporates and students
- Art competitions & exhibitions with/for students
- Yoga, exercise or relaxation classes

Volunteer Guidelines Training: Each volunteer group receives an exhaustive tour of the institution.

Qualification

- Skills to match the activity
- Members should be chosen by the corporate think-tank or be part of the corporate employee engagement programme
- Positive, friendly, lively & energetic attitude

Time commitment: **A structured program factoring in detailed timelines and deliverables is developed to facilitate project tracking and progress. Regular attendance is vital to benchmark project success.**

Corporate Giving: Contributing as a volunteer is an integral extension of both organisational and personal development. Many organizations regularly encourage their employees to volunteer for causes they relate to as it offers numerous potential gains such as improving employee involvement, development of soft skills such as leadership capabilities, etc. The Shiv Nadar Foundation envisions innovative corporate volunteering opportunities at its leadership institutions.

The Shiv Nadar Foundation has set an innovative model for rural and underprivileged students from Uttar Pradesh. The Foundation handpicks meritorious students who are supported and nurtured for seven years in a coordinated academic ecosystem. Corporates rooting for rural talent are welcome to step in to support bright and gifted students to pursue higher education both in India and abroad. This will give them wings to chase their dreams and meet their aspirations.

Global intership programme: SNF Global Internship Programme exposes students to real-world experiences; enabling them to create entrepreneurial solutions specific to the communities they belong to

Programme Objective: To develop a start-up accelerator programme, 'Working on Your Own Venture'. Shiv Nadar Foundation encourages post-graduate students from leading US, UK and Canadian varsities to come to India and explore entrepreneurship through pilot projects at the Vidya Gyan Leadership Academy, a Foundation initiative for meritorious rural under privileged students. Students get to work on critical entrepreneurship aspects by developing, strategizing and executing theme projects for the academy and its beneficiaries.

Kiran Nadar Museum of Arts (KNMA): KNMA is a private modern and contemporary art museum with locations in New Delhi, and Noida.

Established in 2010, it is India's first private museum dedicated to modern and contemporary art. The core collection of the institution comprises post-independence 20th century painters, but the museum holds exhibits of younger, contemporary artists as well.

Inspired by the Guggenheim, MoMA, and the Whitney, which all started out as private museums, art collector and philanthropist Kiran Nadar established the museum in 2010. It started out as a gallery created from the cafeteria of her husband's office outside Delhi. Later, it moved into South Court Mall, a shopping mall, to encourage average mall-goers to enjoy art. The New Delhi location has about 18,000 sq ft of exhibition space and the Noida location has 13,000 sq ft.

Established at the initiative of the avid art collector Kiran Nadar, the Kiran Nadar Museum of Art (KNMA) opened its doors to the public in January 2010, as the first private museum of art exhibiting Modern and contemporary works from India and the sub-continent. Located in the heart of New Delhi, India's capital city, KNMA as a non-commercial, not-for-profit organization intends to exemplify the dynamic relationship between art and culture through its exhibitions, publications, educational, and public programs.

The ever-growing collection of KNMA is largely focused on significant trajectories. Its core collection highlights a magnificent generation of 20th century Indian painters from the post-Independent decades and equally engages the different art practices of the younger contemporaries.

In Kiran Nadar's words, "Though the idea of opening a private art museum occurred with the intention of sharing my art collection with the larger public, I was also acutely aware of the existing dearth of institutional spaces that could bring visibility to modern and contemporary art from India and the subcontinent".

Sponsored by the Shiv Nadar Foundation, KNMA is plugging the lack of art promotion in the public sphere and is working towards encouraging art appreciation. KNMA aspires to become a place for confluence, through its curatorial initiative and exhibitions, school and college workshops, art appreciation discourses, symposiums and public programs. It is focused on bridging the gap between art and the public and fostering a museum-going culture in India. In order to activate the museum as a site for visual and intellectual dialogue, the museum aims to develop innovative programs that seek active collaborations from artists as well as the public.

KNMA is a noteworthy addition to the list of private art museums that are a part of the shift occurring in the art world across the globe with increasing number of collectors bringing out their collections to the public. The 34,000 square feet museum space has housed several critically acclaimed exhibitions that have celebrated Modern and contemporary art in the country and abroad. KNMA upholds the tradition of art patronage and continues to expand that definition through its education initiatives. It also collaborates with schools, colleges, NGOS, trusts this diffusion of knowledge is achieved through regular workshops where adults and children alike get to learn about new art forms and techniques as well as benefit from their interactions with the artists who frequently head these programs. Screenings of films, stimulating curatorial programs, and curated walks form an integral part of the museum's ever expanding itinerary.

Volunteer Programme: KNMA encourages individuals from diverse backgrounds and age-groups to volunteer, contribute, and become part of the museum. Through the Volunteer Programme, individuals are invited to learn and participate actively in various outreach and educational activities, guided tours, workshops, surveys, and research for various community projects. KNMA encourage multi-lingual interactions in the museum, and welcome fresh energy and ideas. Professionals and students who are looking for exciting interactions with art, artists, and community work are encouraged to apply for the programme.

Internship: The internships offered at KNMA are intense and cater to budding art professionals, fresh graduates from the Humanities, young artists who aim to be groomed and trained in the fields ranging from art handling and management, art historical research, curation, publishing, design, archiving, exhibition production, communications and social media, art education, and outreach etc. KNMA Interns are also encouraged to work on individual short-term projects.

Corporate Support: The Kiran Nadar Museum of Art is a leading not-for-profit arts organisation in the country. The museum has gained recognition across the world for its unique vision through regular collaborations with major international museums, loaning of artworks from the KNMA collection to international exhibitions and festivals, and supporting new artistic and cultural production in innovative ways. KNMA has become a place to project and showcase the tremendous cultural potential of the south Asian region. We encourage our vision to be furthered through partnerships with the business community the cultural spaces in India and South Asia such as KNMA can benefit greatly with the support and involvement of corporate organisations. Corporate support for the arts reflects not just their commitment to culture and philanthropy but also a service to knowledge production, skill building, and creating innovative models for public-private partnerships.

Corporate collaborations with KNMA are shared opportunities to associate with the best creative minds and help create platforms where the limits of art making and thinking can be pushed. These partnerships facilitate the strengthening of the socio-cultural eco-system within the country, and lead to a resounding impact globally.

Azim Premji Foundation

Azim Premji Foundation is a not-for profit organisation that has been working since 2000 with the elementary education system in rural government schools. The Foundation began by implementing various programmes to improve educational quality across the country. By 2010 it became clear that working on a "project" mode was inadequate and it takes continuous effort over many decades for any deep-rooted change to happen. This can only be achieved by establishing "institutions" which are embedded in the local context and can collaborate with local government structures. Thus the idea of setting up District Institutes in field locations came into being.

Today, the Foundation with 1000+ employees has field institutes in 40+ districts across 6 states and 1 union territory (Karnataka, Rajasthan, Uttarakhand, Chhattisgarh, Madhya Pradesh, Telangana and Puducherry) reaching more than 3,50,000 schools across the country.

The District Institutes work in collaboration with state governments to engage with teachers, school leaders, teacher educators and other education officials.

The range of work involves efforts to:

- improve the quality of processes and practices within schools,
- facilitate creative approaches to teaching and learning through workshops, teacher forums, seminars, melas, etc.
- build professional networks of teachers and head teachers and
- reform school curriculum, teacher-education curriculum and related issues of education policy.

The Foundation has also set up demonstration schools in Yadgir, Sirohi, Tonk, Dhamtari, Uttarkashi and Udham Singh Nagar to provide quality free education to the local community, at costs and constraints similar to that of rural government schools.

Having successfully built Wipro to be a business leader, Azim Premji felt the need to contribute to a social cause and address the various developmental challenges facing the country. Dileep Ranjekar agreed to assist him with the initial work of setting up a Foundation.

Discussions between them on the various developmental issues Wipro could work on, led to the 'White Paper on Charity' (alternatively titled 'The Social Work Plan of Wipro Corporation') on November 24, 1999. The note identified education, nutrition, healthcare and some initiatives in governance as possible areas of work. Through subsequent discussions, primary education was narrowed down as the Foundation's focus of work because it was a critical factor that significantly impacted other issues in the country.

The Azim Premji Foundation India Private Limited was registered in February 2000. Later it was re-registered as the 'Azim Premji Foundation' on

9th March 2001 under Section 25 of the Indian Companies Act of 1956. The Azim Premji Foundation was to be funded solely by Azim Premji by way of transfer of his personal shares to the Foundation. The objective of the funding was to facilitate universalisation of primary education rather than serve as a constraint in achieving it. The Foundation began its work in Karnataka and Andhra Pradesh in 2001 where the state leadership and education departments were supportive of its mandate.

This history of the Foundation can be divided into three major phases. The first phase was from 2001-2002, the second from 2002-2009 and the third is the current phase from 2009 onwards till now. In the first phase a decision was taken to work in the area of public education on the issues of equity and quality. It was also decided that the Foundation would be an operating entity and not function as a grant making organisation. During the second phase which was from 2002-2009 the Foundation worked intensively in collaboration with state governments across various states in the country. The range of work included assessment, curriculum reform, school textbook development, policy and capacity development of teachers and education functionaries. Towards the end of the second phase a conviction grew within the organisation that it had to commit to school education in a more permanent and sustainable manner.

The learnings from the seven years of working on the ground were consolidated to form the organizing principles of the current entity. The first was that if education has to fulfill its transformative power to society then it has to be a constant and continuous endeavor. Secondly, that while there is a universality to the knowledge and principles of school education, it must be brought to life in a deeply contextual manner. The third principle was that in order to attain systemic improvement it is necessary to work on all aspects of education (teacher education, curriculum, assessment, etcetera); all levels of education (early childhood, primary and secondary school, higher secondary and higher education and research in Universities) and with all stakeholders (with the school, the communities and the different levels of the education system from block to district to state).

The most important implication of the learnings from this phase was that the work of the Foundation had to be organized into institutions since institutions are permanent in nature. In concrete terms, this meant setting up district level institutions which will work on the ground and state level institutions that will work with the state on school education.

During this phase it also became evident that there was a great shortage of talent in the education sector in areas such as curriculum development, assessment reform or teacher education. There was a requirement for a number of Masters level and Ph.D. level programmes in school education. In keeping with the principle of establishing institutions, the Azim Premji University was set up by the passing of the Azim Premji University Act by the Karnataka State legislature in 2010.

The mandate of the University is not limited to school education. It includes other allied fields such as livelihoods, health, governance, and sustainability which contribute to human development as a whole. The University's purpose is to prepare education and development sector professionals who can contribute to a just equitable and humane society.

Major Initiatives (2001- Present)

2001-2008	Computer Aided Learning Programme
2002-2004	Accelerated Learning Programme
2002-2008	Learning Guarantee Programme
2004-2011	Child Friendly Schools Initiative
2003-Present	Policy Planning Unit
2004-2013	Andhra Pradesh Randomized Evaluation Study
2007-2011	Namma Shale
2010-2013	Institutional Capacity Development
2007–Present	Education for Children of Migrant Labour
2012-2015	Namma Shale Plus
2006-2016	Education Leadership Development

APF Vision, Purpose, Mission

Vision: Facilitate a just, equitable, humane and sustainable society.

The primary goal of the Foundation is to contribute to a society that is "a just, equitable, humane and sustainable society" as envisaged in the Constitution

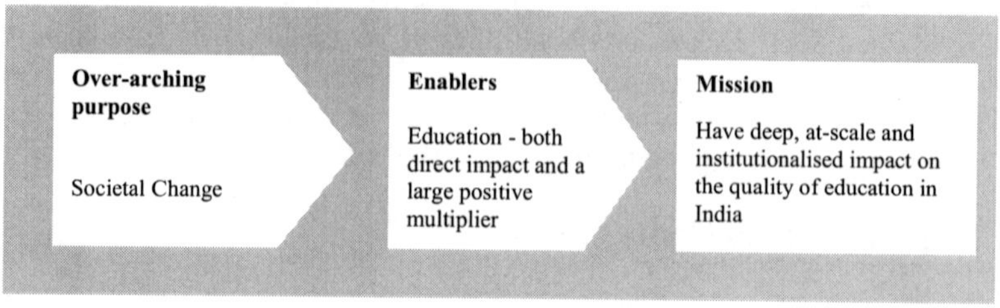

of India. Towards this goal, APU have identified education as a critical area that has direct impact on the economic, social and cultural development of the nation.

In order to concretize Foundation vision APU have established two institutions - Field Institutes and Azim Premji University.

Field Institutes: Most important change leaders for improving education quality are (a) the teacher and (b) the education administrator. The Field Institutes are district level institutions that work in collaboration with the government school system on improving the capacities of teachers, school leaders, teacher educators and other education officials. This is facilitated through multiple modes of engagements - workshops, informal learning groups, Teacher Learning Centres, exposure visits, seminars, melas, etc. In addition Foundation also works at the state-level to create enabling conditions for change.

Azim Premji University (APU): APU was established in Karnataka by the Azim Premji University Act 2010 as a not-for-profit University. The University was founded as one of the key responses to the constraints and challenges that the Foundation encountered in education and as part of a larger strategy to contribute to the education and development sectors in the country. The University administers Masters and Doctorate level teaching programmes, conducts research, and engages with the world of practice. There are close linkages between APU work in the field and the University to ensure a strong two-way connection between theory, research and actual practice.

Education in India – The Context: In the last few decades, India has made tremendous progress in different aspects of education. Access to education has increased dramatically with about 98 percent of rural habitations having a primary school within a distance of 1 km. Youth literacy rate (age group 15-24 years) has increased from 61.9 percent to 86.14 percent during the period 1991-2011.However, equity in and quality of education still remain a challenge resulting in poor learning outcomes and an overall loss of confidence in the public education system.

The sections below list out the some of the issues in different aspects of public education and the Foundation's views on addressing them.

Equity

Challenges

- India's literacy rate is at 74.04 percent (82.14 percent for males and 65.46 percent for females). The global literacy rate for all males is 90.0 percent and the rate for all females is 82.7 percent .
- The Gender Parity Index (GPI) for Gross Enrolment Ratio (GER) in primary education, has been improving steadily but more needs to be done in secondary and tertiary education. The transition rate from elementary to secondary school 94.10 percent for boys and 89.68 percent for girls, and from secondary to higher secondary it is 68.7 percent for boys and 69.3 percent for girls. The data shows a significant number of girls being left behind.
- The estimated number out of school children are 6 million. Among them a higher proportion of females, children from rural areas and ST children are out of school than others. And 28.0 percent children with special needs are out of school.

AP Foundation Views

- Classrooms must offer all students equal access and equal opportunity to achieve desired outcomes.
- Rationalize schools thoughtfully based on population, geographical terrain and safety with the caveat that proximate access in the early years is critical.
- Continue to provide cycles to older children to enable access.
- Provide a transport allowance where necessary for younger children, girls and children with special needs
- Curriculum should be flexible, broad and inclusive reflective of diverse local culture and knowledge.
- Offer a variety of learning experiences to students that help them meet their curricular goals.
- Use learning material beyond the textbook - use the local language and local resources in teaching especially during the early years.

Educational Quality

Challenges

- Several government programmes intended to improve quality have been implemented but most have not really translated into a changed reality for our students.

- The curriculum, classroom environment and pedagogical processes are not learner-centered and are primarily based on rote-learning. The prevailing modes of classroom interaction do not enable the development and unlocking of the imagination, creativity and critical thinking of the child.
- Student learning levels at all stages of education have remained well below expectations. The National Achievement Survey for class 3 conducted by NCERT in 2014 concluded that the national average for performance in language and mathematics were 64 percent and 66 percent , respectively. Though there is some improvement in recent years, much remains to be done to reach the global standard.

Teacher Education

Challenges

- The teacher is central to good education - at its very core, education is the process between the teacher and the student. If education has to improve, teaching has to improve - there is no way around this.
- There are 7.96 million (in 2013-14) school teachers in India. The private sector comprises the lion's share of teacher education Institutions in the country, with the government's share being only 9 percent (2015).
- The quality of academic support, both pre-service and in-service, provided to teachers leaves much to be desired due to poor inputs, lack of resources and a series of professional constraints. Teaching has become mostly uninteresting and routinized, leading to poor classroom processes and little learning.
- Teaching is an intellectually and ethically demanding profession. Teachers must be seen as independent, capable and responsible professionals with respect for his/her professional identity and knowledge.
- Teacher preparation must be a long duration, professional program housed in the University system. Curriculum and pedagogy in teacher education must provide for rigorous theoretical understanding along with strong practical/field connect.
- Opportunities for continuous professional development must be made available to all teachers throughout their careers.

Education Management

Challenges

- Research shows that school leadership is the second largest factor affecting learning outcomes in school. More importantly, it goes on to show that school leadership is even more critical in schools that are under performing. While currently the country invests in teacher development, investments in leadership and managerial capabilities of education functionaries are negligible.
- The system is vexed with problems of hierarchical organisation structure, political interference, uncertain tenures, lack of risk-reward etc. which need to be addressed.

AP Foundation Views

- School leaders need professional preparation, support and mentorship before and after they take on the role. They need platforms or mechanisms to interact with each other as professionals.

Public Education

Challenges

- Public education is still the largest provider of school education in India, with the government's share of schools at 75.51 percent and private schools at 22.09 percent (2013-14). However, recent years have witnessed mushrooming of a large number of private schools across the country promising 'better quality education and English learning'.

APF Views

- Research evidence from India and other countries has shown conclusively that once socio-economic background has been factored in, performance of children is the same in both public and private schools.
- A strong public education system is central to democracy and equity cannot be served by a stratified system.

Assessment

Challenges

- Standardized assessments have begun to be been seen as a way of achieving learning outcomes and teacher accountability.
- There is also an argument being made to scrap the 'No Detention' policy up to the elementary level.

APF Views

- Standardized tests have not worked anywhere in the world to improve learning outcomes – all they have done is cause stress and tension among teachers and students. Assessment is primarily of use to teachers and students as feedback for improvement – it is individual and best done at school.
- Though there are challenges in conceptualizing and implementing Continuous and Comprehensive Evaluation (CCE) - it still remains a pedagogically sound idea.
- There is no evidence to suggest that learning levels have declined since the No Detention policy was put in place - it would be more useful to focus on why learning is not happening since detention neither facilitates nor takes care of learning – though it certainly comes in the way of child continuing in school.

APF work: There are four essential components to APF work:

Developing Talent: Develop a critical mass of people with vision, competence and deep motivation to engage in social action. This includes developing fresh talent (the Azim Premji University has been set up for this purpose) and building capacity in the existing talent (through District Institutes).

Developing Institutions: Establish strong field-level institutions in the most disadvantaged districts of India. The field institutes create avenues for the continuing professional development of teachers and education officials. They also work to reform school curriculum, teacher-education curriculum and related issues of education policy.

Developing Knowledge: Create knowledge and evidence through research to address the challenges in education and development in the Indian context. In many of the states, the Foundation is engaged in large scale educational research work that will create new knowledge and also support evidence based policy making.

Building Social Pressure: Strong networking, advocacy and communications act as a multiplier to facilitate change. APF engage with the state and central governments, with the community, NGOs and industry to build positive social pressure for change.

Operating Principles: A number of key principles inform strategy and approach.

Education and other allied domains: Education is a powerful vehicle for social change and it is the primary focus of APF work. It also has a large positive multiplier effect on other aspects of human life. Related domains like health, nutrition, livelihoods, governance and ecology have a critical bearing on education. However, it is not possible for a single organization to work with equal intensity and focus in all these areas and therefore, calibrate its efforts based on the nature of the specific challenges, own capabilities and ability to work with partners and extended resources.

Operating organization: As an operating organization and not a funding organization. The District Institutes are the operating/ implementing arm of the organization.

At Scale: All work is aimed at creating large scale impact either directly or indirectly. Believe that in a large, complex and diverse country like India, small-scale, intense work in narrow pockets is unlikely to create any significant impact on the system.

Partnership with Government: Seek systemic change and work primarily for India's large underprivileged and marginalized population. Such system wide change which touches the large underprivileged population of India is possible only by working in close partnership with the government. However, seek to supplement the work of the government and not substitute it.

Integrate theory and practice: APF "academia" and "practice" teams work together synergistically. While knowledge through research is critical it must be deeply rooted in practical ground realities for applicability.

Values

APF values describe cultural ethos creating an ethically strong organization. Five values are:

- Catalyze social change with passion
- Act with integrity and courage
- Ensure intense commitment to quality
- Be deeply reflective and rational
- Be open and caring

APF teams

Azim Premji Philanthropic Initiatives (APPI)

Supporting Change makers: At the core of APPI work is the strong culture of social responsibility, ethical action and mutual respect that imbibed from its founders. These values serve as moral compasses for all actions.

While APPI recognises that it cannot solve every problem or address every issue, it aims to bring in fresh perspectives and identify how best change can be achieved so that it can support sustainable solutions.

Impactful Philanthropy: APPI mission is to facilitate a just, equitable, humane and sustainable society. It focuses on effective philanthropy—

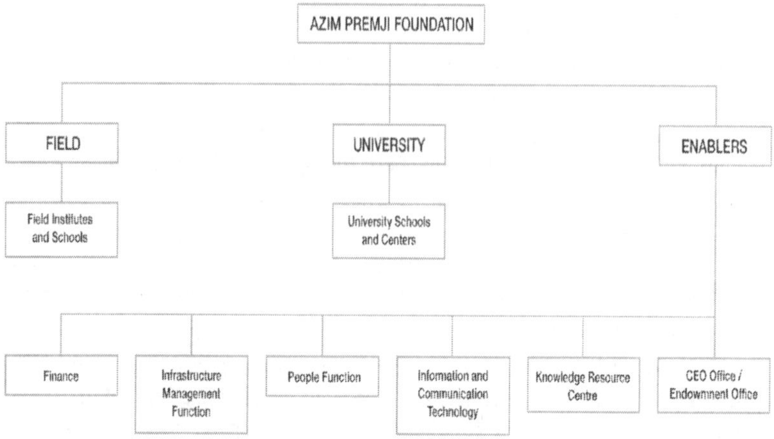

supporting projects across geographies in India, that can transform the lives of the poorest and the most vulnerable who continue to be isolated, unheard and unseen, in modern India. While it aims to meet the urgency of "here and now" needs, it aspires to bring about lasting systemic change. Also seek to contribute to an overall ecosystem that will enhance the effectiveness of all philanthropic capital.

True Partnerships: APPI aspires to build true partnerships with organisations in its chosen field of focus. Partnerships that are based on strongly shared goals and productive relationships. This means being very respectful of our partners' hard-won expertise and experience. The cornerstone of it partnerships is the framework for results that are mutually agreed upon, which clearly state what the grant is going to achieve and in what time frame.

APPI learn by doing and it plays three roles—Funder, Enabler and Orchestrator—in its quest for enduring change at the individual, the community and the system level. As Funder, give out grants to partners whose work adds intrinsic value to vulnerable individuals and communities. They are "good people doing great work", with credibility and a proven track record. A 3-year grant allows them to continue, expand and deepen the great work they already do.

As Enabler, it can offer expertise to build on APPI grant partners' inherent strengths so they can scale their work and reach significantly more people. A 5-year grant supports their organisation development and resource mobilisation capabilities in addition to scaling up the programme.

As Orchestrator, APPI focuses on system change and long-term impact. It develops Special Initiatives that synergistically bring together a number of partners and the government to achieve a particular change in a given sector.

At APPI actively champion those who are disadvantaged, discriminated against or are denied basic freedoms. People who are often overlooked in the development process and are oppressed or let down by the very system meant to benefit them.

Areas APPI work in: APPI supports grant partners with proven expertise, credibility and track record. And it backs issues or initiatives with the potential for both profound and positive impact. Through its largest portfolio of grants, its Vulnerable Groups focus area; it seeks to advance interventions wide ranging in size and scope. Here, it endorses work that is diverse in range, deep in terms of reach, and demonstrable when it comes to impact. Through its Governance focus area, APPI seeks to achieve far reaching reform by energising local communities and enabling sustained people-participation in policy-making at the panchayat level. And create awareness and access to basic freedoms and Constitutionally-guaranteed rights. It funds focused actions such as the Reducing Stunting programme in Odisha under its Nutrition focus area.

Governance: The Constitution of India envisioned a country that is truly democratic and one where citizens expect basic services and enjoy certain rights and freedoms. These are the two pillars of good governance. Unfortunately, there is a large gap between this vision and the reality on the ground. Basic services such as clean drinking water, health, education or even 100 days minimum wage are not met by the state. Here, those especially affected include the marginalised and the most vulnerable. However, the implementation of basic services and access to those services is also partly dependent on citizens holding their elected representatives to account. This is especially important for the disadvantaged. Having a voice, however, is only possible when people and communities are able and capable of being organised, especially at the local level. Similarly, while there exist systems and institutions to implement fundamental rights, there must be a vigilant civil society and an independent media to help every citizen access justice.

Multifaceted Approach: While it will always be true that good governance must ensure participation at all levels, the nature of governance today is changing. Today, many essential needs and services are being met via a public - private partnership, and even, by the private sector. The manner of providing benefits and services can also change—for instance, there can be digital money transfer of say, benefits such as PDS rations. APPI role here is to examine whether these mechanisms and systems actually work, or if going digital will further exclude the vulnerable and underserved sections of society. And to also look at whether there will be built-in accountability systems and active participation from the public within these changing systems. APPI multifaceted approach is to support research, pilot initiatives and contribute to the Government's thinking in this sphere, and inform Government policy and practice. This can be through various means including supporting the provision of better legal aid for under trials, setting up of independent media organisations, galvanising communities by working at the grassroots level, and by backing mechanisms that will produce open source data to tackle air, land and water pollution. APPI shall support grant partners working in these disparate fields, and through strategic grant-making, aim to make democracy function in a truly representative manner.

Local Democracy: The passage of the 73rd and 74th Amendments of the Constitution of India in 1993 granted powers and functions to Local Self Governments or Gram Panchayats at the village level, and Municipalities/ Municipal Corporations, in towns and large cities. They have no voice or agency over finances, allocation or the implementation of social welfare schemes meant to benefit them. APPI can play a more active role, nurture community-level leadership, and hold local representatives accountable. Through grants to partners, community coalitions and networks, it can restore and regenerate a more participative model of democracy in urban and rural areas.

Improving Air Quality: Air pollution is almost at crisis levels in India today resulting in over a million (avoidable) deaths every year from cardiovascular and chronic respiratory diseases. Pollution often tends to affect the quality of life of the poor, the marginalised, the urban poor and migrants harder, as they more exposed to it, unlike the rich who have access to cleaner living conditions. APPI are incubating and supporting an effort to catalyze collective action in the form of Clean Air Platform. This could be a model in showcasing how multi-stakeholder engagement and joint action can turn around the air quality in a city. It will provide support (funding and capacity) to a number of initiatives. It will support initiatives that improve the air quality measurement capabilities, increase community engagement, and improve the capacities of the state and policymakers. To focus the efforts initially, Bengaluru has been chosen, after fine-tuning the model based on the learnings, a city by city approach is being envisaged for improving air quality.

Courts and Criminal Justice: The Indian judicial system is bogged down by huge caseloads-more than 300,000 crore civil and criminal cases pending across the Supreme Court and various High Courts. This is exacerbated by a breakdown of due process in the lower courts. Currently, there are in excess of 200,000 under trials (over 5,000 spending more than eight years in jail) languishing in prison, in violation of their fundamental rights. Most cannot afford legal aid. To ensure justice is not further delayed or denied, APPI believe it is necessary to form legal cells by partnering with civil society organisations. This, however, also requires the close cooperation of law enforcement and judicial agencies. Currently, we are working to support the provision of quality legal aid, speedy bail and redress for under trials.

Marginalised Communities: Its goal is to mainstream and include marginalised communities through strengthening community mobilisation to gain a voice and to seek rights, entitlements and social justice. In order to fulfil this goal, APPI provide grants to Community Based Organisation (CBOs) to ensure their long-term sustainability. The funding allows CBOs to expand their work, achieve organisational and financial sustainability and develop the attributes of a strong CBO. Largely, this thematic grant is being used to enhance and deepen the internal governance and organisational systems to improve non-institutional resource mobilisation (membership fee, individual donations, enterprise development etc.), increase community engagement and conscientisation, strengthen the leadership and participation of youth; women etc. and expand membership base and interventions on the ground.

Impact is at the heart of APPI funding. Studying and assessing impact is a continual and constant process at Azim Premji Philanthropic Initiatives.

Impact is the positive difference in the lives of vulnerable people—as a result of Its partners' efforts. It is also about finding out whether such work has led to systemic change or has had a direct or indirect effect on the sector itself, or on society at large. It also requires learning how to further its funding in a given area and focus APPI strategies in the most meaningful direction so there is maximum benefit.

APPI Approach: APPI Impact practice has a young and growing team. It is tasked with proving and improving the impact of its work. Its organisational approach to impact is:

- APPI intend to be thoughtful about when to evaluate, and its choice of tools and methods
- "Fit for purpose"—primarily based on the purpose to which the outcome of the evaluation will be deployed, and other considerations such as the role APPI plays in the intervention (funder, enabler, orchestrator), the complexity of the grant, the stage of the intervention and the availability of existing evidence
- Its stated position is that it will not consider the generation of evidence on its standalone value but will look for ways that it can take the results meaningfully forward
- Learning is at the core of its impact practice. APPI considers it important to plan and derive learning outcomes early, in order to utilise the findings to improve programmes quickly

While APPI currently considers impact as an aggregate of multiple interventions, its intent is to take an "outside in" view of what impact we intend to see, given APPI mission and choices of domains.

The Azim Premji Foundation has field institutes in 40+ districts across 6 states and one union territory— Chhattisgarh, Karnataka, Madhya Pradesh, Puducherry, Rajasthan, Telengana and Uttarakhand. The district institutes work with government schools to improve the quality of teaching learning processes, build professional networks and reform curriculum along with related issues of education policy. The Foundation through the School of Continuing Education and University Resource Centre of Azim Premji University is also engaged in the North Eastern states and Jammu & Kashmir. Its main area of work is capacity building of senior functionaries at the state or district levels through workshops, courses, curriculum and material development.

The core idea is to improve quality of education and provide better learning experiences for children in government schools through improving the capacities of teachers at multiple levels. This is facilitated through multi-modal engagements - informal learning groups, short discussions, workshops, school visits, exposure visits etc.

The Foundation's work in the field directly leverages and builds upon the rich experience gained through grass roots level engagements for fifteen years. All the work in the field has close linkages with the University to ensure a strong two-way connection between theory, research and actual practice.

Bravo, Azim Premji! CSR gets big boost: Azim Premji has raised the bar for philanthropic commitment by allocating the economic ownership of 34 percent more of the equity base of Wipro to the endowment that supports the activities of the Azim Premji Foundation, which works extensively in the field of education. Already, about 33 percent of Wipro's equity has been allocated to the endowment. This leaves Premji with about 7 percent ownership in the company directly and through entities other than the trust. The trust would now own and be entitled to the economic benefit from 67 percent of Wipro's shares, about 26 percent of the equity being held by the public. Premji has allocated sizeable other assets as well to the Foundation, bringing the value of its corpus to Rs 1,45,000 crore.

The Azim Premji Foundation works extensively with state governments in improving the quality of education. This has a multiplier effect, as compared to ploughing a lonely furrow and hoping others would learn from the success of the Foundation's solitary ventures. This benefit is significant in India's context, where State schools are dysfunctional for the most part and children receive education that fails them and the nation. Strengthening the Foundation's work would augment and extend this benefit. At the same time, this has a downside, which cannot be ignored. Taking 67 percent of Wipro's stake out of any possible contest for ownership would take Wipro outside the market for corporate control. This is potentially a dampener for Wipro's share price and even for the company's eventual performance under whoever succeeds the promoter. A functional market for corporate control is one of the guarantors of high corporate performance.

We hope more of India's captains of industry would come forward to follow Azim Premji's example and spend more money and time on philanthropic activity. Given the limited reach of the State in many sectors of development, there is much that private foundations that deploy business savvy to developmental work can contribute to society. Premji shows how corporate social responsibility transcends a statutory obligation.

ITC Limited

ITC was incorporated on August 24, 1910 under the name Imperial Tobacco Company of India Limited. As the Company's ownership progressively Indianised, the name of the Company was changed from Imperial Tobacco Company of India Limited to India Tobacco Company Limited in 1970 and then to I.T.C. Limited in 1974. In recognition of the Company's multi-business portfolio encompassing a wide range of businesses - Fast Moving Consumer Goods comprising Foods, Personal Care, Cigarettes and Cigars, Branded Apparel, Education and Stationery Products, Incense Sticks and Safety Matches, Hotels, Paperboards & Specialty Papers, Packaging, Agri-Business and Information Technology - the full stops in the Company's name were removed effective September 18, 2001. The Company now stands rechristened 'ITC Limited, 'where 'ITC' is today no longer an acronym or an initialised form.

The Company's beginnings were humble. A leased office on Radha Bazar Lane, Kolkata, was the centre of the Company's existence. The Company celebrated its 16th birthday on August 24, 1926, by purchasing the plot of land situated at 37, Chowringhee, (now renamed J.L. Nehru Road) Kolkata, for the sum of Rs 310,000. This decision of the Company was historic in more ways than one. It was to mark the beginning of a long and eventful journey into India's future. The Company's headquarter building, 'Virginia House', which came up on that plot of land two years later, would go on to become one of Kolkata's most venerated landmarks.

1925: Packaging and Printing: Backward Integration: Though the first six decades of the Company's existence were primarily devoted to the growth and consolidation of the Cigarettes and Leaf Tobacco businesses, ITC's Packaging & Printing Business was set up in 1925 as a strategic backward integration for ITC's Cigarettes business. It is today India's most sophisticated packaging house.

1975: Entry into the Hospitality Sector - A 'Welcom' Move: The Seventies witnessed the beginnings of a corporate transformation that would usher in momentous changes in the life of the Company. In 1975, the Company launched its Hotels business with the acquisition of a hotel in Chennai which was rechristened 'ITC-Welcomgroup Hotel Chola' (now renamed My Fortune, Chennai). The objective of ITC's entry into the hotels business was rooted in the concept of creating value for the nation. ITC chose the Hotels business for its potential to earn high levels of foreign exchange, create tourism infrastructure and generate large scale direct and indirect employment. Since then ITC's Hotels business has grown to occupy a position of leadership, with over 100 owned and managed properties spread across India under four brands namely, ITC Hotels - Luxury Collection, Welcom Hotels, Fortune Hotels and Welcom Heritage.

ITC Hotels recently took its first step toward international expansion with an upcoming super premium luxury hotel in Colombo, Sri Lanka. In addition, ITC Hotels also recently tied up with RP Group Hotels & Resorts to manage 5 hotels in Dubai and India under ITC Hotels' 5-star 'WelcomHotel' brand and the mid-market to upscale 'Fortune' brand.

1979: Paperboards & Specialty Papers - Development of a Backward Area In 1979, ITC entered the Paperboards business by promoting ITC Bhadrachalam Paperboards Limited. Bhadrachalam Paperboards amalgamated with the Company effective March 13, 2002 and became a Division of the Company, Bhadrachalam Paperboards Division. In November 2002, this division merged with the Company's Tribeni Tissues Division to form the Paperboards & Specialty Papers Division. ITC's paperboards' technology, productivity, quality and manufacturing processes are comparable to the best in the world. It has also made an immense contribution to the development of Sarapaka, an economically backward area in the state of Andhra Pradesh. It is directly involved in education, environmental protection and community development. In 2004, ITC acquired the paperboard manufacturing facility of BILT Industrial Packaging Co. Ltd (BIPCO), near Coimbatore, Tamil Nadu. The Kovai Unit allows ITC to improve customer service with reduced lead time and a wider product range.

1985: Nepal Subsidiary - First Steps beyond National Borders: In 1985, ITC set up Surya Tobacco Co. in Nepal as an Indo-Nepal and British joint venture. In August 2002, Surya Tobacco became a subsidiary of ITC Limited and its name was changed to Surya Nepal Private Limited (Surya Nepal). In 2004, the company diversified into manufacturing and exports of garments.

1990: Paperboards & Specialty Papers - Consolidation and Expansion: In 1990, ITC acquired Tribeni Tissues Limited, a Specialty paper manufacturing company and a major supplier of tissue paper to the cigarette industry. The merged entity was named the Tribeni Tissues Division (TTD). To harness strategic and operational synergies, TTD was merged with the Bhadrachalam Paperboards Division to form the Paperboards & Specialty Papers Division in November 2002.

1990: Agri Business - Strengthening Farmer Linkages: Also in 1990, leveraging its agri-sourcing competency, ITC set up the Agri Business Division for export of agri-commodities. The Division is today one of India's largest exporters. ITC's unique and now widely acknowledged e-Choupal initiative began in 2000 with soya farmers in Madhya Pradesh. Now it extends to 10 states covering over 4 million farmers. Also, through the 'Choupal Pradarshan Khet' initiative, the agri services vertical has been focusing on improving productivity of crops while deepening the relationship with the farming community.

2002: Education & Stationery Products - Offering the Greenest products: ITC launched line of premium range of notebooks under brand Paperkraft in 2002. To augment its offering and to reach a wider student population, the Classmate range of notebooks was launched in 2003. Classmate over the years has grown to become India's largest notebook brand and has also increased its portfolio to occupy a greater share of the school bag. Years 2007-2009 saw the launch of Practical Books, Drawing Books, Geometry Boxes, Pens and Pencils under the 'Classmate' brand. 'Paperkraft' offers a diverse portfolio in the premium executive stationery and office consumables segment.

2000: Lifestyle Retailing - Premium Offerings: ITC also entered the Lifestyle Retailing business with the Wills Sport range of international quality relaxed wear for men and women in 2000. The Wills Lifestyle chain of exclusive stores later expanded its range to include Wills Classic formal wear (2002) and Wills Clublife evening wear (2003). ITC also initiated a foray into the popular segment with its men's wear brand, John Players, in 2002. In 2006, Wills Lifestyle became title partner of the country's most premier fashion event -Wills Lifestyle India Fashion Week - that has gained recognition from buyers and retailers as the single largest B-2-B platform for the Fashion Design industry. To mark the occasion, ITC launched a special 'Wills Signature', taking the event forward to consumers.

2000: Information Technology - Business Friendly Solutions: In 2000, ITC spun off its information technology business into a wholly owned subsidiary, ITC Infotech India Limited, to more aggressively pursue emerging opportunities in this area. Today ITC Infotech is one of India's fastest growing global IT and IT-enabled services companies and has established itself as a key player in offshore outsourcing, providing outsourced IT solutions and services to leading global customers across key focus verticals - Banking Financial Services & Insurance (BFSI), Consumer Packaged Goods (CPG), Retail, Manufacturing, Engineering Services, Media & Entertainment, Travel, Hospitality, Life Sciences and Transportation & Logistics.

2001: Branded Packaged Foods - Delighting Millions of Households: ITC's foray into the Foods business is an outstanding example of successfully blending multiple internal competencies to create a new driver of business growth. It began in August 2001 with the introduction of 'Kitchens of India' ready-to-eat Indian gourmet dishes. In 2002, ITC entered the confectionery and staples segments with the launch of the brands mint-o and Candyman confectionery and Aashirvaad Atta (wheat flour). 2003 witnessed the introduction of Sunfeast as the Company entered the biscuits segment. ITC entered the fast growing branded snacks category with Bingo! in 2007. In 2010, ITC launched Sunfeast Yippee! to enter the Indian instant noodles market. In September 2014, ITC launched Gum On Chewing Gum marking the entry into the category of gums. The Company entered the Fruit-based juices and beverages market with the launch of B Natural Fruit beverages in January 2015. ITC's forayed into the dairy segment with the launch of Aashirvaad Svasti Ghee in November 2015. Launched in April 2016, Fabelle chocolates are ITC's premier offering in the luxury chocolate space. ITC forayed into the branded coffee category in July 2016 with the launch of Sunbean Gourmet Coffee. In February 2017, ITC launched ITC Master Chef super safe spices - the first-of-its-kind spices launched in India, offering export quality super safe spices to the Indian homemaker. ITC MasterChef Prawns were launched in June 2017 as the Company entered the Frozen foods segment. ITC's first foray into fresh fruits and vegetables segment was marked with the launch of Farmland Potatoes in November 2017.

In just over a decade and a half, the Foods business has grown to a significant size under numerous distinctive brands, with an enviable distribution reach, a rapidly growing market share and a solid market standing.

2002: Agarbattis & Safety Matches - Supporting the Small and Cottage Sector: In 2002, ITC's philosophy of contributing to enhancing the competitiveness of the entire value chain found yet another expression in the Safety Matches initiative. ITC now markets popular safety matches brands like iKno, Mangaldeep and Aim.

ITC's foray into the marketing of Agarbattis (incense sticks) in 2003 marked the manifestation of its partnership with the cottage sector. Mangaldeep is a highly established national brand and is available across a range of fragrances like Rose, Jasmine, Bouquet, Sandalwood and 'Fragrance of Temple'.

2005: Personal Care Products - Expert Solutions for Discerning Consumers: ITC entered the Personal Care Business in 2005 and the portfolio has grown under 'Essenza Di Wills', 'Fiama', 'Vivel' 'Superia' brands which have received encouraging consumer response and have been progressively extended nationally. In May 2013, the business expanded its product portfolio with the launch of engage deodorants. ITC marked its foray into the health space with the acquisition of the brand Savlon and Shower to Shower in 2015. In 2017, the business acquired the brand Charmis to enhance its skincare portfolio.

2010: Expanding the Tobacco Portfolio: In 2010, ITC launched its hand rolled cigar, Armenteros, in the Indian market. Armenteros cigars are available exclusively at tobacco selling outlets in select hotels, fine dining restaurants and exclusive clubs.

ITC's Core Values are aimed at developing a customer-focused, high-performance organisation which creates value for all its stakeholders.

Corporate Strategies: ITC is a board-managed professional company, committed to creating enduring value for the nation and the shareholder. It has a rich organisational culture rooted in its core values of respect for people and belief in empowerment. Its philosophy of all-round value creation is backed by strong corporate governance policies and systems.

ITC's corporate strategies are:

- Create multiple drivers of growth by developing a portfolio of world class businesses that best matches organisational capability with opportunities in domestic and export markets.
- Continue to focus on the chosen portfolio of FMCG, Hotels, Paper, Paperboards & Packaging, Agri Business and Information Technology.
- Benchmark the health of each business comprehensively across the criteria of Market Standing, Profitability and Internal Vitality.
- Ensure that each of its businesses is world class and internationally competitive.
- Enhance the competitive power of the portfolio through synergies derived by blending the diverse skills and capabilities residing in ITC's various businesses.
- Create distributed leadership within the organisation by nurturing talented and focused top management teams for each of the businesses.
- Continuously strengthen and refine Corporate Governance processes and systems to catalyse the entrepreneurial energies of management by striking the golden balance between executive freedom and the need for effective control and accountability.

Corporate Governance

Preamble: Over the years, ITC has evolved from a single product company to a multi-business corporation. Its diverse businesses include fast moving consumer goods, hotels, paperboards, paper & packaging and agri business. The Company's investments in its different businesses are structured in the nature of in-house divisions, subsidiaries, joint ventures, associate companies and trade investments.

The task of governing a corporation of ITC's size and diversity was rendered more complex in post liberalisation India, which began experiencing the intense impact of globalisation. In order to address its own unique organisational context and prepare itself for the global Indian market, ITC, as early as in 1999, fashioned a unique corporate governance model that would enable it to 'focus' on its multiple businesses, while maximising shareholder value.

This governance policy has not only stood the test of time, but also supported ITC's rapid growth in the last two decades since its formulation. In the intervening years, ITC has not only widened its diversity with the launch of several new businesses in its chosen strategic arena, but has also responded to the growth challenge by creating new internal structures like shared services and business verticals, designing broad-band roles like Line CMC Members, Chief Operating Officers of Business / Vertical, and enabling operating decision making powers at empowered levels.

Definition and Purpose: ITC defines Corporate Governance as a systemic process by which companies are directed and controlled to enhance their wealth generating capacity. Since large corporations employ vast quantum of societal resources, ITC believes that the governance process should ensure that these companies are managed in a manner that meets stakeholders aspirations and societal expectations.

Core Principles: ITC's Corporate Governance initiative is based on two core principles. These are:

- Management must have the executive freedom to drive the enterprise forward without undue restraints; and
- This freedom of management should be exercised within a frame work of effective accountability.

ITC believes that any meaningful policy on Corporate Governance must provide empowerment to the executive management of the Company, and simultaneously create a mechanism of checks and balances which ensures that the decision making powers vested in the executive management is not only not misused, but is used with care and responsibility to meet stakeholder aspirations and societal expectations.

Cornerstones: From the above definition and core principles of Corporate Governance emerge the cornerstones of ITC's governance philosophy, namely trusteeship, transparency, empowerment and accountability, control and ethical corporate citizenship. ITC believes that the practice of each of these leads to the creation of the right corporate culture in which the company is managed in a manner that fulfils the purpose of Corporate Governance.

Trusteeship: ITC believes that large corporations like itself have both a social and economic purpose. They represent a coalition of interests, namely those of the shareholders, other providers of capital, business associates and employees. This belief therefore casts a responsibility of trusteeship on the Company's Board of Directors. They are to act as trustees to protect and enhance shareholder value, as well as to ensure that the Company fulfils its obligations and responsibilities to its other stakeholders. Inherent in the concept of trusteeship is the responsibility to ensure equity, namely, that the rights of all shareholders, large or small, are protected.

Transparency: ITC believes that transparency means explaining Company's policies and actions to those to whom it has responsibilities. Therefore transparency must lead to maximum appropriate disclosures without compromising the Company's strategic interests. Internally, transparency means openness in Company's relationship with its employees, as well as the conduct of its business in a manner that will bear scrutiny. ITC believes transparency enhances accountability.

Empowerment and Accountability: Empowerment is an essential concomitant of ITC's first core principle of governance that management must have the freedom to drive the enterprise forward. ITC believes that empowerment is a process of actualising the potential of its employees. Empowerment unleashes creativity and innovation throughout the organisation by truly vesting decision-making powers at the most appropriate levels in the organisational hierarchy.

ITC believes that the Board of Directors are accountable to the shareholders, and the management is accountable to the Board of Directors. The Company believes that empowerment, combined with accountability, provides an impetus to performance and improves effectiveness, thereby enhancing shareholder value.

Control: ITC believes that control is a necessary concomitant of its second core principle of governance that the freedom of management should be exercised within a framework of appropriate checks and balances. Control should prevent misuse of power, facilitate timely management response to change, and ensure that business risks are pre-emptively and effectively managed.

Ethical Corporate Citizenship: ITC believes that corporations like itself have a responsibility to set exemplary standards of ethical behaviour, both internally within the organisation, as well as in their external relationships. The Company believes that unethical behaviour corrupts organisational culture and undermines stakeholder value.

Code of Conduct

Applicable to all directors, senior management and employees of the Company: ITC's Code of Conduct is derived from three interlinked fundamental principles, viz. good corporate governance, good corporate citizenship and exemplary personal conduct.

Philosophy: ITC is a professionally managed organisation and the core value underlying our corporate philosophy is "trusteeship". We believe this organisation has been handed to us by the various stakeholders in "trust" and we as professionals are the "trustees" of these stakeholders. It is therefore our responsibility to ensure that the organisation is managed in a manner that protects and furthers the interests of our stakeholders. We recognise society as an important stakeholder in this enterprise and therefore it is part of our responsibility to practice good corporate citizenship.

It is also our belief that in order to serve the interests of our stakeholders in perpetuity, we must build ITC into an institution whose dynamism and vitality are anchored in its core values.

Corporate Governance Policy: The Corporate Governance Policy is the apex level instrument guiding conduct of the affairs of the Company and clearly delineates the roles, responsibilities and authorities of the key entities in the governance structure of the Company. This Code forms an integral part of the Company's Governance Policy. The directors, senior management and employees must adhere to the Corporate Governance Policy of the Company.

Good Corporate Citizenship: In the conduct of the Company's business, the practice of good corporate citizenship is a prerequisite and embraces the following:

Dealing with People in the Organisation: In dealing with each other, directors, senior management and employees shall uphold the values which are at the core of our HR Philosophy - trust, teamwork, mutuality and collaboration, meritocracy, objectivity, self respect and human dignity. Indeed, these values form the basis of our HR management systems and processes. In selection and recruitment, while meritocracy will be a prime criterion, managers will scrupulously consider all factors that go towards securing the interests of the Company. ITC will focus on meritocracy, equity and upholding of Company values in all people processes including performance management systems, appraisals, remuneration and rewards.

A Gender Friendly Workplace: As a good corporate citizen, ITC is committed to a gender friendly workplace. It seeks to enhance equal opportunities for men and women, prevent/stop/redress sexual harassment at the workplace and institute good employment practices.

Sexual harassment includes unwelcome sexually determined behaviour such as: unwelcome physical contact; a demand or request for sexual favours; sexually coloured remarks; showing pornography and any other unwelcome physical, verbal or non-verbal conduct of a sexual nature.

ITC maintains an open door for reportees; encourages employees to report any harassment concerns and is responsive to employee complaints about harassment or other unwelcome and offensive conduct. A committee has been constituted to enquire into complaints and to recommend appropriate action, wherever required.

ITC demands, demonstrates and promotes professional behaviour and respectful treatment of all employees.

Relationships with Suppliers and Customers: All directors, senior management and employees shall ensure that in their dealings with suppliers and customers, the Company's interests are never compromised. Accepting gifts and presents of more than a nominal value, gratuity payments and other payments from suppliers or customers will be viewed as serious breach of discipline as this could lead to compromising the Company's interests.

Legal Compliance: It is the Company's policy to comply fully with all applicable laws and regulations. Ensuring legal and regulatory compliance is the responsibility of the Chief Executives of the Businesses and the Divisional Management Committees. The Company cannot accept practices which are unlawful or may be damaging to its reputation. Divisional Management Committees must satisfy themselves that sound and adequate arrangements exist to ensure that they comply with the legal and regulatory requirements impacting each business and identify and respond to developments in the regulatory environment in which they operate. In the event the implication of any law is not clear, the Company's Legal Department shall be consulted for advice.

Health and Safety: The Company attaches great importance to a healthy and safe work environment. ITC is committed to provide good physical working conditions and encourages high standards of hygiene and housekeeping. Particular attention should be paid to training of employees to increase safety awareness and adoption of safe working methods, particularly designed to prevent serious or fatal accidents.

Environment Policies: The Company believes that commitment to sustainable development is a key component of responsible corporate citizenship and therefore deserves to be accorded the highest priority. Accordingly, the Company is committed to Best Practices in environmental matters arising out of its business activities and expects each business to fully demonstrate this commitment.

In addition to complying with applicable laws and regulations, Businesses must establish procedures for assessing the environmental effects of their present and future activities. They should adopt Best Practices in their environmental policies and procedures.

Personal Conduct: All directors, senior management and employees have the obligation to conduct themselves in an honest and ethical manner and act in the best interest of the Company at all times. They are expected to demonstrate exemplary personal conduct through adherence to the following:

Avoidance of Conflict of Interest: All directors, senior management and employees must avoid situations in which their personal interest could conflict with the interest of the Company. This is an area in which it is impossible to provide comprehensive guidance but the guiding principle is that conflict, if any, or potential conflict must be disclosed to higher management for guidance and action as appropriate.

Transparency and Auditability: All directors, senior management and employees shall ensure that their actions in the conduct of business are totally transparent except where the needs of business security dictate otherwise. Such transparency shall be brought about through appropriate policies, systems and processes, including as appropriate, segregation of duties, tiered approval mechanism and involvement of more than one manager in key decisions and maintaining supporting records. It shall be necessary to voluntarily ensure that areas of operation are open to audit and the conduct of activities is totally auditable.

Protection of Confidential Information: No director, senior management and employee shall disclose or use any confidential information gained in the course of employment/ association with the Company for personal gain or for the advantage of any other person. No information either formally or informally shall be provided to the press, other publicity media or any other external agency except within approved policies.

Dealing in Securities of the Company by Employees: Employees, who are granted Stock Options under the Company's Employee Stock Option Schemes (ESOS) shall not buy and / or sell any shares of the Company.

This restriction, however, will not apply to exercise of Options granted by the Company under ESOS and sale of resultant shares arising out of such exercise.

- Employees, who are not, granted Stock Options under ESOS, and their 'Immediate Relatives', and also the 'Immediate Relatives' of Employees who are granted Stock Options shall not buy and / or sell shares of the Company in excess of 10,000 shares in aggregate in a calendar quarter.
- Employees and their 'Immediate Relatives' shall not enter into any derivative transactions with respect to the shares of the Company.

(Immediate Relative for this purpose means spouse, and includes parent, sibling, and child if they are financially dependent on the employee.)

Company Facilities: No director, senior management and employee shall misuse Company facilities. In the use of Company facilities, care shall be exercised to ensure that costs are reasonable and there is no wastage.

Leading by Example: The organisation's directors and senior management set the professional tone for the Company. Through both their words and their actions, the organisation's leadership conveys what is acceptable and unacceptable behaviour. ITC's directors, senior management and employees must constantly reinforce through their actions and behaviour that ITC's stated beliefs of responsible corporate citizenship are rooted in individual conviction and personal integrity.

Waivers: Any waiver of any provision of this Code of Conduct for a director, senior management or employee must be placed for approval before the Company's Board of Directors / Corporate Management Committee, as appropriate.

Non Adherence: Any instance of non-adherence to the Code of Conduct should be brought to the attention of the immediate reporting authority, with copies to the relevant Divisional Chief Executive / Head of Corporate

Department and the Head of Corporate Human Resources. In respect of senior management, any such instance should be brought to the attention of the Chairman of the Audit Committee with a copy to the Company Chairman.

Duties of Independent Directors: The duties of Independent Directors of the Company, as laid down under Schedule IV to the Companies Act, 2013, are incorporated herein pursuant to Clause 49 of the Listing Agreement with Stock Exchanges. It shall be the duty of Independent Directors to:

(a) undertake appropriate induction and regularly update and refresh their skills, knowledge and familiarity with the Company;

(b) seek appropriate clarification or amplification of information and, where necessary, take and follow appropriate professional advice and opinion of outside experts at the expense of the Company;

(c) strive to attend all meetings of the Board of Directors and of the Board Committees of which they are a member;

(d) participate constructively and actively in the Board Committees in which they are chairpersons or members;

(e) strive to attend the general meetings of the Company;

(f) ensure, where they have concerns about the running of the Company or a proposed action, that these are addressed by the Board of Directors;

(g) keep themselves well informed about the Company and the external environment in which it operates;

(h) not to unfairly obstruct the functioning of an otherwise proper Board or Board Committee;

(i) pay sufficient attention and ensure that adequate deliberations are held before approving related party transactions and assure themselves that the same are in the interest of the Company;

(j) ascertain and ensure that the Company has an adequate and functional vigil mechanism and ensure that the interests of a person who uses such mechanism are not prejudicially affected on account of such use;

(k) report concerns about unethical behaviour, actual or suspected fraud or violation of the Code of Conduct;

(l) act within their authority and assist in protecting the legitimate interests of the Company, shareholders and its employees;

(m) not to disclose confidential information, including commercial secrets, technologies, advertising and sales promotion plans and unpublished price sensitive information, unless such disclosure is expressly approved by the Board of Directors or required by law.

Whistleblower Policy

Philosophy: ITC believes that every employee is a trustee of its stakeholders and must adhere to the Company's Code of Conduct (hereinafter referred to as 'ITC Code') and conduct himself or herself at all times in a professional and ethical manner.

Purpose: The "Whistleblower Policy" encourages Directors and employees (hereinafter referred to as 'employees') to bring to the Company's attention, instances of unethical behaviour, actual or suspected incidents of fraud or violation of the ITC Code, that could adversely impact the Company's operations, business performance and / or reputation. The Company will investigate such reported incidents in an impartial manner and take appropriate action to ensure that the requisite standards of professional and ethical conduct are always upheld.

Policy: It is ITC's Policy:

(a) To create an environment where every employee feels free and secure to report specific incidents of unethical behaviour, actual or suspected incidents of fraud or violation of the ITC Code;

(b) To investigate such reported incidents in a fair manner;

(c) To take appropriate disciplinary action against the delinquent employee(s);

(d) To ensure that no employee is victimised or harassed for bringing such incidents to the attention of the Company.

The practice of this Policy will be overseen by the Audit Committee.

Reporting Mechanism

(a) Employees are encouraged to bring to the attention of the Company incidents pertaining, inter alia, to:

- Illegal or unethical conduct including that which adversely affects investors, shareholders, customers, suppliers, other employees, or the business performance or image or reputation of the Company;
- Violation of any law or regulation including actual or suspected fraud;
- Conflict of interest with the Company;
- Leaking of confidential or proprietary information of the Company;
- Any other violation of the ITC Code.

(b) A Whistleblower complaint may be made by any employee (hereinafter referred to as the 'complainant'). Such complaint should be sent to his or her immediate reporting authority, with copies to the relevant Divisional Chief Executive / Head of Corporate Department and the Head of Corporate Human

Resources. Anonymous complaint will not be entertained. If the complainant has reasons to believe that the concerned immediate reporting authority or his / her superior is involved in the suspected violation, the complaint may be addressed directly to the Head of Corporate Human Resources.

Complaint by or against senior management (as defined in the ITC Code) should be made to the Chairman of the Audit Committee with a copy to the Company Chairman.

(c) Complaint shall be made in writing and must include as much information about the suspected violation as the complainant can provide. It should describe:

- the nature, period of commission and details of the alleged violation;
- the identities of the persons suspected to have committed the alleged violation; and
- a description of the documents that would prove or relate to the suspected violation.

(d) Employees are encouraged to report such incidents as early as possible, in any case within 30 days of the suspected violation / breach noticed by him / her, so that timely action can be taken.

Investigation

(a) Upon receipt of a complaint (other than by or against senior management), the Head of Corporate Human Resources, who should keep the Line Director informed, will make an assessment thereof and on being satisfied as to the seriousness and credibility of the complaint, direct the complaint for investigation, in consultation with the General Counsel, to the Internal Audit Department of the Company.

(b) All employees have a duty to cooperate in an investigation.

(c) All information disclosed during the course of an investigation, including the identity of the complainant, will be kept confidential, except as necessary or appropriate to disclose for the purposes of the investigation or where required to be statutorily disclosed.

(d) The report of the investigation shall be submitted by the Internal Audit Department to the Corporate Management Committee along with reasoning and supporting material. Depending on the materiality, the investigation findings will be reported to the Audit Committee.

(e) Complaint by or against senior management will be investigated as directed by the Audit Committee.

(f) If the Corporate Management Committee / the Audit Committee determines that a violation has occurred, the Company will take appropriate action which may include disciplinary proceedings against the violator, including termination of employment.

No Retaliation

(a) This Policy is intended to encourage and enable employees to raise bonafide concerns. No employee who reports a violation shall suffer any harassment, retaliation or adverse employment condition as a consequence of such reporting.

(b) Any employee who retaliates against a person reporting a violation will be subject to disciplinary proceedings, which may extend to termination of employment.

Complaint to be made in good faith

(a) A complainant must act in good faith and have reasonable grounds for forming a belief that his or her complaint constitutes a violation as described under Clause 4(a).

(b) This Policy must not be used as a tool for victimisation, making false allegation or acting malafide.

(c) Any person who is found to be making baseless, reckless, malicious or deliberately false allegation, shall be subject to disciplinary proceedings, which may extend to termination of employment.

Corporate Social Responsibility

ITC's overarching aspiration to create significant and sustainable societal value is manifest in its CSR initiatives that embrace the most disadvantaged sections of society, especially in rural India, through economic empowerment based on grassroots capacity building. Towards this end, the Company has adopted a comprehensive CSR policy outlining programmes, and plans to undertake projects and activities to create a significant positive impact on identified stakeholders. All these programmes fall within the purview of Schedule VII of the provisions of Section 135 - Companies Act, 2013 and the Companies (Corporate Social Responsibility Policy) Rules, 2014. The footprint of the Company's Social Investments Programme (SIP) projects is spread over 25 states covering 188 districts.

The Company believes that an effective stakeholder engagement process is necessary for achieving its sustainability goal of inclusive growth.

The Company's stakeholders are confronted with multi-dimensional and inter-related issues, at the core of which is the challenge of securing sustainable livelihoods. Accordingly, it anchors its stakeholder engagement on the following principles:

MATERIALITY	COMPLETENESS	RESPONSIVENESS
Prioritised consideration of the economic, environmental and social impacts identified	Understanding key concerns of stakeholders and their expectations	Responding coherently and transparently to such issues and concerns

Areas listed under Schedule VII to the Companies Act, 2013	***ITC's interventions (including through Trusts established by the Company)***
(i)Eradicating hunger, poverty and malnutrition, promoting health care including preventive health care and sanitation including contribution to the Swach Bharat Kosh set-up by the Central Government for the promotion of sanitation and making available safe drinking water	• Health & Sanitation • Drinking Water • Eradication of Poverty
(ii) Promoting education, including special education and employment enhancing vocation skills specially among children, women, elderly, and the differently abled and livelihood enhancement projects	• Education • Vocational Training • Livestock Development • Livelihood Generation
(iii) Promoting gender equality, empowering women, setting up homes and hostels for women and orphans; setting up old age homes, day care centres and such other facilities for senior citizens and measures for reducing inequalities faced by socially and economically backward groups	• Women Empowerment
(iv) Ensuring environmental sustainability, ecological balance, protection of flora and fauna, animal welfare, agroforestry, conservation of natural resources and maintaining quality of soil, air and water including contribution to the Clean Ganga Fund set up by the Central Government for rejuvenation of River Ganga	• Environment Sustainability • Soil & Moisture Conservation • Social Forestry
(v) Protection of national heritage, art and culture, including restoration of buildings and sites of historical importance and works of art, setting up public libraries, promotion and development of traditional arts and handicrafts	• Protection of national heritage, art and culture
(vi) Rural Development Projects	• Agri Development

ITC's e-CHOUPAL: The ITC e-Choupals are designed to deliver enhanced value to all participants in the value chain, including farmers, by leveraging the power of Information Technology. With a judicious blend of click and mortar capabilities, ITC e-Choupals have triggered a virtuous cycle of higher productivity, higher incomes, enhanced capacity for farmer risk management, larger investments and better quality of produce.

Village internet-kiosks managed by lead farmers, called 'sanchalaks', facilitate information access to other farmers, in their local language. Real-time information on weather forecasts and market prices, customised knowledge on scientific farm practices and risk management are supplemented by the availability of quality farm inputs and price discovery of farm produce within the village. Such crucial information and inputs enhance the ability of farmers to take informed decisions, align their farm output with market demand and ensure higher quality and productivity. The aggregation of demand for farm inputs from individual farmers gives them access to high quality inputs from established manufacturers at fair prices.

Launched in June 2000, ITC e-Choupal is today the largest initiative among internet based interventions in rural India. Its services reach out to more than 4 million farmers in over 35,000 villages through 6,100 kiosks spread across 10 states.

ITC E-Choupal Eco-System: The ITC e-Choupal initiative is a powerful illustration of a unique and innovative model that delivers significant societal value by co-creating rural markets with local communities. A network of village internet kiosks - e-Choupals - enable even small and marginal farmers in rural India, who are de-linked from the formal market, to access real-time weather and price information, and relevant knowledge and services to enhance farm productivity, quality and command better prices - improving their competitiveness and capacity to manage risk.

Complementing this digital infrastructure is Choupal Pradarshan Khet - customised agri-extension services, demonstration plots and training programmes that promote best practices and assist farmers to diversify crop portfolios.

The ITC e-Choupal initiative has emerged as an efficient two-way channel for a variety of goods and services, raising farm incomes and making farming more profitable. The Company leverages the e-Choupal platform to support holistic development of rural communities in and around e-Choupal catchments through a number of initiatives - dairy management, agarbatti manufacturing and skills development - aimed at stimulating non-farm incomes and creating sustainable livelihood opportunities. This endeavour also includes the Swasthya Choupal initiative that focuses on enhancing awareness on maternal and child care through a network of Village Health Champions.

Launched in 2000, ITC e-Choupal is today the largest initiative among Internet-based interventions in rural India. Its services reach out to more than 4 million farmers in over 35000 villages through 6100 kiosks spread across 10 states. ITC e-Choupal's achievements have been well documented as case studies in premier institutions like the Harvard Business School, references in World Bank reports and in eminent publications like The Economist.

e-Choupal is an initiative of ITC Limited, a conglomerate in India, to link directly with ruralfarmers via the Internet for procurement of agricultural and aquaculture products like soybeans, wheat, coffee, and prawns. e-Choupal tackles the challenges posed by Indian agriculture, characterized by fragmented farms, weak infrastructure and the involvement of intermediaries. The programme installs computers with Internet access in rural areas of India to offer farmers up-to-date marketing and agricultural information.

Effects of e-Choupal: ITC Limited has provided computers and Internet access in rural areas across several agricultural regions of the country, where the farmers can directly negotiate the sale of their produce with ITC Limited. Online access enables farmers to obtain information on mandi prices, and good farming practices, and to place orders for agricultural inputs like seeds and fertilizers. This helps farmers improve the quality of their products, and helps in obtaining a better price.

ITC Limited kiosk with Internet access is run by a sanchalak — a trained farmer. The computer is housed in the sanchalak's house and is linked to the Internet via phone lines or by a VSAT connection. Each installation serves an average of 600 farmers in the surrounding ten villages within about a 5 km radius. The sanchalak bears some operating cost but in return earns a service fee for the e-transactions done through his e-Choupal. The warehouse hub is managed by the same traditional middle-men, now called samyojaks, but with no exploitative power due to the reorganisation. These middlemen make up for the lack of infrastructure and fulfill critical jobs like cash disbursement, quantity aggregation and transportation.

Since the introduction of e-Choupal services, farmers have seen a rise in their income levels because of a rise in yields, improvement in quality of output, and a fall in transaction costs. Even small farmers have gained from the initiative. Farmers can get real-time information despite their physical distance from the mandis. The system saves procurement costs for ITC Limited. The farmers do not pay for the information and knowledge they get from e-Choupals; the principle is to inform, empower and compete e-market place for spot transactions and support services to futures exchange.

Socio-Economic Environment: The global cyclical upswing that began midway through 2016 gathered strength during 2017. As per latest IMF estimates, World GDP grew by 3.8 percent in 2017 representing a marked improvement over 2016, which at 3.2 percent was the weakest year of growth since the global financial crisis of 2009. The pick-up in growth was supported by synchronous growth in the Advanced Economies which grew by 2.3 percent in 2017 against 1.7 percent in 2016, and Emerging Markets & Developing Economies which recorded a growth of 4.8 percent in 2017 against 4.4 percent in 2016.

Within the Advanced Economies, the US posted a strong growth of 2.3 percent in 2017 against 1.5 percent in 2016, led by robust recovery in Private Investment and expansion in consumer spending. The Euro Area also expanded by 2.3 percent during the year compared to 1.8 percent in 2016. In the Emerging

Markets & Developing Economies, acceleration in growth was mainly attributable to Brazil and Russia achieving positive growth after two successive years of decline. The Chinese economy also grew faster at 6.9 percent in 2017 compared to 6.7 percent in 2016.

The synchronised growth momentum in Advanced and Emerging Economies is likely to sustain going forward resulting in a further pick-up in global economic growth to 3.9 percent in 2018 and 2019. The US economy is projected to grow at 2.9 percent in 2018 aided by an expansionary fiscal policy, positive investment and private consumption outlook and 'full employment' of its workforce. At 4.9 percent growth in 2018, the strong growth momentum in the Emerging Markets & Developing Economies is likely to sustain and improve marginally mainly due to robust performance of commodity exporting countries such as Brazil, South Africa, Saudi Arabia and an anticipated pick-up in growth in India. Growth in China, however, is projected to slow down to 6.6 percent in 2018, reflecting the ongoing rebalancing of the economy towards a more sustainable and broad-based consumption and services led growth. However, the increasing trend of protectionist policies in the developed world, faster pace of increase in US interest rates and progressive tapering of quantitative easing in the EU could impact capital flows and weigh on the nascent recovery in commodity-exporting emerging economies.

The Indian economy witnessed another challenging year, with Real GDP growth slowing down sharply to 6.6 percent compared to 7.1 percent in 2016-17, reflecting the short-term disruptions caused by GST implementation, residual impact of cash crunch and deceleration in Net Exports. It is pertinent to note that Nominal GDP growth in 2017-18 stood at 9.8 percent - the lowest in six years. The Industry sector decelerated further during the year, recording the slowest growth in four years.

The anticipated pick-up in Consumption remained elusive with Private Final Consumption Expenditure (PFCE) growing by only 6.1 percent during the year against 7.3 percent in 2016-17. Likewise, recovery of the capex cycle did not fructify with deceleration in Fixed Capital Formation growth to 7.6 percent . Data on new project announcements, new capacity commissioned and stalled/abandoned projects during the year point to the subdued investment climate in the country. The 'twin deficits' came under pressure as well – higher expenditure and lower net tax collections resulted in Fiscal Deficit touching 3.5 percent of GDP against a target of 3.2 percent while the Current Account Deficit expanded to about 1.9 percent of GDP (Vs. 0.7 percent in 2016-17) due to pick-up in imports even as growth in exports remained subdued.

On the positive side, India remains the fastest growing major economy in the world. Inflation remained largely within the comfort zone of the RBI during the year with the Consumer Price Index (CPI) declining to 3.6 percent in 2017-18 against 4.5 percent in 2016-17, prompting the RBI to reduce policy interest rates by 25 bps during the year. However, with rising crude oil prices, anticipation of commodity prices firming up in the ensuing year and Core CPI steadily rising for the past several months, the scope for further reduction in interest rates seems limited. Foreign capital flows into the country remained robust leading to stability in the Indian Rupee and sustained buoyancy in the capital markets with the Sensex advancing by 11 percent in 2017-18 after a 17 percent rise in 2016-17.

As per median estimates, based on the Survey of Professional Forecasters conducted by RBI, GDP is likely to grow by 7.3 percent in 2018-19 on the back of improvement in the Net Exports position and normalisation of private consumption growth levels, partly aided by a favourable base effect. The green shoots of recovery in investments witnessed towards the end of the year especially in the infrastructure sector along with expectations of a normal monsoon augur well for the economy in the near term. Rising crude oil prices, revenue collections, external capital flows and rural demand recovery are the key monitorables in 2018-19. The pace of GDP growth is expected to gather momentum in the medium term on the back of favourable global economic tailwinds, pick-up in Private Investment and implementation of key policy reforms.

While India remains one of the fastest growing major economies in the world, the pace of economic growth in recent years has remained below the desired levels and the country's potential. Stagnation in the manufacturing sector needs to be reversed at the earliest towards the creation of sustainable livelihoods and absorption of millions of Indians entering the job market every year.

The successful implementation of structural initiatives identified by the Government towards improving the ease of doing business in the country by enhancing transparency, speeding up the approvals process, resolving policy issues and fostering greater levels of value addition within the country would be crucial to boost the performance of the Indian economy and realise its true potential. Enhancing agricultural productivity and value addition to international standards while simultaneously improving market linkages remain critical for the growth of the agricultural sector. In this context, it is pertinent to note that anywhere between 5 percent and 40 percent of food is wasted along the chain in India, depending on the inherent perishability of the crop and the season. India processes only 8 percent of its total food production as compared to 23 percent in China, 65 percent in USA and 78 percent in Philippines. A big thrust on India's Food Processing sector can lead to significant job creation, enhance rural incomes and help manage food inflation. Similarly, supportive policies in the area of agro-forestry would go a long way in creating sustainable livelihoods while simultaneously augmenting the nation's environmental capital.

Over the last four years, your Company has implemented an integrated pilot programme towards doubling farmer incomes in four districts of

Allahabad, Chandauli, Ghazipur and Varanasi, reaching out to nearly 2,00,000 farmers. The programme seeks to enhance productivity, crop quality and price realisation through specific interventions such as adoption of new high yielding varieties of wheat, introduction of short duration paddy to enable timely sowing of wheat in rabi season, promotion of value-added crops as well as educating farmers on best practices, knowledge and know-how transfer through the Choupal Pradarshan Khet initiative and, in particular, through practices like zero till sowing. Over 28,000 farmers, who have adopted all the initiatives under the integrated programme, have already reported doubling of incomes. Your Company is also engaged in enriching the potato value chain through its subsidiary, Technico Agri Sciences Ltd, which is a leading player in the production of early generation seed potato.

The interventions in this area include introduction of better quality and improved variety of seed potato and supporting potato farmers in upgrading their produce to chip grade potato for enhanced value realisation. With a view to scaling up your Company's contribution to the national goal of improving farmer incomes, your Company has recently entered into a partnership with the NITI Aayog to boost agricultural and allied activities in 25 districts under the Aspirational Districts programme launched to further the Honourable Prime Minister's vision to transform such areas. Under this initiative, your Company will collaborate with NITI Aayog and the district administration to train 2,00,000 lead farmers to enable them to reduce costs / enhance farm productivity across major crops in the identified districts.

The forward linkages to domestic agricultural value chains provided through your Company's Branded Packaged Foods Businesses stood further strengthened during the year with the recent foray into branded packaged potatoes & apples for the retail segment under the 'Farmland' brand, and 'Super Safe' spices, frozen prawns and dehydrated onions under the 'ITC Master Chef' brand.

Given India's disproportionately low share of global natural resources relative to its large population and where millions continue to live in abject poverty, the focus both at the national and corporate level should be on fashioning strategies that foster sustainable, equitable and inclusive growth. Differentiated and preferential incentives, in the form of fiscal or financial benefits to companies that adopt sustainable business practices would act as a force multiplier in achieving this critical national goal. It is your Company's belief that businesses can bring about transformational change by pursuing innovative business models that synergise the creation of sustainable livelihoods and the preservation of natural capital with enhancing shareholder value. This 'Triple Bottom Line' approach to creating larger 'stakeholder value', as opposed to merely ensuring uni-dimensional 'shareholder value', is the driving force that defines your Company's sustainability vision and its growth path into the future.

Your Company is a global exemplar in 'Triple Bottom Line' performance and is the only enterprise in the world of comparable dimensions to have achieved and sustained the three key global indices of environmental sustainability of being 'water positive' (for 16 years), 'carbon positive' (for 13 years), and 'solid waste recycling positive' (for 11 years). The focus on creating unique business models that generate substantial livelihoods across the value chains has led to your Company's Businesses supporting six million sustainable livelihoods, many of whom belong to the weakest in society. The following sections outline your Company's progress in pursuit of the 'Triple Bottom Line'.

Piramal Foundation

Piramal Foundation (PF), the philanthropic arm of the Piramal Group, is a Section 8 company that develops innovative solutions to resolve issues that are critical roadblocks towards unlocking India's economic potential.

The Foundation believes that bringing impact at scale across diverse geographies and communities can be achieved through partnerships with governments and like-minded organisations. Therefore, all of its projects are in conjunction with state and central governments, like-minded philanthropists, corporates, donors, NGOs and social delivery organisations.

In line with the Millennium Development Goals, Piramal Foundation is committed towards improving primary healthcare and nutrition, universal primary education and enabling access to safe drinking water.

Each social initiative nurtured by Piramal Foundation, addresses one of the three focus areas that include -

- Primary Health & Nutrition - Piramal Swasthya
- Education - Piramal Foundation for Education Leadership
- Clean Drinking Water - Piramal Sarvajal

The Foundation's initiatives are a reflection of the Group's core values and corporate philosophy of 'Doing Well and Doing Good'.

Offices in over 30 countries Brand presence in over 100 global markets Team of over 15,000 people from 21 diverse nationalities

Valued at US$ 10 Billion, Piramal Group is a global business conglomerate with diverse interests in Pharma, Financial Services, Information Management, Real Estate and Glass Packaging. The Group has offices in over 30 countries and a global brand presence in more than 100 markets.

Under the aegis of Mr. Ajay Piramal, the Chairman, Piramal Group is a torchbearer of trusteeship and responsible business ethos. Based on the philosophy of 'Doing Well and Doing Good', the Group continues to create long-term value for its stakeholders and the community at large.

In the three decades of its existence, Piramal Group has pursued a twin strategy of organic and inorganic growth.

Driven by its core values, Piramal Group steadfastly pursues inclusive growth, while adhering to ethical and values-driven practices. Piramal Foundation, the philanthropic arm of the Piramal Group develops innovative solutions to resolve issues that are critical roadblocks towards unlocking India's economic potential. Its sustainable development programmes in healthcare, education and clean drinking water across 21 Indian states, largely in partnership with the central and state governments have impacted over 90 Million lives.

Purpose: The values that guide our culture are embodied in PF purpose - 'Doing Well and Doing Good'. PF believes that individual success and organisational growth cannot be mutually exclusive from responsible and ethical business practices. PF purpose provides clear guidance to PF people and ensures that it identifies the right partners to create mutual, enduring value.

Rooted in values, driven by passion: The philosophy of 'Doing Well and Doing Good', along with its core values of Knowledge, Action, Care & Impact have been constant in its journey and serve as guideposts to help PF become the company we would like to be.

PF stay true to its purpose of 'Doing Well and Doing Good' by following three basic tenets:

Healthcare Insights & Analytics: Healthcare Insights & Analytics, a business division of Piramal Enterprises Limited, is a cohesive portfolio of companies that offers best-in-class, high-value healthcare analytics, data and insight products & services to the world's leading pharma, biotech and medical technology companies, enabling them to take informed business decisions.

Over the last 3 years, the business division has compiled a strong, rich and informative data repository that is amongst the largest in the US. Today, it covers over 90 percent of the healthcare ecosystem, enabling the business to deliver deep and relevant insights to clients.

Based on the Group's core values, the business division continues to create value for all its stakeholders.

Piramal Foundation for Education Leadership Transforms the Education Ecosystem through its 'School Excellence Program' in Surat: The initiative has impacted over 2000 teachers and headmasters, leading to improved Student Learning Outcomes. In Surat, the Cluster Resource Coordinators (CRCs) and Urban Resource Coordinators (URCs) contributed and collaborated with school headmasters to train and support the teaching community.

Piramal Foundation for Education Leadership the School Excellence Program was introduced to address the need of improving student learning outcomes in Surat Municipal Corporation (SMC) schools that were run by Nagar Prathmik Shikshan Samiti (NPSS).

During the 4 years of this School Excellence Program, various training and fellowship initiatives were introduced to enhance the knowledge base of the teachers and headmasters, for imparting better education to students. For example, Teachers Instructional Practices and Processes System (TIPPS), one of the key initiatives undertaken by the Programme, recorded lesson deliveries by teachers for creating a peer learning environment through open feedback sessions. Tools such as 'Building as Learning Aid' (BaLA), were promoted in schools for a healthy learning environment. Libraries were set-up by the headmasters and teachers for inculcating reading habits which enriched the holistic learning and comprehension skills of students. Learning Centers were set-up for students for their lessons and homework after school, by engaging the community youth.

In collaboration with NPSS, several initiatives were implemented to increase the enrollment in schools, through participation in events such as 'Pravesh Utsav', where the Gandhi Fellows, with the support of headmasters and teachers performed 'Nukkad Nataks' and organized rallies. Implementation of the 'Swachh Bharat Abhiyan' campaign sensitized the community dwellers on the awareness of health, hygiene and cleanliness.

The Piramal Foundation for Education Leadership (PFEL), an initiative of the Piramal Foundation, has been crafting, implementing and offering leadership training programmes for school headmasters, youth and education administrators in the government system by collaboratively improving processes, deploying tools and integrating technology through various programmes.

PFEL has signed long-term MoUs with 12 states across India in collaboration with the state and central governments. PFEL believes in causing behaviour change at scale in government officials across the value chain. This is achieved by building Meaning, Learning, Joy and Pride along with improving processes and integrating technology in the government education system of India.

Piramal Foundation is a Section 8 company that develops innovative solutions to resolve issues that are critical roadblocks towards unlocking India's economic potential. The Piramal Group's core values of Knowledge, Action Care and Impact guide the organisation in carrying out its responsibilities towards society. It believes that considerable positive change can occur when we collaborate with like-minded partners and nurture projects that are scalable, ensuring a long-term impact. In line with the Strategic Development Goals, the Piramal Foundation is focused on universal primary education, empowering women, reducing child mortality rates, improving maternal health and improving access to safe drinking water.

Recently, Piramal Foundation partnered with NITI Aayog to transform 25 aspirational districts across 7 states in India.

The Foundation currently works across 21 states and has impacted over 90 million lives, mostly in partnership with state governments. It has developed innovative approaches and programs in every vertical and has built strong partnerships with governments, technology partners and international organisations, including with Michael & Susan Dell Foundation, Harvard Graduate School of Education and World Diabetes Foundation. The projects are implemented through Piramal Swasthya, Piramal Sarvajal and Piramal Foundation for Education Leadership.

Piramal Enterprises Limited is the flagship company of the Piramal Group.

Piramal Enterprises Limited (PEL) is one of India's large diversified companies with presence in Pharma, Financial Services and Healthcare Information Management. The company generates ~46 percent of its revenues from international markets. Driven by both organic as well as inorganic strategy, PEL has steered dynamic business growth over the three decades of its existence.

Anticipating the potential of financial services in India, PEL built a platform with innovative financial solutions that cater to the needs of varied industry verticals.

It made its foray into the financial services sector with Piramal Capital & Housing Finance Limited (PCHFL), a housing finance company registered with the National Housing Bank (NHB) that is engaged in various financial services businesses. It provides end-to-end financing solutions in both wholesale and retail funding opportunities across sectors such as real estate and infrastructure, renewable energy, hospitality, logistics, industrials, auto components etc. Through its group companies, the platform has strategic partnerships with leading global pension funds such as Canadian Pension Plan Investment Board (CPPIB), APG and Ivanhoe Cambridge.

India Resurgence Fund (IndiaRF), an equal joint venture by Piramal Enterprises Limited and Bain Capital Credit, invests capital in the form of both debt and equity in India's distressed asset space.

When the Indian pharmaceutical industry was focused on international generics, PEL saw an opportunity to expand its pharma business and invested in the domestic formulation business.

Today, its Pharma division has end-to-end manufacturing capabilities across 13 global facilities and a large global distribution network in over 100 countries. PEL sells a portfolio of niche differentiated pharma products and provides an entire pool of pharma services (including the areas of injectables, Highly Potent Active Pharmaceutical Ingredients (HPAPI) etc).

When the world was talking about critical healthcare, PEL realised the power of data and information and invested in healthcare analytics.

PEL's Healthcare Insights & Analytics business division is the premier provider of healthcare analytics, data & insight products and services to the world's leading pharma, biotech and medical technology companies and enables them to take informed business decisions.

PEL's corporate ethos, a reflection of its core values –Knowledge, Action, Care and Impact, has enabled the company to develop and consolidate a coveted international business network of strong partnerships with global market leaders, committed to creating long-term value to all stakeholders.

Piramal Swasthya: India is a country of diversity and nearly 70 percent of its population resides in rural and remote areas with very limited or no availability of Healthcare services. Distance to Healthcare facilities, geographical constraints and tough terrain adds on to the challenges of Healthcare in India. To alleviate this challenge, Piramal Swasthya Remote Health Advisory and Intervention Service seeks to provide round the clock health advice to remote and vulnerable sections of the community and Community Outreach Program aims at tackling barriers faced by rural people in accessing Primary Healthcare. Remote Health Advisory and Intervention Service (RHAI).

104 Health Helpline | 24×7 Healthcare Advises: A beneficiary, anywhere in a given state, can dial 104 Health Helpline toll-free number through phone and connect to a Health Advisor and/or doctor who could address the health query through use of advanced medical algorithms and disease summaries accessed easily through medical health software while referring to patient's Electronic Health record online. 104 service is a 24 x 7 contact center that aims to reduce the minor ailment load on public health system by offering medical information and advice, virtually. Patient can avail counseling services; request directory information like list of Hospitals and services offered and can lodge a complaint against any Public Health system facility.

1097 HIV AIDS Helpline | Nationwide Call Center: On world AIDS day, 1st December 2014, India's first HIV AIDS Counseling Helpline Service – 1097 called as National Aids Helpline 1097 was launched by National Aids Control Organisation and supported by Population Service International. It is implemented by Piramal Swasthya.

1097 assists in achieving NACP goal of reducing new infections by 50 percent and providing comprehensive care, support and treatment to all persons living with HIV/AIDS i.e. prevention of those who are not infected and care, support & treatment for those who have been infected.

Mother & Child Tracking System (MCTS) Call Center: Piramal Swasthya's Mother & Child Tracking System call center aims to track all pregnant women and their children to provide awareness about healthy practices, government schemes and benefits and ensuring co- ordination between healthcare functionaries and the beneficiaries. The call centre make outbound calls and offer information about antenatal care, Government healthcare schemes for mothers and children, institutional deliveries, immunisation, iron and folic acid tablets received etc.

Core Services: Outbound calls, Grievance redressal, connecting mothers with respective ASHA, Tracking of mothers and children.

Telemedicine Services | Specialist Advice through audio and video: Telemedicine services offer specialist advice to the most remotest of places through high quality sophisticated software. It focuses upon bringing much needed specialist Healthcare to remotest of areas where there are very few or no health workers. It virtually connects doctor to patients and addresses the need of highly skilled health workers where they are scarce.

Community Outreach Program (COP)

- **Mobile Medical Units**

Nurse led Model | Sanjeevani Village Health Outreach program | PPP – Assam | 2012

Sanjeevani – Village Health Outreach Program is once-a-month, fixed date outreach initiative that will result in converged health services at the Village level. Sanjeevani is operating throughout the state with 80 Mobile Medical Units (MMU). Each MMU is manned by Registration & Measurement Officer, Lab Technician, Pharmacist, Auxiliary Nurse cum Midwife (ANM) and Pilot.

The services aim in early identification, Screening, referral, follow-up and free medicines for effective Chronic disease management. Based on the screening done in VHOP, the beneficiaries are referred to the nearest PHC for confirmation, prescription and commencement of treatment. Each MMU has a pre-defined calendar and a route plan for delivering the services covering 2 villages and a population of 3000 each day on an average and 48 villages in a monthly cycle of 24 days.

Doctor led Model | Chandranna Sanchara Chikitsa | PPP – Andhra Pradesh | 2016: State of Andhra Pradesh envisions the overall health and wellness of the state population. Piramal Swasthya's one of the largest Mobile Medical Units (MMUs) program in Andhra Pradesh is acting as a force multiplier to existing health centers. These MMUs are making healthcare service delivery available, accessible and affordable for remote and underserved population.

CSR intervention: Mobile Health services are also operated for several public sector and private sector organizations eg: Department of Atomic Energy, ILFS and BPCl etc. These services aim at enabling access to primary health care to the employees and their families around their major manufacturing facilities and often cover tough terrains and far flung habitations with communities that are vulnerable and in of quality Healthcare services.

Shriram Transport Finance Company Limited – Mobile Medical Units and Clinics: Truck drivers in India have to travel long distances on an extensive spread of National and State highways. Their occupation exposes them to a multitude of risk factors resulting to various health problems that are generally neglected. Shriram Transport Finance Company Limited (STFC) in partnership with Piramal Swasthya has launched a unique primary healthcare programme for the truckers community which aims to provide primary healthcare services at no cost through Seven (07) Mobile Medical Units and One (01) day care Clinic. The mobile healthcare camps through MMUs in and around the strategically planned service points are an endeavor to make quality primary healthcare services available, accessible and affordable to the transport fraternity at large.

Core Services:

- Primary healthcare camps at strategically identified locations
- Day Clinic at trucker's parking hub (Mumbai).
- Screening, diagnosis, treatment and referral for Non-Communicable Diseases (Diabetes & Hypertension), Communicable Diseases and minor ailments.
- Awareness, education and counselling on healthy life style practices, life style modifications, Non-Communicable disease management.

This Programme is funded by STFC as part of its CSR Initiative and managed by Piramal Swasthya. Currently it is operational at Jaipur, Mumbai, Bhubaneswar, Vijaywada, Chennai, Bangalore and Hyderabad and the day clinic operates at truckers parking hub at Kalamboli, Navi Mumbai.

Non-Communicable Disease Management | ASHWAS | CSR -Telangana | 2016: A community based Non Communicable Disease intervention program focused on timely screening, identification and treatment of Diabetic and Hypertensive patients. Program also aims to reduce the incidence of Non Communicable Diseases (Diabetes & Hypertension) through preventive, predictive and promotive means of Healthcare service delivery.

Tribal Health Program

ASARA: Started in 2010, ASARA is a Unique model ending preventable deaths in extremely remote, hilly and difficult to access terrain of Araku valley, Andhra Pradesh. The model aims to provide access to specialist consultation in remotest of the areas where there is no or limited availability of Healthcare resources.

The project has now been expanded to Paderu and Chintapalle mandals. The expansion aims to cover the 2.5 lakh-plus population, including women, children and adolescents in 1179 hard-to-reach habitations across the entire tribal belt of Vishakhapatnam district, starting with Paderu and Chintapalle.

Gosthani – Community Nutrition Hub: Emphasis on nutrition is an important dimension of this program. A community-based approach to nutrition has been adopted at dedicated 'Nutrition Hubs' to educate communities about a healthy and nutritious diet. The hubs are being set up to help prepare, process and preserve nutritional – traditional and locally available – food items for families.

Cancer Screening Program

D.E.S.H. – Detect Early Save Her & Him: Piramal Swasthya has launched its community-based screening programme – D.E.S.H. for oral, breast and cervical cancers in Kamrup. The programme components include creating community awareness, screening for the cancer of oral cavity, breast and cervix through mobile cancer screening units, mobility for the patients detected positive to a treatment centre and tracking and follow-up.

Equipped with the best equipment, including a mammography unit and staffed by doctors, nurses and radiographers, the Mobile Cancer Screening Unit screens the local population for oral, breast and cervical cancer. Patients identified with cancer are referred to Dr. B. Borooah Cancer Institute for treatment.

Integrated Electronic Medical Records

Accessible Medical Record via Integrated Technologies (AMRIT): AMRIT is a platform built by Piramal Swasthya, which will act as a foundation or the first step in achieving transformed health care. The uniqueness of AMRIT is, it will allow disparate systems to be able to connect to it and use the Patients Health Records, thereby creating a unified and ubiquitous presence of Health Data of the patient across India with unique Beneficiary ID's. This in healthcare and that to primary healthcare is a boon as the beneficiaries visiting different locations for healthcare advice and treatment will not have to worry about carrying their health records, be it prescriptions, lab tests or radiology test like MRI, USG etc. AMRIT as a platform is built to capture data for ANC, PNC, NCD (including cervical, breast and oral cancer).

104 Arogyavani | PPP – Karnataka | 2013: Piramal Swasthya's one of the largest health helpline centres in India providing validated health advice to vulnerable population of Karnataka State. Arogyavani Karnataka has received over 1.6 crore calls and has provided Medical advice to 6.9 lakh cases. The helpline has served around 12.7 percent cases belonging to communicable diseases, around 56.6 percent Non-Communicable disease cases.

Chandranna Sanchara Chikitsa | PPP – Andhra Pradesh | 2016: State of Andhra Pradesh envisions the overall health and wellness of the state population. Piramal Swasthya's one of the largest Mobile Medical Units (MMUs) program in Andhra Pradesh is acting as a force multiplier to existing health centers. These MMUs are making healthcare service delivery available, accessible and affordable for remote and underserved population.

Mobile Medical Services | PPP – Sri Ganganagar, Rajasthan | 2016: Piramal Swasthya, in partnership with the National Health Mission, Govt. of Rajasthan, has been operating 6 Mobile Medical Units across 6 blocks in Ganganagar district of Rajasthan serving 120 villages each month since April 2015. Each of these MMUs conduct health camps at the pre-designated fixed set of 20 villages in a month. Each MMU is staffed by a Doctor (MBBS), a Nurse (GNM), a Pharmacist, a Lab Technician and a driver. In the MMU along with a free doctor consultation, free basic laboratory tests are performed as well as free medicines are provided. The services are provided with special focus on ANC and PNC checkups and screening, diagnosis and management of NCDs.

Prevention of Parent to Child Transmission of HIV (PPTCT) | PLAN International | iNGO – Rajasthan | 2015: Prevention of Parent to Child transmission (PPTCT) of HIV AIDS – "AHANA" program is a program initiated by PLAN International (India Chapter) in partnership with Piramal Swasthya in 17 districts of Rajasthan to increase the uptake of PPTCT services. The program is supported by the Rajasthan State Aids Control Society (RSACS) and National Health Mission, Govt. of Rajasthan. The Project specifically looks at building skills (facilitate) at institutional and community levels to increase uptake of PPTCT Services in a sensitive manner in the selected districts. The Program aims to build the skills among peripheral health workers under general health system in PPTCT and to conduct outreach and follow-up of HIV Positive Women and HIV Exposed infants.

Comprehensive Type 2 Diabetes Mellitus Project | World Diabetes Foundation | iNGO – Assam | 2016: The Comprehensive Type 2 Diabetes Mellitus project was introduced to fulfil the need for diabetes screening, treatment, and management in Assam. World Diabetes Foundation partnered with Piramal Swasthya to train key human resources with a focus on prevention, management, pregnancy, children, and complications. A major thrust was also put towards affecting positive behavioural changes among the target population.

Social Media Policy: This policy aims at setting guidelines for sharing content across all online Platforms that may influence how the general public perceives Piramal Swasthya.

The term "social media" refers to blog sites, wikis, social networks, content sharing sites and any kind of online communication between two or more entities, (collectively referred as "Social Media").

This policy:

- Is applicable to all employees (core, contract, retainer, consultant or any other category) of Piramal Swasthya while at the workplace or outside the work place.
- Is applicable to access of Social Media sites from Piramal (Group, Foundation, Swasthya)/client systems or personal systems; and is subject to country specific laws and regulations. Relevant country specific laws and regulations shall supersede this policy wherever applicable.

Piramal Sarvajal: Piramal Sarvajal, seeded by the Piramal Foundation in 2008, is a mission driven social enterprise which designs and deploys innovative solutions for creating affordable access to safe drinking water in underserved areas. Sarvajal is at the forefront of developing technologies and business practices in the safe drinking water sector that are designed to make a purely market-based model sustainable in both rural and urban deployment conditions. Currently, PF are reaching out to about 4,30,000 consumers daily, through 1000 touch-points across 16 states. To Innovate, Demonstrate, Enable and Promote affordable safe-drinking water solutions.

Piramal Sarvajal sets up community level solutions that are locally operated but centrally managed on a market based pay per use system. While PF are purification technology agnostic, PF leverage cloud based technology for greater operational oversight. As such, its initiatives are low cost for high impact.

Two thirds of the Indian terrain has no perennial river flowing through it, creating overdependence on ground water. Even today three quarters of India still drinks untreated water, inadvertently leading to losses ranging from diarrheal deaths to permanent fluorosis.

This was particularly poignant in the Piramal hometown of Bagar, situated in a water scarce region of Rajasthan. To change this, Sarvajal founder Anand Shah gave genesis to a program aimed at achieving low-cost scalable solutions serving "safe water for all."

Since the initiative was bound to be a multi-location affair, distributed operations posed a serious challenge to efficiently and (cost) effectively managing the project. Also, generating sufficient demand meant breaking existing taboos around buying water by educating consumers about water-health linkages. Sarvajal's team therefore innovated a solution that could be customized for the water contamination profile of any location with pioneering remote monitoring technology. It also invested in community awareness activities while tapping into local entrepreneurial drive and resources by adopting a franchise model.

Innovative Elements: Piramal Sarvajal (PS) is committed to reducing the burden of disease while creating local livelihood in village ecosystem. PS design and deploy community level sustainable solutions for creating affordable access to safe drinking water in underserved areas.

Piramal Sarvajal pioneered last-mile operational accountability by developing and deploying remotely monitored and controlled drinking water purification systems. This in turn has resulted in a more transparent data backed system that let's us track social impact in real-time. Piramal Sarvajal's other popular innovation is the Water ATM: a solar powered, cloud-connected, smart card based automatic water vending machines.

Purification: Because the water profile of each community is unique, the innovation is purification technology agnostic. PS generally use 5 step purification machines where you can customize which parts you need in accordance with the local needs. Depending on the local need, PS pick up existing, off-the shelf purification technology to address the local water context.

All PS purification machines equipped with remote monitoring and information layering.

Different types of water contamination

Geogenic Contamination: This refers to elevated concentrations of certain naturally occurring elements in groundwater which have a negative health effect on humans consuming this water. In northern India, the main geogenic contaminant is flouride, which effects the groundwater at dangerously high levels causing chronic health problems.

Pathogenic contamination: This refers to disease-causing bacteria, viruses and protozoa that contaminate groundwater and infect people with water-borne diseases such as cholera, typhoid fever and bacillary dysentery. In developing countries like India, the pathogenic contaminant Escherichia coli, the main bacteria present in human and animal feces has a crippling effect on public health.

Soochak: The Soochak is a remote monitoring device which can be mounted on a commercial-scale water purification plant. This patented device captures minute-by-minute machine status on the technology backend and allows Piramal Sarvajal to sustainably bring affordable, safe drinking water to underserved communities in the most far-flung reaches of India. At the same time, it's touch screen guides local operators on the daily functioning of the plant in the local language.

Water ATM: Water ATMs are automated water dispensing units, which provide communities with 24/7 safe water access. They are solar powered and cloud connected, thus enabling remote tracking of the water quality and of each pay per use transaction.

Purifying Chilling Dispensing Unit (PCD): Purifies, Cools & Dispenses 100 percent safe drinking water at any place, any time. PCD units are suitable for offices, showrooms, hotels, hospitals, public places like railway stations, bus stations, gardens, malls, community areas etc.

Features

- 5 Stage Purification Process
- Self-Cleaning System
- Remote Monitoring
- Real time data
- 24 X 7 Water Dispensing
- Optional Payment Mode
    - (a) RFID prepaid card
    - (b) Coin issued by Govt of India
- Efficient After-Sales Service personnel across the country

Partner Solution: Piramal Sarvajal has been a pioneer in deploying remotely tracked community-level drinking water purification systems by bringing accountability to day-to-day operations. By being technology-driven, PS ensures better machine and operator accountability, meaning better service for the communities.

Piramal Sarvajal provides safe drinking water through customized decentralized drinking water solutions at selected urban / rural locations. This is achieved through installation of a state-of-the-art community level purification plant for delivery of safe drinking water at affordable prices to the beneficiaries.

The project is operated in partnership with a local entrepreneur or the local Panchayat/ Community Based Organization; thereby creating sustainable livelihood opportunities within the chosen community. To address the issue of effective post-purification water distribution, Piramal Sarvajal has innovated a unique Water ATM model that uses smart cards to create price transparency and quality accountability to the last mile.

Operating Models

Model 1:
Single Unit Community Solution

- One purification plant installed in any community (village, school, construction site etc.).
- Optional installation of Water ATMs to track water consumption by beneficiaries
- Piramal Sarvajal trains an operator/entrepreneur who manages local daily operations
- Piramal Sarvajal provides regular maintenance support and community awareness drives

- All partners have access to daily and monthly performance reports using real-time data from the ground

Model 2:
Hub and Spoke Model

- One centrally located purification plant with access to raw water and power
- Water ATMs installed at nearby community (slum, school network), increasing Piramal Sarvajal's impact radius
- Water ATMs are solar-powered and can operate off-grid, providing 24/7 access to safe drinking water
- Filtered water is transferred from the central purification plant to the ATMs using a hygienic water carrying vehicle
- Piramal Sarvajal provides regular maintenance support and community awareness drives
- All partners have access to daily and monthly performance reports using real-time data from the ground

Adopt a village

The problem

- India has a population of 1.2 billion of which 68 percent is rural.
- 77 million Indians lack access to safe drinking water
- 85 percent of country is dependent directly on groundwater as its main source of water, yet the Central Ground Water Board estimates that over half of India's groundwater is contaminated with poisonous substances
- According to World Bank estimates, 21 percent of communicable diseases in India are related to unsafe water

PS Solution:

- Strategically designed for remote, off-grid locations with central oversight and management.
- Low-footprint public facing Water ATMs provide 24x7 availability of water at an transparent, affordable price.
- Continuous monitoring of real time field data and vital process parameters means stakeholders are guaranteed of water quality and project management.
- Field teams provide business handholding for local entrepreneur, engage community leaders and lead door to door health awareness campaigns.

Sarvajal Impact

- Villagers have access to drinking water of assured quality
- Incidences of waterborne disease are reduced as health is improved
- Changes perception of drinking water and health linkages to create informed consumers
- Community members, particularly women and children, need not waste time in fetching water from remote sources

Adopt a School

The problem

- Around 30 percent of rural schools in India lack access to safe drinking water on school premises. Currently, students are either required to carry water from home or they miss class because they are sent to fetch water during the school hours.
- Although 93 percent of schools have drinking water facilities within campus, it is functional in only 50 percent of these schools
- Illness due to water borne diseases is the primary reason for absenteeism from schools in rural India
- More than 40 percent of diarrhea cases in schoolchildren are contracted at school rather than at home.

PS Solution

- Around 30 percent of rural schools in India lack access to safe drinking water on school premises. Currently, students are either required to carry water from home or they miss class because they are sent to fetch water during the school hours.
- Although 93 percent of schools have drinking water facilities within campus, it is functional in only 50 percent of these schools
- Special school awareness drives for students
- Social impact for each installations clearly substantiated with data
- Ownership Structure – Government Owned or Sarvajal Owned (Pay-per-use).

Sarvajal Impact in Schools

Socially

- Students have access to drinking water of assured quality.
- Changes perception of drinking water and health linkages at a young age.

- Students need not waste time in fetching water during school hours.

Economically

- Reduce school absenteeism due to water related illnesses.
- Students convey the importance of safe drinking water to their parents.
- Potential to expand the model to become self-sustaining, even after the philanthropic start-up funds expire.

Sustainably

- Invested capital is used judiciously and efficiently to fund a local initiative.
- Provides real time data monitoring services to measure social impact.
- Data driven transparency to the last mile assures optimized productivity of sponsored projects.

Adopt a Slum

The problem

- 65 million people live in India's 33,510 urban slums
- Indian urban water managers often experiences system losses of up to 50 percent , causing huge environmental inefficiencies and financial losses.
- Providing piped water access to these densely populated areas is often not an option. Tanker trucks, the current government alternative, are unreliable and unable to serve the large population.
- India's poor ultimately pay more than the middle class does for basic water services because of forced bribes and being disproportionately affected by direct taxes on consumption.

PS Solution

- Strategic Hub and Spoke design takes advantage of the dense population and to serve the maximum number of people.
- Low-footprint public facing Water ATMs provide 24x7 availability of water at an transparent, affordable price.
- Continuous monitoring of real time field data and vital process parameters means stakeholders are guaranteed of water quality and project management.

- Field teams provide business handholding for local entrepreneur, engage community leaders and lead door to door health awareness campaigns.

Sarvajal Impact in Slums

- Slum inhabitants have reliable access to drinking water of assured quality.
- Incidences of waterborne disease are reduced as health is improved.
- Changes perception of drinking water and health linkages to create informed consumers.

Economically

- Families save burdensome cost of healthcare to treat waterborne diseases.
- Work absenteeism due to water related illnesses is reduced.
- Sustainable local jobs are created through Sarvajal's operation.
- Success of Sarvajal's work inspires other entrepreneurs to enter the decentralized drinking water sector, bolstering the local market.
- Model is economically self-sustaining.

Sustainably

- Invested capital is used judiciously and efficiently to fund a local initiative.
- Provides real time data monitoring services to measure social impact.
- Data driven transparency to the last mile assures optimized productivity of sponsored projects.
- Donors create lasting legacy by investing in long term sustainable ventures with local buy-in.

Jal Katha

Take PS to the waterspout – safe and clean: With the mission to find the right school to create access to safe drinking water for children, the Sarvajal team set out with an open mind. The secondary data search took the team to the district of Mewat in Haryana. Apportioned as a separate district from Gurgaon in 2005, Mewat had alarmingly low indicators of education, health, standard of living, public infrastructure and services.

Being a semi-arid region with highly saline ground water, there is an acute drinking water shortage in the villages in Mewat, to the extent that they are dependent on the neighboring villages for water. The district also grapples with an unhygienic environment and appalling living conditions. This, together with minimal health infrastructure, further weighs down on its population's health.

In comparison to the rest of Haryana, Mewat's sex ratio indicated a favorable trend in the last census, but in contrast to it, the literacy rate among females is far lower than that of the males in the same district. The conservative families of the region preferred to bestow an edge to their male children by sending them off to other districts or private schools for education. As usual, a girl child is often burdened with household choresor married early and may not get to see the lights of a classroom. A study commissioned by Niti Aayog also cited the reason for girls dropping out of school, as the burden of fetching water for the family. This sets the vicious cycle of a girl's life, in motion. Only girl children who are fortunate enough would find their way to a government school. Given this, odds are that PS still would find more girl children in the Government Primary Schools than boys.

All that was not right in the district of Mewat made it just the right choice for a Sarvajal intervention – the school that was selected was the Government Primary School in Nagina.

Located in Nagina, one of the 5 blocks of Mewat, the school was established in 1964. The school has 830 students, 23 class rooms, 18 teachers (in the place of 32) and 8 cooks to take care of noon meal scheme. A broad range of issues prevents the school from thriving — the infrastructure, dilapidated toilets, furniture that needed fixing and more. The school had just the bare minimum – the head master's room is a witness to it.

But the greatest of the hazards to health of the children was the large dumping ground in front of the school - stagnant water from sewages modeled a home to many a pig family. Swarms of houseflies that enveloped everything around could send a chill down any unsuspecting visitor's spine. It reminds you of the hard task that rests squarely on the Swachh Bharat Abhiyaan with our Prime Minister as the key champion. It also reminds you of the indifference that plagues our society – the resultant inaction.

The water sources are two, a tubewell with 2000 TDS and water from supply stored in a reservoir. When these were not enough school bought tanks of water. The school did not have enough assistance to buy water all the time. Arun from VI standard has a great smile but dental fluorosis has already made his teeth opaque with a brown stain a sign of degeneration of teeth. His father works as a peon in the bank, he lives in a joint family and has around 14 members in it. He does not bring water from home but he drinks many times from the plant, since his class is the closest to the water spout. Many children in the school have opaque teeth like his, though it is not reversible, further erosion can be prevented if they avoid water with high fluoride.

Sarvajal through a CSR partnership with Dr. Lal Path Lab established a 500 LPH purification plant at this school on April 26 2018. The water is purified with RO and UV/UF technology and made available for children to drink through the day.

Sarvajal Acts two fold: The school has been struggling to ensure that it receives prominence in the eyes of the government to attract financial support to keep it functional. The Headmaster, Mr. Hari Chand invited the key stakeholders the community leaders, Block Education Officer and Pachayat leaders for the inauguration, to advocate for the different needs of the school. The Headmaster said, "Today we have pure drinking water from Piramal Sarvajal through their CSR partner and we are positive that it will improve the lives for children, I am looking forward for support from all of you to improve the school."

He articulated the benefit "To know there is an unrestricted supply of drinking water at school will help the school gain recognition in the eye of community. If the parents know the children will get safe drinking water round the clock we will be able to retain children in the school."

Children are not deterred to play in the scorching sun anymore: Generally, children of primary school age need at least 3-4 glasses of water during the day with the number going higher in summers when the temperature is at its peak. The scorching sun seldom deters the spirited young children from running around in rigorous catch-me-if-you-can-games during lunch break. Bare feet, and hot sand notatall a matter. This is all the more reason to situate drinking water at a convenient, easy-to-run-to and safe location. The ease has to be from an access point of view that encourages these young sun-braving hearts to drink regularly. With the safety highlight, the water needs to lure them in taste and motivate them to return to it many times a day – it truly sounds like a mother's job. "Paani peethe rahna beta – dhoop tej hai"

Even running in groups from one building to another aimlessly pulling at each other and huddling together at the end of the run seems to be so much fun. Oblivious to sweat gleaming on the temples, and trickling down the nape, the drying lips and the parching throats, they are engrossed in play. Soon the little body start sending signals to run to a water spout – Sarvajal's safely housed purification plant and the water dispensed at the right height for children welcomes them. The sight of children in a row cupping their palms to drink from the flowing stream of water from the tap, with steady gulping sounds, with an 'ah! 'that puts a satisfying end to that perfect drink, wiping the lingering water from their faces with the back of their little hands, is heartening. The water quenches their thirst and their wet palm cools their face. The satiated look on the face of these little ones is precisely why Sarvajal is here.

While this plant is located in the primary section of the school, opportunity to serve is doubled since the premises also houses higher secondary school which has around 250 students the benefit of access of safe drinking water also can be utilized by these adolescent girls.

Many a reason to keep a child from school, water should never be one!

When private schools distinguish between the world of haves and have-nots, Government schools hold the safety net for every child who has already fallen through the sieves of privilege and fortune. While the opportunity to serve girls resonates at the hearts, not to forget are the boys who are here due to social and economic situations of their parents. Among those girls and boys are many who have stunted growth due to nutritional deficiencies, many living with conditions attributed at birth and many differentially abled- the school with its minimum facilities have welcomed them and is providing them education.

Safe water can keep them in good health, prevent them from falling ill with water borne illness, help children achieve some of their developmental milestones, continue to study and rise above their current predicament – support them to have a dream and pursue it.

Help a village and a like – minded corporate

Adopt a Village: Piramal Sarvajal and HDFC ERGO partnered to launch the Sarvajal Kendra (Sarvajal Hub) in Peeth, in October of 2013. Peeth is a village in the heart of the Aravallis in Rajasthan. It is one of the most backward districts of the country and is severely water stressed. In Peeth, most people (84 percent) get their drinking water from the local well, contaminated with dangerously high levels of fluoride and other heavy minerals. Although surveys showed that the local residents were aware of danger of their water posed to their health, but the only alternative was a single private drinking water supplier, who charged 2 rupees per litre and only catered to 40 families.

Thus, the market welcomed the Sarvajal Kendra, as a much needed solution. Today, the facility serves more than 200 families daily, ensuring they get safe water delivered at their doorstep. In fact, since the Sarvajal Kendra 2 more local suppliers have been inspired to replicate the drinking water business model. All together, the 4 suppliers now reach at more than 500 families.

No Power, No Water

Adopt a School: The Desh Bandhu & Manju Gupta Foundation has a boarding school in the Dhule district of Maharashtra. This school was primarily for children of tribal families who wouldn't otherwise have access to formal education. However, the children's academic performance was being affected by the significant number of sick days due to diarrhea and other waterborne illnesses.

For such a worthy cause Piramal Sarvajal was happy step in and install a purification unit to serve the children with clean water. The Sarvajal water would keep the kids healthy and fully functioning for learning.

In fact, only 6 months after installation, the Desh Bandhu & Manju Gupta Foundation reached back out to thank Sarvajal. They eagerly shared that, since the plant's installation, absences due to waterborne illness has decreased by 90 percent .

Slums can be smart as well

Adopt a Slum: Despite living in India's national capital, many households in Delhi still do not have access to piped water. Indeed, even those who have piped water are not guaranteed safe water quality, making drinking municipal water hazardous for health. Recognizing the dire need of the citizen, Delhi Jal Board (DJB), Government of NCT of Delhi partnered with Piramal Sarvajal to create India's 1st Decentralized Drinking Water Project for Urban Slums. Under this Public-Private Partnership model, PS are creating access for over 10,000 low income families in each of the 6 slum communities.

Public service as a safe and sustainable service

Adopt a public place: The dearth of low-cost, good-quality safe drinking water options in Delhi's public places was blight on a city that is increasingly modernizing as a sustainable global center. In fact, even when authorities installed traditional safe water facilities, there was no way to monitor the upkeep and quality at different locations across the sprawling city. Piramal Sarvajal stepped in with a more efficient, low cost public utility. In partnership with Delhi Transport Corporation (DTC) and Delhi Integrated Multimodal Transit System (DIMTS), and the government of NCT of Delhi PS provided sustainable access to safe drinking water through a network of Water ATMs. Now, authorities know how their facilities are working from a remote central management position and can guarantee quality to the citizen of Delhi.

Multilateral organization partnered projects

Adopt a School: On a typical 45°C summer day, each of the 100 students at Goner Girls' School used to carry a 1 litre bottle filled with drinking water to school, which had to be carefully rationed for the entire school day. Working with the Michael and Susan Dell Foundation, Akshaypatra and Jaipur Zila Parishad, Sarvajal sought to change this. Now that Sarvajal's Water ATM is installed in their school, they no longer have to carry water with them or worry about having enough to stay healthy and hydrated during their lessons.

Govt. partnered (PPP) projects

Adopt a Slum: Kavita ji is a housewife who lives about 200 metres away from Sarvajal's site office in Delhi's Sawda Ghevra JJ Colony. Just prior to Sarvajal's arrival in Sawda, Kavita ji's newest family member Bharti (then 7 months old) had a severe case of diarrhea, leading to hospital bills of more than Rs 5,000. On the doctor's recommendation, Kavita ji started buying

15 litres of Sarvajal everyday for the entire family. She says proudly, "We can go without TV for a few days but not Sarvajal. We are proud to be a Sarvajal gali (Sarvajal lane).

Rural franchise project

Franchise Model: Before we met him, Sandeep was an educated but unemployed 30 year old. His town, Taranagar, lies in the heart of the Churu belt, an area rife with water contamination due to heavy minerals. That's why Sandeep and his uncle, Hanumanji jumped at the opportunity to open a safe water business with Sarvajal. Today, they have been successfully running their franchise for 5 years, employing 12 local youngsters to help serve 3000 people every day. Through referrals, they've helped set up 3 other Sarvajal Franchises across Rajasthan and the success of their business in Taranagar encouraged 3 other local competitors.

Serving underserved construction labourers

Adopt a Community: L&T Realty reached out to Sarvajal to install a drinking water solution for their Crescent Bay, Bhoiwada construction site in Parel East, Mumbai. The 1700 labourers working on site needed a safe water source to hydrate from the daily heavy labor. Sarvajal installed Water ATMs across the living camps to give the workers and their families 24/7 access to clean water. "In just 2 months this system has benefitted the labourers and the staff substantially," claims site supervisor, Mr. Mahamoni. "Earlier we used to get packaged drinking water at times, and we find the quality of Sarvajal to be even better" We are able to see improvement in the health of the labour. They use this water for drinking as well as cooking and particularly stomach-related ailments have almost become very few.

Birla Foundations

Aditya Birla Group is an Indian multinational conglomerate, head quartered in Mumbai, India. It operates in 35 countries with more than 120,000 employees worldwide. The group was founded by Seth Shiv Narayan Birla in 1857. The group has interests in sectors such as viscose staple fibre, metals, cement, viscose filament yarn, branded apparel, carbon black, chemicals, fertilisers, insulators, financial services, telecom, BPO and IT services.

The group had revenue of approximately US$45 billion. It is the third-largest Indian private sector conglomerate behind Tata Group with revenue of just over US$100 billion and RIL with revenue of US$74 billion.

Non-ferrous metals: The Group's, non-ferrous metals are under Hindalco Industries. Its manufacturing locations are primarily in India and it owns mines in Great Sandy Desert, Australia near Nifty Airport called Birla Nifty Copper Operation (Nifty Copper Mine). On 11 February 2007, the company entered into an agreement to acquire the Canadian company Novelis for US$

6 billion, making the combined entity the world's largest rolled-aluminium producer. On 15 May 2007, the acquisition was completed with Novelis shareholders receiving $44.93 per outstanding share of common stock. The Group plans to close a part of its aluminium foil making mill in UK and shift that to its plant near Nagpur.

Cement: The Group's cement business was earlier under Grasim Industries and UltraTech Cement. The two entities have now been merged into UltraTech Cement to form India's largest cement company. UltraTech Cement was acquired from L&T in 2004.

Carbon black: After purchasing Columbian Chemicals Co the Group is now the largest manufacturer of Carbon black worldwide.

Textile business: The Aditya Birla Group is the world's largest producer of Viscose staple fibre. It operates from India, Laos, Thailand, Malaysia and China. It owns the Birla Cellulose brand. Apart from viscose staple fibre, the group also owns acrylic fibre business in Thailand, viscose filament yarn businesses and spinning mills in India and South East Asia. The group has pulp and plantation interests in Canada and Laos. It also owns the Domsjö factory in Sweden which exports viscose today. The Swedish government is hoping to negotiate further investments in Sweden, in particular in the hyper-modern future biorefinery in the city of Örnsköldsvik. Its two companies i.e. Aditya Birla Nuvo Ltd and Grasim Bhiwani Textiles Ltd which is a subsidiary of Grasim Industries are in textile business. Grasim Industries was recently placed 154th in a list of the world's best regarded firms compiled by Forbes.

Planet Fashion: Planet Fashion is a men's clothing brand. Commencing in 2001, Planet Fashion now has more than one hundred fifty retailers in 100 cities throughout India. Planet Fashion, right now, is an acronym being a menswear getaway giving comprehensive loset alternatives for all those occasions, around price things, while using greatest brands throughout each category.

The Aditya Birla Group's retail store enterprise – Madura Fashion & Lifestyle – is one of the strongest developing brand clothes corporations throughout The Indian subcontinent. Global marketing involves models like Van Heusen, Allen Solly, Peter England and Louis Philippe. Madura Fashion & Lifestyle has 1607 shops, covering 2.2 sq. ft. connected with retail store room. It has 1,500 premium multi-brand shops along with 320+ departmental shops worldwide. The company out sources engineering, textiles and apparel.

Telecom services: Aditya Birla Group is the majority shareholder of Idea Cellular. Idea Cellular was started as a joint venture with the AT&T and the Tata Group. After an IPO on the Indian stock markets, Idea Cellular now accounts for a third of the group's market capitalisation. The company is headquartered in Mumbai. On 31 August 2018 Idea Cellular completed its merger with Vodafone India and thereby became largest telecom company in terms of subscribers and revenue, surpassing Airtel.

Financial services: Aditya Birla Capital (ABC) is the umbrella brand for all the financial services business of The Aditya Birla Group. ABFSG ranks among the top 5 fund managers in India (including LIC) with an AUM of US$23 billion. Having a strong presence across the life insurance, asset management, lending (excluding Housing), housing finance, equity & commodity broking, wealth management and distribution, online money management portal—Aditya Birla Money My Universe, general insurance advisory and private equity and health insurance businesses. ABFSG reported consolidated revenue from these businesses at just under 70 billion (US$ 970 million) and profits of about 7.5 billion (US$100 million). The financial services arm of the group is currently headed by Ajay Srinivasan.

K. K. Birla Foundation: The K.K. Birla Foundation was established in 1991 by Krishna Kumar Birla in Delhi. Its mission is to promote literature (especially Hindi literature) and the arts, as well as education and social work. It regularly gets mentioned in the media for the awards it confers, including:

- the Saraswati Samman Rs. 500,000 (US$7,000) for literary work in any Indian language(22),
- the Vyas Samman Rs.250,000 (US$3,500) for prose/poetry work in Hindi,
- the Bihari Puraskar Rs.100,000 (US$1,400) for prose/poetry work in Hindi/Rajasthani, only authors from Rajasthan are eligible,
- the Shankar Puraskar Rs.150,000 (US$2,100) for a work in Hindi concerning Indian philosophy, culture and/or art,
- the Vachaspati Puraskar Rs.150,000 (US$2,100) for any work in Sanskrit, the G.D. Birla Award for Scientific Research Rs. 150,000 (US$2,100).

G. P. Birla Scholarship: The Trust has been established to carry forward the cherished dream of Late Shri G. P. Birla, the renowned Industrialist and Philanthropist, to promote education, develop human resources and empower the youth of the Country. With this objective, the Trust proposes to grant Scholarships to meritorious students, male or female, from West Bengal, who have in the year 2018, passed class XII examination and have secured 80 percent marks or more from State Board or 85 percent or more from Central Board and are in need of financial help to pursue further studies.

Further studies may be in any stream including Science, Humanities, Engineering, Medicine, Architecture, Commerce, Law, Chartered Accountancy, Company Secretaryship and Cost Accountancy Course in any recognized University/Institution in India. Scholarship amount will be to cover Tuition Fees and Hostel Fees, [where applicable], subject to a ceiling of Rs.

50,000/- per student per year. The Scholarship will be granted to 100 selected students for one year at a time and to be continued upon satisfactory performance by the Student in the preceding year, as evaluated by the Trust, up to completion of the Course subject to a ceiling of 4 years, on yearly basis. Additional onetime payment of Rs. 7000/- towards purchase of Books in 1st Year shall also be given.

For selection of Students for Scholarship, an Expert Panel of the Trust will review the applications received and interview shortlisted prospective candidates. The decision of the Expert Panel will be final. Applications may be forwarded through the Head of the Institution from which the Student has passed Class XII or where he has taken admission.

Mission

- To promote education, develop human resources and empower the youth of the Country.
- To support meritorious and needy Students to pursue further studies and fulfill their dreams.
- To produce future leaders of the Country.

Values: Acting and taking decisions in a manner that is fair and honest. Following the highest standards of professionalism and being recognised for doing so. Integrity for the group means not only financial and intellectual integrity, but encompasses all other forms as are generally understood.

Heritage: The values and the success of the Aditya Birla Group can be traced back to the inspiring ideals and vision of two legendary leaders, who established the foundation of the Group in India and overseas. The roots of the Aditya Birla Group date back to the 19th century in the picturesque town of Pilani set amidst the Rajasthan desert. It was here that Seth Shiv Narayan Birla started trading in cotton, laying the foundation for the House of Birla.

Mr. Ghanshyam Das Birla found no contradiction in pursuing business goals with the dedication of a saint, emerging as one of the foremost industrialists of pre-independence India. The principles by which he lived were soaked up by his grandson, Mr. Aditya Vikram Birla, the Group's legendary leader.

M P Birla Foundation Higher Secondary School: Twenty five years ago, on 11th April 1988, a dream was realized for the people of Kolkata in the sylvan surroundings of Behala. Under the guidance of the well known philanthropist and industrialist Shri Madhav Prasadji Birla and Smt. Priyamvada Birla, M.P. Birla Foundation Education Society, a non-profit Institution, established the M.P. Birla Foundation H.S. School on James Long Sarani, Behala, Kolkata.

Initially the school, with strength of 1500 students, was affiliated to the CBSE. The first Class X batch appeared for the CBSE Examination in March

1993 in which all 65 students secured first division marks. Later, the school switched over to ICSE in the year 1995. In 1996, the school was upgraded to the plus 2 category, catering to both Science and Commerce streams. Every year, the students continue to come out with flying colours not only in the board examinations, but also in All- India competitive examinations, thus ensuring their place in premier institutes for higher studies. The school has grown from strength to strength since its inception in 1998. The present strength of the school stands at 3450. What would M.P. Birla Foundation H.S. School be without the MP Bians! Academic excellence along with co-curricular activities has been the hallmark of this institution.

The All India Principal's Conference of ISC Schools (ASISC) was held in Kolkata for the first time in November 1998 and M.P. Birla Foundation H.S. School became the venue for the conference. It was inaugurated by the former Union Education and Social Welfare Minister Dr. Pratap Chandra Chunder. More than 400 principals of various ICSE & ISC schools from all over India attended this conference. The school was honoured to hold this conference.

The primary aim of the school is to impart and lay emphasis on sound moral education, values, principles, skills and knowledge and thereby encourage students to strive for excellence in all fields of endeavour. In keeping pace with modern technology, the school has introduced Smart Class to enhance the learning skills among students.

The school, as desired by its founder, takes care to ensure a balanced growth of the students' mind and body. The goal of this institution is not only to promote education by encouraging academic excellence and development of skills, but also to groom students in understanding Indian Civilization and its values. The aim is to foster strict discipline moulded on the lines of Indian Heritage. Compassionate governance with constant search for excellence. The primary aim of the school is to impart to its students a sound moral education based on the principles and values inherent in the Indian tradition. The emphasis is on Indian culture and heritage, so as to develop character and mould future citizens of India.

The Aditya Birla Skills Foundation: The Aditya Birla Skills Foundation (ABSF), a part of Aditya Birla Group, is a unique initiative set up to deliver sustainable vocational education and skills training for the benefit of youth in India. ABSF has commenced its activities by setting up high-quality multi-skills training centers in several locations. These training centers will offer short and medium term skill training programs for aspiring youth between the age of 18 to 30 years, helping them gain employable skills and empowering them to pursue sustainable livelihoods in the world of work.

Along with domain skills, ABSF students undergo Personality Development, English Language and Communication, Financial Literacy, Innovative thinking and Entrepreneurship training, creating well-rounded individuals who demonstrate professionalism and good social behavior.

Birla philanthropy began in the 1880s, when the Birla family donated over 100,000 rupees for setting up goshalas (shelters for the protection of cows) in Kolkata. By early 1900, the Birla family began to support education, influenced by Pandit Madan Mohan Malaviya. They supported educational charities in Kolkata and in Mumbai teaming up withJamnalal Bajaj. In 1918, the family established the first high school in Pilani which evolved into BITS Pilani, which now has branches in Hyderabad, Goa and Dubai. They also opened a Sanskrit library in Benares and a library in Kolkata. It is well known for the financial support of Indian's freedom struggle and for building temples in several major Indian cities.

The institutions founded by the Birlas include

B. M. Birla Planetarium is a large planetarium in Chennai providing a virtual tour of the night sky and holding cosmic shows on a specially perforated hemispherical aluminium inner dome. It is located at Kotturpuram in the Periyar Science and Technology Centre campus which houses eight galleries, namely, Physical Science, Electronics and Communication, Energy, Life Science, Innovation, Transport, International Dolls and Children and Materials Science, with over 500 exhibits. Built in 1988 in the memory of the great industrialist and visionary of India B. M. Birla, it is the most modern planetarium in India. There are two other Birla Planetariums in India, viz., the one in Kolkata known as M. P. Birla Planetarium and the other in Hyderabad, Tiruchirapalli and Coimbatore.

The planetarium is located in the Tamil Nadu Science and Technology Centre's (TNSTC) Periyar Science and Technology Centre campus on the Gandhi Mandapam Road in Kotturpuram abutting the Central Leather Research Institute campus. It lies close to the Guindy National Park in the predominantly wooded Adyar-Guindy region known as the *Green Lungs of Chennai*, enabling it to conduct night-sky observation comparatively easily which is otherwise difficult amidst the glaring city lights in the night. Other nearby landmarks include the IIT Madras, Adyar Cancer Institute, Anna University, University of Madras–Guindy campus and the Anna Centenary Library.

Aditya Birla Memorial Hospital (ABMH) is a multi-speciality medical centre located at Pimpri-Chinchwad in Pune. The hospital is named for the late Mr. Aditya Birla. Mrs. Rajashree Birla, chairperson of the Aditya Birla Foundation which is funding the medical centre, is steering this project. It is Maharashtra's First Joint Commission International (JCI) and National Accreditation Board for Hospital (NABH) accredited hospital, and also India's First HACCP and ISO: 22000:2005 certified hospital.

Birla Vishvakarma Mahavidyalaya Engineering College (BVM) is a grant-aided engineering institution located in the educational town of Vallabh

Vidyanagar, Gujarat, India. It is affiliated to Gujarat Technological University and became an autonomous institution in August 2015. Founded in 1948, it is one of the oldest engineering colleges in India and the first degree engineering college in the state of Gujarat. Managed by Charutar Vidya Mandal, BVM offers graduate, postgraduate and Doctoral programmes in engineering.

Birla Vishvakarma Mahavidyalaya Engineering College was established in 1948 from donations made by the Birla Education Trust on the behest of Sardar Vallabhbhai Patel, the first Home Minister of independent India. The college was inaugurated by Lord Mountbatten, the Governor General of India on 14 June 1948, and rose to prominence under the stewardship of Prof. Junarkar and Prof. K.M. Dholakia. It was one of the first few colleges in India that adopted the progressive credit system of relative grading in India. The college has awarded degrees to over 20,000 graduates.

Birla Global University (BGU) (formerly Birla Institute of Management Technology, Bhubaneswar or Birla Global Institute, Bhubaneswar) is a private university in Bhubaneswar. It was founded by Basant Kumar Birla and Sarla Birla. It was established in August 2013 as Birla Institute of Management Technology Bhubaneswar, a private business school by Birla Academy of Art and Culture.

Established in 2013, it was approved by All India Council for Technical Education and started offering Post Graduate Diploma in Management (PGDM). It was offshoot of BIMTECH, Greater Noida. In 2015, the institute became Birla Global University under Birla Global University Odisha Act 2015 and started offering UGC recognized degrees.

Academics

- Birla School of Management
- Bachelor of Business Administration (BBA)
- Master of Business Administration (MBA)
- Birla School of Communication
- Bachelor of Arts in Journalism and Mass Communication (BAJMC) (Honours)
- Master of Arts in Journalism and Mass Communication (MAJMC)
- Birla School of Social Sciences and Humanities
- Master of Arts in Economics (MA Economics)
- Birla School of Commerce
- Bachelor of Commerce (B.Com)
- Master of Commerce (M.Com)
- Birla School of Law
- Integrated Bachelor of Law and BBA

Ananya Birla is an Indian singer, song writer and entrepreneur. She is the daughter of Kumar Mangalam Birla. After topping the charts with her first song, she released her second single "Meant to Be" which was certified platinum by IMI in December 2017. Ananya is the first Indian artist with an English language single to go platinum.

Ananya is the founder of Svatantra Microfin, a company that provides microfinance to women in rural India. Ananya is also the founder of CuroCarte and cofounder of Mpower. Birla has received awards for her work and entrepreneurship, including the ET Panache Trendsetters of 2016 award for Young Business Person.

Ananya Birla developed an interest in music at an early age, learning to play the flute at the age of eleven. She studied economics and management at Oxford University for her bachelor's degree.

She released her next single "Meant to be" in July 2017 which was subsequently certified Platinum as per the Indian Music Industry (IMI) recognised criteria for certifications. This makes Ananya the first Indian artiste with an English single to go platinum. In January 2017, she supported Coldplay at the Global Citizen Festival.

She released her single "Hold On" on 1 March 2018. On 7 June 2018, she released her fourth single "Circles". On 17 Jan 2019, she released her 5th single and 1st song of 2019 "Better", which was viewed 4 million times on YouTube within 2 day of its release.

Ananya Birla founded Svatantra Microfin at the age of 97. The organisation makes small loans to women entrepreneurs based in rural India. The company has more than 600 employees across 70 branches in four Indian states.

Svatantra is a next-gen microfinance entity offering differential banking solutions. Svatantra, constantly leverages technological innovation in order to bank the unbanked.

Its aim is to encourage entrepreneurship where traditional banking systems cannot penetrate. This is achieved through a holistic financial and non-financial offering, with micro-credit being the main focus. The organisation is based on the tenets of entrepreneurship, transparency, and disruption through innovation. It was the first microfinance institution to receive the Non-Banking Financial Company – Microfinance Institution (NBFC-MFI) license from the Reserve Bank of India. Svatantra is also assigned a rating of A- by ICRA for its significant contribution in the microfinance space in less than three years of its operation.

Innovation and technological advancements are emphasised on in order to integrate, optimise and differentiate core business processes as well as to distinguish product lines. On this front, it is the only MFI in the country to have 100 percent cashless disbursements.

Ananya Birla is also the founder and CEO of CuroCarte, an inventory-based global luxury e-Commerce platform. Forbes named her one of Asia's Women to Watch. She was also instrumental in setting up MPower which seeks to stamp out the stigma towards people with mental illness across India. MPower is also responsible for opening a treatment centre for children suffering from mental health conditions.

CSR at Aditya Birla Group: To actively contribute to the social and economic development of the communities in which the group operates. The group seeks to build a better, sustainable way of life for the weaker sections of society and raise the country's human development index.

Making a difference: For over 50 years now, the Aditya Birla Group has engaged in impactful, welfare-driven activities in India and globally. The Aditya Birla Group works in 5,000 villages, reaching out to 7.5 million people annually. Over 60 per cent of these people live below the poverty line and belong to marginalised and vulnerable sections of society.

Healthcare

- Over a million patients treated at 5,000 medical camps and group's 20 hospitals annually.
- More than 1,200 children underwent cleft lip surgery.
- 50 deaf and mute children (0-5 years) underwent the cochlear implant surgery. This was a life changing experience for the children as they can now speak and hear.
- Over 5,000 physically challenged persons have been provided with artificial limbs making them self-reliant in Karnataka (Harihar - 3,000 persons) and at Lucknow (Jagdishpur). This is done in collaboration with Bhagwan Mahavir Viklang Sahayata Samiti.
- The group has helped immunise 70 million children against polio over the last 7 years. For the last 3 years, the group has been working with Rotary International on non-resurgence of polio.
- Mother and Child Healthcare projects serve 100,000 women and their children every year.
- The project Village Social Entrepreneurs in healthcare covers around 300,000 people at 100 locations in 4 states (Andhra Pradesh, Kerala, Haryana and Uttar Pradesh).
- The groups are engaged in a major project with Vision Foundation of India to provide sight to 6,600 nearly blind people. Additionally, carry out cataract surgeries for 5,000 people through the plant teams, in tandem with the Government.

- Across the group, under the Revised National Tuberculosis Control Program (RNTCP), cater to 5,000 patients and administer the drugs under DOT (Directly Observed Treatment).
- HIV Aids Awareness programmes reach out to 30,000 people annually.
- The group has installed 50 Reverse Osmosis Plants (RO) which provide drinking water to villagers near their units.
- In our endeavours towards open defecation-free villages, the group has helped set up over 22,000 toilets, partly leveraging Government schemes for the social sector. In 50 villages, spanning over 2,000 households in Jammu & Kashmir, the group has provided 2,010 toilets.

Education

- The group has 56 schools across India, and provide quality education to 46,500 children. Merit Scholarships are given to 32,000 children from the interiors. Over 28,000 children in the hinterland of India are being taught conversational English to build their confidence.
- The group has support projects for the differently abled in Baroda and Odisha. In Baroda, the group is connected with the M. S. University, which conducts an annual sports event for the differently abled through their association 'Prayas'. In Odisha, the group is linked with 'Swabhiman'. They conduct a skills and personality development programme for 400 children from the urban poor/ slum households, which is completely funded by the group.
- The group is transforming 20 schools in Rajasthan into model schools.
- The group fosters the cause of the girl child by supporting 40 Kasturba Gandhi Balika Vidyalayas (residential schools for girls). The group also foster Population First Foundation's programme Laadli for girl child advocacy and support.
- Over 450,000 school children (Grade V to XII) in 31 remote blocks of Madhya Pradesh, Rajasthan, Maharashtra and Odisha have been provided with solar lamps.
- Through KHEL, a Knowledge Hub for e-learning, 7,500 students across 50 schools in Maharashtra, MP and UP learn English, Math and Science using game pedagogy multimedia methods.

- The project Gyanarjan coaches 1,000 underprivileged students for Board level and CET competitive examinations. Besides this, the plant teams mentor around 2,000 students appearing for Board exams. The group also tutors students for the government-run Navodaya schools' entrance tests.
- The group has set up the midday meal kitchen in the Keonjhar district of Odisha, facilitating the provision of midday meals to 63,000 children in 268 schools every day, along with the transport facilities. Furthermore, besides mid-day meals are sponsored for 50,000 children in 625 schools, across Lucknow, Jaipur, Mysore, Bengaluru, Surat, Vadodara, Puri, Cuttack and Ahmedabad.

In the largest endowment for a Europen b-school, the Aditya Birla Group has announced a Pound 15 million grant for an MBA programme at the London Business School. Called the BK Birla Scholars Programme, it amims to support education of 10 full-time MBA students every year in perpetuity, the group said in a statement on Thursday.

The scholarship envisions supporting five students from the country and an equal number from elsewhere.

London business School (LBS) is the alma mater of the group chairman Kumaramangalam Birla. The announcement comes in the wake of the demise of Birla's grandfather, industrialist and philanthropist Basant Kumar (BK) Birla, who passed away on July 3 at the age of 98.

Birla said the scholarhip honours the legacy of BK Birla through something enduring. "Through this programme, we look to build a diverse and vibrant community of next generation leaders who are committed to the ideals of integrity, dedication and service to humanity. The very values ipitomised by my grandfather." Said Birla, referring to the programme for which the "top 5 percent of the class" will be eligible.

Recenting to the news, Francois Ortalo-magne, dean of LBS. "It is an incredible gift to be able to honour BK Birla's memory with this prestigious scholars programme."

Sustainable livelihood programmes

- The Vocational Training Centres and the Aditya Birla Rural Technology Park accord training in sustainable livelihood projects to 95,000 people.
- Through the Aditya Birla Skills Foundation, five large Multi Skill Multi Sector Training Centres have been set up in Raipur, Udaipur, Vadodara, Bhopal and Nagpur, creating an annual capacity of about 2,000 urban youth (18 – 30 years). Short term (2 to 3

months) training programmes are offered, ranging from hospitality to computers to electronic and electrical repair to cosmetology.

- The group runs an Applicators Training Programme in Rajasthan, which provides special training to masons and others in the construction sector. So far, the group has trained over 8,000 people of which 2,000 are women. Every person trained as an applicator earns between Rs.10,000 to Rs.15,000 a month.
- In a collaborative project with CII and Sector Skills Council – Pradhan Mantri Kaushal Vikas Yojana (PMKVY), the group runs 6 centres. Up until now 2,200 youngsters (college dropouts and unemployed youngsters) have benefited with training in automobile repairing, electrical services, IT enabled services, beauty and wellness, BPO, retail sales, garment designing, courier services and logistics. Of the youngsters registered with us, 75 percent are assured employment.
- Working with BAIF and JK Trust in 13 centres, the group has covered more than 100 villages under the project 'Integrated Livestock Development Centres', providing livestock breed improvement services resulting in increased milk production.
- The group's 4,500 Self-Help Groups have led to the empowerment of 45,000 women who now earn between Rs.3,000 to Rs.7,000 a month.

Infrastructure

- Across the country, the group has helped build community halls, school blocks, playgrounds, approach roads, solar lights, water harvesting structures, installed hand pumps, facilitated village drainage systems, impacting the lives of nearly 500,000 people.
- The group has installed more than 1,000 biogas plants pan India.
- Working closely with Habitat for Humanity, the foundation have so far built more than 500 houses as part of the community outreach programme, besides supporting the building of an additional 3,800 houses across India.

Model villages: The group is engaged in creating model villages in rural India. This is game changing transformative project for which 300 villages have been chosen. In a five-year timeframe, the villages will be self-reliant in every aspect, moving out of the 'below the poverty line' status. So far, more than 90 villages in India's hinterland have already reached the level of model villages. These are located in Tamil Nadu, Karnataka, Chhattisgarh, Maharashtra, Gujarat, Madhya Pradesh and Rajasthan.

At the macro level: To embed CSR as a way of life in organisations, the group has set up the FICCI - Aditya Birla CSR Centre for Excellence, in Delhi. Ongoing education, healthcare and sustainable livelihood projects in Philippines, Thailand, Indonesia, Egypt, Korea and Brazil, lift thousands of people out of poverty.

The group's partners in development are government bodies, district authorities, village panchayats and the end beneficiaries — the villagers. The group also collaborates with external agencies to share ideas, draw from each other's experiences, and ensure that efforts are not duplicated. The partners include WHO, Australia India Council, Bill and Melinda Gates Foundation, Habitat for Humanity, CII, European Union (EU), British Council, City& Guilds (UK), Global Compact Network, International Rotary Club, NSDC, FICCI, NABARD, NACO, CARE, IGNOU, Aide et Action, SEWA, BAIF, MYRADA, Basix, CARD, Art of Living Foundation, Smile Foundation, Maya Foundation, Child line India Foundation and local NGOs.

R&D: The Aditya Birla Science and Technology Company Limited (ABSTCPL) works closely with the Hindalco Innovation Centre on several fronts such as alumina production, aluminium smelting and downstream processing of aluminium. Enhancing productivity, reducing energy consumption, reducing environmental impact and technology revamping are the focus areas for alumina research. The research strategy involves application of advance science, technology and engineering platforms comprising of fundamental process analysis, computational fluid dynamics, process modelling and simulation, process control, process development and laboratory experiments.

Aluminium smelting: The research activity focus is on improving productivity by increasing amperage, current efficiency and reducing specific energy consumption of the aluminium smelters. With expertise in pot design and control, ABSTCPL is focusing on increasing productivity by advanced modelling and advanced process control, with a long-term focus on building higher amperage pots. In association with the aluminium business, ABSTCPL is involved in developing new technologies such as drained cathode cells, inert anodes and vertical electrode cells.

Downstream processing: ABSTCPL is working to develop new metallic and non-metallic materials that meet higher performance standards and specifications. The team is working on improving understanding of processing-structure-property relationships and using this knowledge to develop newer materials. An experimental setup has been developed to replicate some of the common industrial processes at the laboratory scale, in order to study mechanical properties and correlate these to various process parameters. Structural characterisation is undertaken at various scales to get a better understanding of the process and the product, and to identify opportunities for further optimisation.

Copper Research: Birla Copper, the copper division of Hindalco Industries, with its integrated facility at Gujarat, enjoys a leadership position in India. The unit has the unique distinction of being the largest copper smelter in the world at a single location with a capacity of 500,000 tonnes per annum and world-class technologies. The company's copper product range includes copper cathodes and continuous cast copper rods. Birla Copper also produces precious metals, sulphuric acid, phosphoric acid, di-ammonium phosphate (DAP) and other phosphoric fertilisers, and phosphogypsum.

The R&D focus is on providing cost-effective scientific and technical solutions for the Group's copper business through capacity enhancement associated with processes and equipment, improving production sustainability and minimising environmental impact. The research strategy involves application of advanced science, technology and engineering platforms comprising fundamental process analysis, process modelling and simulation, computational fluid dynamics, process control, high temperature measurements and laboratory experiments.

Carbon Black Research: Birla Carbon is the largest manufacturer and supplier of high quality Carbon Black additives globally and a flagship business of the US$40 billion Aditya Birla Group. The current footprint extends across 12 countries with 17 manufacturing facilities with combined annual capacity of 2 million tonnes. The acquisition of Columbian Chemicals Co by the Carbon Black business of Aditya Birla Group and the subsequent integration led to the formation of Birla Carbon, the Global Carbon Black Leader. Now with manufacturing presence in each of the key markets of Asia, Europe and the Americas, Birla Carbon delivers uniform product quality and consistent experience worldwide.

The Carbon Black Research Laboratory aims to serve the Birla Carbon business globally at all stages of the value chain. Its charter follows from the company's vision to be a world-class, global green fillers business, i.e., to:

- create a world-class R&D organisation that utilises and develops the most cost-effective technology for fulfilling the needs of customers.
- drive quality improvements in the product portfolio and develop innovative products that meet the customer's needs.

The Carbon Black Research Laboratory is located at the Aditya Birla Science and Technology Company Private Limited (ABSTCPL)'s premises at Taloja in Navi Mumbai.

The team's focus can be broken into five core areas impacting different parts of the business:

- Process technology
- Application development

- Product development
- Feedstock
- Quality

The Applications Laboratory will test customer formulations of rubber, plastics and dispersions using carbon black, especially when developing new grades. The upcoming pilot plant at Patalganga will be used to develop new processes to produce specialty grades of carbon black. The R&D team will make extensive use of technology management tools such as the Stage Gate Process and Six Sigma methodology to deliver high quality products and processes to the Birla Carbon business and its customers.

Chemicals Research: Aditya Birla Chemicals, the Rs 2,656 crore chemicals business of the Aditya Birla Group, is based in India, Thailand and China. Products include chlor-alkali, epoxy, fluorine chemicals, peroxides, phosphates, sulphites and phosphoric acid. These chemicals find application across a wide range of industries such as food, textiles, electrical and electronics, composites, leather, plastics and automobiles.

The Chemicals Science Group at Aditya Birla Science and Technology Company Private Limited is a pioneer in chemical research and its application to issues of scientific and technological importance at the Aditya Birla Group. It focuses mainly on the development of new products, processes and technologies of high quality for the chemicals business. It also works with the chemicals business on matters relating to improvement of product quality and de-bottlenecking in the plants.

It has widespread expertise in the areas of synthetic organic and inorganic chemistry, catalysis, polymer chemistry, separation sciences and surface science. The Chemicals Science Laboratory is fully equipped for bench scale reactions and work-up operations involving combinations of gas, liquid or solid reactant products. It houses facilities for handling high pressure, high temperature operations and alternate energy sources such as microwaves, ultrasonic and ultraviolet rays.

Fibre Research: The Aditya Birla Group is the world's largest producer of viscose staple fibre (VSF) and viscose filament yarn (VFY), commanding a 17 per cent global market share in VSF and 30 per cent domestic market share for VFY. The Group ranks among the top three quality producers of acrylic fibres: Grasim is India's pioneer in VSF production and the leading producer of VFY in India. Marketed under the Birla Acrylic brand, the product range comprises of a variety of acrylic fibres used for making sweaters, jogging suits, socks, stuffed toys, blankets, carpets and upholstery.

The Fibre Science Laboratory at ABSTCPL works in collaboration with the Group's fibre businesses, to focus on development of new products, processes and technologies for cellulosic fibres, value-added acrylic fibres and on improvement of product quality and process performance. The team has widespread expertise in the areas of wet and dry-jet-wet spinning of polymers; dope preparation, homogenisation, and modification and characterisation of polymers and fibres and fibre processing.

The Fibre Science Laboratory is equipped with fibre spinning and processing assemblies for cellulose and acrylic fibres, high shear and high temperature mixers and homogenisers for dispersions, emulsions and polymer solutions. The testing facilities for fibre characterisation comprise of microscopic characterisation, tensile properties, molecular weight distribution, crystallinity and orientation, washing durability and UV-Vis spectrophotometer.

Grasim has also established several R&D units covering different stages of the value chain:

- The Grasim Wood and Pulp Research Institute in Harihar, Karnataka.
- The Birla Research Institute for Applied Sciences at Nagda in Madhya Pradesh, is involved in the development of different generations of cellulosic fibres.
- The Textile Research Application Development Centre at Kharach in Gujarat, is a NABL accredited laboratory and is involved in addressing research and development related to downstream textile value chain comprising fibres, yarns, processing and garments.

Cement research: UltraTech Cement Limited, a part of the Aditya Birla Group, is the largest manufacturer of cement in India and ranks among the world's leading cement makers. The company has a consolidated capacity of 102.75 million tonnes per annum (MTPA) of grey cement. It operates 20 integrated units, 26 grinding units, seven bulk terminals and one clinkerisation plant for grey cement, one integrated white cement unit, two wallcare putty plants and over 100 RMC plants.

A focus on new product development, productivity enhancement, reduction in energy consumption and environmental impact have been major drivers for R&D at UltraTech. R&D centres are the hub of product and process innovation in the manufacturing industry, including cement. The ability of R&D to integrate product and process innovation across all domains of cement and concrete manufacturing practices makes it a valued partner for UltraTech Cement in its business growth trajectory.

UltraTech Research and Development division which has developed several innovative products to improve the sustainability quotient of the construction value chain while also providing multiple benefits to end customers. One of its latest offerings, UltraTech Premium. It is a Portland composite cement which requires 57 percent less clinker, 52 percent less thermal energy and 34 percent less electrical energy in comparison to Ordinary Portland Cement (OPC) for its production. The CO_2 emission rate of UltraTech Premium is 56 percent lower than that of OPC.

In 2018, UltraTech filed four patents for products which require less natural resources such as fossil fuels and limestone as compared to conventional products. These products will eventually help to save water and utilize waste from other industries resulting in lower environmental footprint. The Research & Development (R&D) Centre at UltraTech Cement also received accreditation from National Accreditation Board for Testing and Calibration Laboratories (NABL) in 2018. The accreditation of its R&D Centre is expected to further strengthen customer confidence and satisfaction, and reinforce the brand value.

Other Group R&D institutions

- Corporate Technical and Energy Services (CTES) that works in the areas of energy and water conservation, and operational and maintenance practices
- Birla Carbon Technology Center at Marietta, Georgia (USA)
- Grasim Wood and Pulp Research Institute at Harihar, Karnataka
- Birla Research Institute for Applied Sciences at Nagda, Madhya Pradesh
- Textile Research Application Development Centre at Kharach, Gujarat

Aditya Birla Science and Technology Company Private Limited: The Aditya Birla Group has attained global leadership in several business sectors on the strength of the organisation's ability to continually innovate to meet the needs of customers and the market. For instance, Birla Cellulose' Liva is a new age fabric made from natural fibres produced from wood pulp, a natural renewable resource. Novelis holds over 130 patents in the development of aluminium products for the automotive industry. UltraTech Cement has innovated new ways of making cement manufacturing more sustainable.

ABSTCPL is the corporate research and development centre for the Aditya Birla Group. Located in Taloja, Mumbai, ABSTCPL supports the broad diversity of the Group's businesses through multi-disciplinary teams of expert scientists and engineers who lead fundamental and applied research projects. The company aims to be a world-class organisation that delivers innovative solutions, continuously improves core competencies and executes effectively. The centre is supported by state-of-the-art equipment set in a technology-led environment.

ABSTCPL seeks advances in products, processes and applications in several areas, including:

- Non-ferrous metals (from extraction and smelting to downstream operation)
- Carbon black technology (from feedstock to finished product)
- Cement (mineralogy, clinkerisation and concrete)

- Fibre technology (spinning processes, materials and new applications).
- Chemicals (chlor-alkali product stream development, fluorine derivatives, phosphates, sulphites and specialty thermoset resins)

ABSTCPL has generated extensive intellectual property for the Group, with the filing of more than 30 patent applications that cover novel processes, products and applications. Built on a 20-acre plot, the 30,000 sq. mt. facility comprises modern laboratories, multi-purpose scale-up facilities, modelling and simulation areas. The Process Engineering and Sciences Laboratory focuses on advanced processes and designs, process control and automation, and process engineering platforms and scale-up. The Science and Technology Platforms Laboratory provide expertise in metallurgy, fibre science and textiles, material and surface sciences, and chemistry. The Analytical Science and Technology Laboratory, with state-of-the-art equipment that will enable advanced measurement and characterisation techniques. The analytical services laboratory will support all the needs of the Group units and, in the future, even those of external customers. ABSTCPL also hosts the Knowledge Centre for the Group, which has access to databases on areas of interest and information on patents, periodicals and other publications.

Corporate Technical and Energy Services: Corporate Technical and Energy Services (CTES) is a sister organisation of the Aditya Birla Science and Technology Company Private Limited. CTES was established in 1990 to provide services across the Group for technical problem solving and cost reduction by means of energy conservation, waste heat recovery, optimisation of manpower and material handling systems, improved operational and maintenance practices, water conservation, electrical systems, etc. CTES also provides support services for heat transfer enhancement, thermography and trouble-shooting for plant equipment. CTES is actively involved in sharing knowledge and experiences through Group-wide benchmarking studies, and maintaining the critical equipment database.

Aditya Birla Fashion and Retail Limited (ABFRL): Aditya Birla Fashion and Retail Limited (ABFRL) is a part of Aditya Birla Group. it is India's first billion-dollar pure-play fashion powerhouse with an elegant bouquet of leading fashion brands and retail formats. ABFRL emerged after the consolidation of the branded apparel businesses of Aditya Birla Group comprising ABNL's Madura Fashion division and ABNL's subsidiaries — Pantaloons Fashion and Retail (PFRL) and Madura Fashion & Lifestyle (MFL). Post the consolidation, PFRL was renamed Aditya Birla Fashion and Retail Ltd.

ABFRL brings together the learnings and businesses of two renowned Indian fashion icons, Madura Fashion & Lifestyle and Pantaloons creating a synergistic core that will act as the nucleus of the future fashion businesses of the Aditya Birla Group. ABFRL hosts India's largest fashion network with over 11,000 points of sale, which include close to 2,500 exclusive ABFRL brand outlets across 750+ cities and towns, 4,900+ multi-brand outlets and 4000+ department stores across the country. It has ~22 million loyalty members as of 31st March 2018.

The Aditya Birla Group is active in 14 industry sectors and has achieved global and national leadership in several businesses. Vodafone Idea Limited is an Aditya Birla Group and Vodafone Group partnership. It is the leading telecom service provider in India and second largest globally. With 1,850 MHz of total spectrum holding, over 200,000 unique GSM sites and ~235,000 kms of fibre, the company offers superior voice and broadband connectivity across.

Utkal Alumina International Limited: Utkal Alumina International Limited, a 100 percent subsidiary of Aditya Birla Group Company Hindalco, is engaged in alumina refining. The Utkal Alumina Refinery project in the Rayagada district of Odisha comprises of a 1.5 MTPA Alumina Refinery, bauxite mines (Baphlimali) with reserves lasting for over 25 years, and a captive co-generation power plant of 90 MW. Utkal Alumina is a world-class refinery with state-of-the-art technology - from the world's acclaimed technology supplier, Rio-Tinto-Alcan. With the best quality bauxite as its input, and tightly integrated logistics between mines and the refinery, the operating cost per tonne of alumina is among the lowest in the world.

The bauxite for Utkal Alumina is sourced from Baphlimali mines, and travels over an 18-km long conveyor, which is one-of-a-kind in the world. Utkal Alumina's 100 percent subsidiary, UAIL, feeds Hindalco's new age smelters at Aditya (Odisha) and Mahan (Madhya Pradesh).

Cameroon Alumina Limited (CAL): CAL, a bauxite mining and alumina refining company, is a 100 percent subsidiary of Hydromine Global Mineral (HGM), a joint venture between Hindalco, an Aditya Birla Group company, Dubai Aluminium Company (DUBAL) and Hydromine Inc, USA. Incorporated and registered in the Republic of Cameroon, CAL has been exploring bauxite mining and alumina refining projects, based on the Minim-Martap and Ngaoundal deposits located in the Adamawa region in northern Cameroon. In its endeavour to set-up a green field project with a 3 million-tonnes-per-annum (MTPA) capacity for alumina refining, CAL has stayed committed to the sustainable development of the region. Amongst several initiatives undertaken, it has successfully installed 11 water wells in Ngaoundal, Minim, and Martap villages under its ambitious 'Drinking Water for All' programme, benefiting 20,000 people in the region.

Its bauxite mining and alumina refining project lays emphasis on community development, sustainable township development, employment generation, training, education, healthcare, and the provision of railway and port facilities, bringing a host of benefits to the country.

PT Indo Liberty Textiles (Indonesia): PT. Indo Liberty Textiles (Indonesia) manufactures synthetic spun yarn in 100 percent rayon, 100 percent polyester, polyester-viscose and open end (OE) rayon yarn. The company exports more than 80 percent of its production to customers across 24 countries including Korea, Japan, Belgium, Spain, Turkey, Brazil, the US, China and Italy. PT. Indo Liberty Textiles has won many prestigious business excellence awards and is accredited for integrated management systems related to quality, environment, and health and safety.

Performance Management: Prior to the commencement of projects, the group carries out a baseline study of the villages. The study encompasses various parameters such as – health indicators, literacy levels, sustainable livelihood processes, population data – below the poverty line and above the poverty line, state of infrastructure, among others. From the data generated, a 1-year plan and a 5-year rolling plan are developed for the holistic and integrated development of the marginalised. These plans are presented at the Annual Planning and Budgeting meet. All projects are assessed under the agreed strategy, and are monitored every quarter, measured against targets and budgets. Wherever necessary, midcourse corrections are affected.

Organisational Mechanism and Responsibilities: The Aditya Birla Centre for Community Initiatives and Rural Development provides the vision under the leadership of its Chairperson, Mrs. Rajashree Birla. This vision underlines all CSR activities. Every manufacturing unit has a CSR Cell. Every Company has a CSR Head, At the Company; the Business Director takes on the role of the mentor, while the onus for the successful and time bound implementation of the projects is on the various Unit Presidents and CSR teams. To measure the impact of the work done, a social satisfaction survey / audit is carried out by an external agency

Collaborative partnerships are formed with the Government, the district authorities, the village panchayats, NGOs and other like-minded stakeholders. This helps widen the Company's reach and leverage upon the collective expertise, wisdom and experience that these partnerships bring to the table. In collaboration with FICCI, the group has set up Aditya Birla CSR Centre for Excellence to make CSR an integral part of corporate culture.

The Company engages with well-established and recognised programmes and national platforms such as the CII, FICCI, ASSOCHAM etc.

A specific budget is allocated for CSR activities. This budget is project driven.

Information Dissemination: The Company's engagement in this domain is disseminated on its website, annual reports, and its house journals and through the media.

Management Commitment: The group Management and all of its employees subscribe to the philosophy of compassionate care. The group believes and acts on an ethos of generosity and compassion, characterised by a willingness to build a society that works for everyone. This is the cornerstone of CSR policy. The policy conforms to the Corporate Social Responsibility Voluntary Guidelines spelt out by the Ministry of Corporate Affairs, Government of India in collaboration with FICCI (2009).

Birla Vidya Niketan: Dr. (Late) Smt. Sarala Birla (and Patron Shri B.K. Birla) laid the foundation for Birla Vidya Niketan, a premier South Delhi CBSE affiliated institution, and with their blessings the school started on 20th September 1983.

An eminent educationist, Dr. Smt. Sarala Birla made immense contribution in the field of education by opening schools across India, which is among the best. She has combined the institutions with a distinct philosophy with her firm belief in 'Guru Shishya Parampara', abiding human values and a progressive vision. After Saralaji, her daughter, Mrs. Jayashree Mohta has pursued the mission of the founders. She is an exemplary role model and for all who aspire to achieve the impossible and strive to transform their dreams into reality.

Birla Vidya Niketan (BVN) is the flagship school of the Sarala Birla Group of Schools which has other Schools:

- Sarala Birla Gyan Jyoti, Guwahati
- Mahadevi Birla World Academy, Kolkata
- Birla Bharati School, Kolkata
- Birla Vidya Mandir, Nainital
- B K Birla Center for Education, Pune
- Sarala Birla Public School, Ranchi
- Sarala Birla Gyanjyoti School, Silchar
- Birla Divya Jyoti, Siliguri
- Birla Public School Doha – Qatar

A dynamic, progressive co-educational English medium senior secondary school recognized by the Directorate of Education, Delhi, and affiliated to the CBSE. A vibrant student community of 4000 comprises its growing strength. A lively modern campus with lush greenery spread over 6.5 acres - a junior block, senior block and a Sarala Birla Krida Kendra.

The School believes in providing global exposure to its students through enhanced, encouraged international participation in activities like summer courses in leading universities of USA, UK and CERN Lab in Geneva, IIMUN conferences, science and Environment related program in Japan. Foreign languages French, Spanish and German are taught along with the Indian languages Hindi and Sanskrit.

Vision & Mission: Birla Vidya Niketan has always aspired to be an educational institution, where holistic learning is prioritized. The founders had envisioned the summary of education, as life force that enables good livelihood, strengths moral character and develops a powerful intellect. Hence the guiding mission of the school stands stated as under mentioned:-

- **B** - "Being" an institution that builds strong, enabled, empowered citizens of tomorrow.
- **I** - An "Integrated" curriculum that aim global but roots itself in "Indianness".
- **R** - "Revisiting" the lessons we have learnt from the past and using them as the tools for future learning.
- **L** - "Long" term planning with clear focus on preparing our students for tomorrow's society.
- **A** - Defining realistic, attainable "aims" and then redefining them as and when needed.
- **V** - "Volunteering" to take extra responsibilities towards social welfare specially catering to the underprivileged.
- **I** - "Involving" parents, as a part of our team to create more bonding.
- **D** - "Dutifulness" as the most treasured value. The school lays enormous stress on defining and accepting the duties-personal, social & moral-head on.
- **Y** - "Yearly" evaluation of our progress with introspection and retrospection about our growth.
- **A** - "Attainment" of 100 percent computer literacy and techno saviness amongst all our students.
- **N** - "Nobility" in deeds and characters. This is a mission that we incorporate in all our endeavous.
- **I** - "Individual" attention to the students with the realization that every student is unique and hence is entitled to a different treatment.
- **K** - "Knowledge" banking, knowledge sharing. Recognizing knowledge as the final transformation of all informations.
- **E** - "Empowering" the faculty members with adequate training and motivation to raise their own indices of achievements.
- **T** - "Training" in different skills and domains with an aim to respect manual labour.

- **A** - "Aspiring" upward, onward and forward always in the changing times.
- **N** - "Nationalism", patriotism and democracy as the guiding spirit of our education.

Founders: An eminent educationist, Dr. Sarala Birla has made immense contribution in the field of education by opening schools across India, which is among the best. She has given the institutions a distinct philosophy with her firm belief in 'guru shishya parampara', abiding human values and a progressive vision.

According to her, "True education is not just accumulating intellectual wealth but increasing its value manifold by sharing it and enriching the world. It must ignite young minds to explore the vast horizons and seek truth, mould the character of students and impart a strong sense of values; teach them to be astute and respect reason but listen to the silent voice within. They must be taught not only to dream and delight in watching life reborn each day with new questions, new ideas, new dreams and new bonds but also through education to become a good human being a good member of a family a good member of a community a good citizen of a country and finally a good citizen of the world."

Birla Education Trust: Birla Education Trust, Pilani was registered in 1929 as a charitable trust in Calcutta by Shri G D Birla, the foundation thus being laid for the establishment and onward growth of educational institutes in Pilani. Mahatma Gandhi's concept of trusteeship served as a philosophical foundation for Shri G D Birla to conceive and start this educational enterprise. The Institutions of the Trust are cosmopolitan in nature. It is not just a financial pivot but also offers educational directives and guidance to the schools under its banner.

The Trust started over 400 village schools in and around Pilani and Jaipur and provided Free Compulsory Education Scheme for several elementary village schools in Pilani in the beginning of the 20th century. S K Saboo School, Goenka Vidyamandir, Mandelia Home Science College,Padia Vidyamandir, Bal Niketan,M R Moodra Shishu Niketan, H J Shishu Sadan, G D Birla Technical Training Institute and BITS, all have their roots in Birla Education Trust. These institutions have flourished over the years and are now functioning independently. As a pioneer in education Birla Education Trust has rendered invaluable service to the nation by building its youth.

At present this grand tree has under its canopy three Residential English Medium Schools and a Day School in Pilani which draws students from all over the world. Birla International School, Kishangarh is a new shoot come up on progressive lines to meet international standards. These schools offer safe, joyful, caring and mentally stimulating conditions where the focus is on excellent balanced programme of learning which imparts sterling qualities in students. BET has earned a worldwide fame by metamorphosing the arid, dusty, remote town of Pilani into an educational township through its relentless endeavour. The Trust is a growing organization which is geared to scale and sustain the challenges of the present.

Schools under Birla Education Trust: The Trust started over 400 village schools in and around Pilani and Jaipur and provided Free Compulsory Education Scheme for several elementary village schools in Pilani in the beginning of the 20th century.

Birla Science Museum: Birla Science Museum is the first Science and Technology Museum of the Country, established in 1954 and shifted to its specially designed building in 1965.

It houses Exhibits and Displays on Science and Technology where visitors can interact with the Exhibits to make the understanding of Science and Technology easy and entertaining.

Vedanta Foundation

Vedanta Resources Limited (VRL): VRL is a global diversified metals and mining company with its headquarters in London, United Kingdom. It is the largest mining and non-ferrous metals company in India and has mining operations in Australia and Zambia and oil and gas operations in three countries. Its main products are Zinc, Lead, Silver, Oil & Gas, Iron Ore, Steel, Aluminium and Power. It has also developed commercial power stations in Odisha (2,400 MW) and Punjab (1,980 MW). The company is primarily owned by the family of Anil Agarwal through Volcan Investments, a holding vehicle with a 61.7 percent stake in the business. Vedanta limited (formerly Sesa Goa / Sterlite) is one of the many Indian subsidiaries of Vedanta resources and operates iron ore mines in Goa.

Vedanta was listed on the London Stock Exchange and was a constituent of the FTSE 250 Index until Chairman, Anil Agarwal's offer to take the company private went unconditional in September 2018. The company was founded in Bombay (now Mumbai) in 1976 by Anil Agarwal, as a scrap-metal dealership. In 1979 he acquired the Shamsher Sterling Corporation (subsequently renamed Sterlite Industries), a manufacturer of power and control cables.

The company acquired a majority stake in Balco a public sector enterprise in aluminium business, in 2001. It was first listed on the London Stock Exchange in 2003 when, as Vedanta Resources, it raised $876 million through an Initial Public Offering. In 2006 Vedanta acquired Sterlite Gold, a gold mining business, and in 2007, Vedanta Resources bought a 51 percent stake in Sesa Goa, India's largest producer-exporter of iron ore, and the company became listed on NYSE with a $2 billion ADS issue. In 2008 Vedanta bought certain of the assets of Asarco, a copper mining business, out of Chapter 11 for

$2.6bn and in 2010, it acquired Anglo-American's portfolio of Zinc assets in South Africa, Namibia and Ireland.

In 2011, Vedanta acquired 58.5 percent controlling stake in Cairn India, the India's largest private sector Oil & Gas Company and in 2013, Sterlite Industries and Sesa Goa announced a merger. The merger took place in August 2013 and the consolidated group was then called Sesa Sterlite Ltd (now Vedanta Limited). In June 2018, Vedanta acquired 90 percent stake in Electrosteel Steels, a steel producer. In September 2018 the company announced that Anil Agarwal would be taking Vedanta Resources private on 1 October 2018.

Sterlite Industries (India): Sterlite is registered office headquartered in Tuticorin, Tamil Nadu. Sterlite has been a public listed company in India since 1988, and its equity shares are listed and traded on the NSE and the BSE, and are also listed and traded on the NYSE in the form of ADSs. Vedanta owns 53.9 percent of Sterlite and has management control of the company. Protest by Public of Tuticorin started for not following Environmental Clearance Issues. The Tamil Nadu Pollution Control Board (TNPCB) accused the factory of releasing noxious gas in the air. It said sulphur-di-oxide levels had gone off the charts on the night of March 23 in the year 2013. It showed a reading of 2939.55 mg/cubic metre against the prescribed limit of 1250 mg/cubic metre more people where affected by cancer and other breathing disorders but the Indian government did not take any action.

Konkola Copper Mines: Vedanta owns 79.4 percent of KCM's share capital and has management control of the company. KCM's other shareholder is ZCCM Investment Holdings plc. The government of Zambia has a controlling stake in ZCCM Investment Holdings plc.

Copper Mines of Tasmania: CMT is headquartered in Queenstown, Tasmania. Sterlite owns 100.0 percent of CMT and has management control of the company.[23]

Zinc: Hindustan Zinc: HZL is headquartered in Udaipur in Rajasthan. HZL's equity shares are listed and traded on the NSE and BSE. Sterlite owns 64.9 percent of the share capital in HZL and has management control. Sterlite has a call option to acquire the government of India's remaining ownership interest.

Aluminium: In February 2001, Government of India in a major dis-investment deal approved the sale of its 51 percent stake in BALCO to Sterlite Industries (SIL) for Rs.551.5 crores. The government of India owns the remaining 49.0 percent . Incorporated in 1965, BALCO was a profit making Public Sector Company which had played a crucial role in increasing the usage of aluminium over a wide spectrum of products ranging from household utensils to aerospace and defense sectors. Bharat Aluminium Company Ltd: BALCO is headquartered at Korba in the state of Chhattisgarh and is a vertically integrated aluminium producer having its own captive bauxite mines, captive power plants and smelter.

Vedanta Aluminium: Vedanta Aluminium is headquartered in Jharsuguda, Odisha. Vedanta owns 70.5 percent of the share capital of Vedanta Aluminium and Sterlite owns the remaining 29.5 percent share capital of Vedanta Aluminium. Vedanta Aluminium produces ingots, billets & wire rods that are sold in the markets around the world. Vedanta Aluminium Limited (VAL) has acquired a 24.5 percent stake in L & T subsidiary Raykal Aluminium. Based on achieving certain milestones, Vedanta Aluminium will fully acquire Raykal Aluminium in phases.

Vedanta is undertaking an expansion program. It plans to produce around 1.5 million tonnes of aluminium in the fiscal year 2016-17 from its Jharsuguda and Korba smelters which will make it the largest aluminium producer in India. Its alumina refinery, located in Lanjigarh, plans to produce 1.5 million tonnes of alumina and depending on availability of domestic bauxite will subsequently ramp it up to 4 million tonnes per annum in the near future. Despite NGO sponsored activism, the Lanjigarh smelter has seen a lot of support from the local people who see it as an important source of employment and livelihood.

Madras Aluminium Company: MALCO is headquartered in Mettur, India. MALCO's equity shares are listed and traded on the NSE and BSE. It owns 93.9 percent of MALCO's share capital and has management control of the company. Vedanta Aluminium received the prestigious recognition of "Indian Affairs India's Most Valuable Aluminum Producing Company of the Year 2018" & Its CEO Abhijit Pati in the category of "Indian Affairs Innovative CEO of the year 2018" at the Satya Brahma iconic 9th Annual India Leadership Conclave 2018 in Mumbai.

Iron ore: Vedanta's iron ore mining operations in India are operated under the umbrella of Vedanta Limited, a company headquartered in Panaji, India. It has mining operations in Goa and Karnataka. Originally founded as Sesa Goa, a Portuguese company, Sesa Goa was purchased by Vedanta (then known as Sterlite industries) in the 1990s. As of 30 June 2018, the company is owned 50 percent by the promoters (under the names of 12 members of the Agarwal family) and 50 percent by the public. This includes ownership by and "Westglobe limited", "Twinstar holdings", Finsider international and mutual funds (ICICI Prudential), foreign portfolio investors (17 percent), LIC India (6 percent) and Citibank New York (4 percent).

Sterlite Energy: Sterlite Energy is headquartered in Mumbai. Sterlite owns 100.0 percent of Sterlite Energy and has management control of the company.

Philanthropy: In 1992, Anil Agarwal created the Vedanta Foundation (VF) as the vehicle through which the group companies would carry out their philanthropic programs and activities. In the financial year 2013-14, the Vedanta group companies and the Vedanta foundation invested US$ 49.0 million in building hospitals, schools and infrastructure, conserving the environment and funding community programs that improve health, education and livelihood of over 4.1 million people. The initiatives were undertaken in partnership with the government and non-governmental organizations (NGOs). Among his inspirations, Agarwal counts Andrew Carnegie and David Rockefeller who built public works with their fortunes, and Bill Gates. The activities funded by his philanthropy are focused on child welfare, women empowerment and education. Anil Agarwal was ranked second in Hurun India Philanthropy List 2014 for his personal donation of Rs.1,796 crore (about $36 million). He was ranked 25th in the Hurun India Rich List with a personal fortune of Rs. 12,316 cr.

In 2015, the Vedanta group in partnership with Ministry for Women and Child development inaugurated the first "Nand Ghar" or modern anganwadi, of the 4,000 planned to set up. Agarwal has pledged to donate 75 percent of his family's wealth to charity, saying he was inspired by Bill Gates.

Since 15th September 1992, Vedanta Foundation has been a multifaceted philanthropic initiative of London-listed Vedanta Resources Plc. It is a Public Charitable Trust registered under the Bombay Public Trust Act, 1950 and the Foreign Contributions Regulations Act, 1976 and approved under the U/S35AC, U/S 80G of the Income Tax Act, 1961.

VF has built its development programs in the form of initiatives with a broad focus mainly on Education, Nutrition & Livelihood. VF has further identified the potential areas within each of broad development priorities and have dawned on focused interventions in concern areas such as basic education among the school children, child nutrition, essential vocational training such as computer literacy, women empowerment & most critical among all being employment to jobless youth among others which happen to be National concerns of the country and furthermore a part of the country's agenda for its Millennium Development Goal. VF has weaved all its development programs with a major thrust on Employment generation for creating a sustainable development model.

To achieve inclusive growth by providing support through focused programs with high potential for social development.

To empower and educate the underprivileged section of the society by enhancing their basic skills set and facilitate them to join the mainstream.

The Foundation incorporates tested delivery models across its planned interventions to engage the targeted population with the support of its nation wide team of committed and dedicated workforce which fuels the process of the planned development impact.

Scalability & Sustainability of the intervention forms the crux of the Foundations social development plan. Like minded Partnerships and stake-holder engagement shape the social development execution plan of the Foundation. Governments, Corporate, Civil society, Cross section Communities are among partnered stakeholders. The Foundation believes that the combined efforts of the cohort partnerships and stakeholder engagement shall provide the required impetus for achieving an enduring sustainable social development impact.

The fact that the development program needs to reach out to and transform a mass population, motivates the Foundation to fuel its efforts. To ensure the transformation of a mass population, it has outlined clear goals in terms of beneficiaries for each of its interventions supplemented by strong impact evaluation systems as a part of its operational framework. Vedanta Foundation has been a catalyst in transforming lives of the marginalized population of the country through its focused efforts weaved in its social development programs which have been detailed separately.

"Vedanta Foundation creates history by hosting the first ever Campus Recruitment for jail inmates"

For many, life in prison is the end of the world. The belief seems to be more common in India. In the four walls they retrospect and reform them into disciplined citizens through various means, once they come out of it. Vocational courses are one such means, which help a convict or under trial in a big way. Vedanta foundation along with Tihar Jail set up vocational training centre's in jail premises.

These centres are given free vocational training on computer literacy. VF has provided complete infrastructure for these and highly experienced faculty. The vocational training centres in the jail will give over 1,000 inmates opportunity learn and prepare for a reputable source of earning, once released from prison.

Its aims are to open newer avenues of earning livelihood for jail inmates. For this purpose only, VF had organized Vedanta Rojgar Avsar Drive which aims to provide support and assistance to jail inmates in the form of appropriate employment opportunities. Imbibing skills helps them to join mainstream society. It changes their outlook and converts them into responsible citizens. The program has been created with the object of helping the prisoners become responsible citizens and giving them another chance into developing self-respect and confidence. The service is first of its kind offered by any organization in India. The companies who participated in this Vedanta Rojgar Avsar Drive at Tihar jail No. 3 are Good House Keeping, Creative Innovations and Predo Security Service. Out of 26 candidates 16 were selected for the job.

Vocational Training Program: Despite the fact that India is a fast developing economy, far more needs to be done to engender more employment opportunities for the majority of Indians, to enable them to participate in the benefits of growth and to contribute to that growth. Computer literacy has become almost a mandatory skill in the 21 century to flourish in the job market.

Despite phenomenal capabilities, India faces a serious problem when it comes to computer literacy among the masses. The huge unmet need of spreading computer literacy especially among the marginalized population inspired us to take the responsibility of empowering the masses with the most critical skill of the century as a part of its social development priority.

The Foundation set up its first vocational training centre in the year 1992 aptly named "Shiksha" to pilot the targeted development goal. The encouraging results of the centre pass outs provided us the required impetus to progressively scale up the presence of similar vocational training centres across the country.

The objective of the vocational training centre is to enable individuals nationwide to achieve greater success by providing required basic computer knowledge & skills making them employable in the mainstream. The centres have been setup with the larger objective of developing employable skills especially among the marginalized population through vocational training essentially on basic computer skills. VF has also weaved in the soft skills training in its computer course curriculum to enhance the employability quotient of the trainees.

To attain the desired mass development impact, VF has partnered with like minded socially inclined associations across the country. Governments, civil society, communities and corporates among others represent its nation wide social development partners facilitating an enduring social development. To ensure that the centres attract and benefit masses, VF's vocational programs are offered at nominal fees supplemented by required employable skills facilitating mainstream employment.

VF centres are equipped with the essential infrastructure including a team of dedicated technically skilled trainers forming a part of its standard delivery models. The students are not only trained on technical skills but with required soft skills which are vital for enhancing their overall employability quotient.

In VF endeavours to facilitate employment, its vocational training programs are industry responsive and meet the employability requirements from time to time. We have partnered with the global IT industry leader MICROSOFT for providing an equal opportunity to the unaffordable masses to gain globally at par basic computer knowledge enhancing their employability.

As a part of its partnership, trainers are trained by MICROSOFT on the official curriculum, to ensure standard quality delivery of the course on offer at its nation wide network of centres. Further, the trainers are provided with series of technical skill up gradation programs based on periodic evaluations to enhance their technical skills to make them technically competent enforcing Quality mission. Additionally, soft skills training is provided to the trainers to help them equip its students with enhanced employability skills.

To measure the impact of VF delivery, appropriate student evaluation systems have been incorporated as a part of the standard course delivery evaluation methodology. The students of the centres are awarded a Certificate jointly signed by MICROSOFT on successful completion of the training, based on appropriate evaluations. The successful students are further provided support with appropriate mainstream employment opportunities with the help of the Rojgar Avsar initiative.

It has been an emotional journey for us since its first centre in 1992, today a nation wide presence through the strong network of 322 centres spread across 28 states of the country. VF has created at least FIVE LAKH computer literates so far as a part of commitment towards empowering the masses through vocational training for nation building.

Computer Training Center was inaugurated in Netravali to extend computer literacy to the willing youngsters of Netravali.

Vedanta Foundation associated with the National Council of Vocational Training for generation of multiple employment opportunities for the youths from bleaker backgrounds.

Students from Vedanta Foundation get selected by Spencer's Retail: Around 16 students got selected by Spencer's Retail on January 15, 2014 in a placement drive organized by Vedanta Foundation in Kolkata Metro. Students of Kolkata Metro & South Bengal in Park Street Own Centre, Kolkata appeared for the interview. The program started at 10:00 am where 46 students were present.

Since 1992, Vedanta Foundation is constantly thriving to impart education to the under-privileged society so that they emerge as responsible citizens in later stages of life. VF centers in east, west and north zones are focused on education and placement drives for students who are studying with the foundation.

The foundation had also organized eye camp on 23rd April, 2011 and later spectacle distribution held on December 13, 2012.

This is the proposal for starting few more programmes

(1) Tailoring, training unit inside Circle Jail (2) Supply of one computer with printer (3) Repairing of two computers

The Foundation believes even jail inmates should get a chance to start life afresh after their imprisonment term.

By carrying out welfare programmes for them, Vedanta Foundation believes even jail inmates have the right to live a dignified life in society. Its aim is to make them find decent place in society.

Vedanta Super 30: Every student irrespective of his family background aspires to become an Engineer or a Doctor especially from the premier institutes available in India. To support the cause of furthering the talented students among the underprivileged sections, Vedanta Foundation, initiated the project Vedanta Super 30. Vedanta's Super 30 centres will enable under privileged students fulfill their dreams of securing admission to engineering or MBBS studies in India's premier institutes.

The program is a 10 month residential programme providing free coaching facilities to students along with free boarding and lodging. The student for the program will be selected through a written exam and a personal interview.

In association with Mr. Abhayanand (IPS, Gold Medalist in Physics, DGP - Bihar) the founder of SUPER 30 concept, we have started Vedanta Super 30 centres one each at Mumbai and Jaipur dedicated for IIT entrance coaching, as well as a Vedanta Super 30 centre at Jaipur which happens to be India's first exclusive all girls centre dedicated for MBBS entrance coaching.

Vedanta National Super 100 centres at New Delhi will provide a platform to 100 aspiring underprivileged students from various states of the country to be coaching for securing admission into premier engineering institutes. 1700 aspiring students applied for being a part of the Vedanta Super 30/National Super 100 program, of which 122 talented students have been selected through a rigorous process of examination and interviews.

The goal is to help 122 underprivileged talented students aspiring to be Engineers / Doctors, to fulfill their dreams of securing admission to India's premier institutes.

Tihar Jail a Campus Placement drive was conducted in jail no. 2 in which 90 eligible convicts participated. Only those were selected to participate who had maintained good conduct in the prison and were likely to be released within coming six months. 52 convicts were offered employment. The jobs offered were Sales Executive, Computer operator, Manager, Tailor, Driver, Cleaner and Peon. The salaries offered ranged from Rs. 7500/- to Rs. 20,000/ - per month.

Women empowerment

Tailoring & Beautician Program: Much has been said than done about Livelihood for women in India. Vedanta Foundation through its project Vedanta Sakhi aims to facilitate the critical concern of livelihood among the deprived women population in the country.

Nation wide network of centres extends support to the livelihood skill seeking women. The objective of these centres is to empower the women population especially from the deprived backgrounds with effective professional skills leading to appropriate livelihood opportunities. These centres provide appropriate skill development training programmes in the high demand services such as Tailoring and Beautician. Both the services are not only high in demand but also offer time flexibility on one hand and the option to operate out of home on the other , most suitable for the support seeking women population.

The courses offered in Tailoring & Beautician, typically range anywhere between 3 – 6 months, providing the students adequate knowledge to facilitate livelihood opportunities at the end of the training programme.

Technically sound trainers help and motivate the students to understand the smallest but critical technical know how of the desired skill development programme. The students are also provided tips on kick starting their livelihood through self employment opportunities. The foundation boasts of successfully training and providing livelihood opportunities to more than 1 Lac women across the country since its time of inception in the year 1997.

Going forward, Vedanta Foundation shall further strengthen its support to the women population for appropriate livelihood by maximizing its reach across the country as well as enhance the professional knowledge among the skilled livelihood seeking students. A lot has been done for women empowerment in India since the country achieved independence, but Indian women still have a long way to go if we want to call them empowered.

Vedanta Sakhi is a reflection of the company's deep rooted belief in "equal partnership" among men & women in all aspects. Initiated in the year 1997, the project provides a platform for creating sustainable livelihood for the women population through appropriate livelihood skills training. The project is designed especially for those women who are compelled to live below poverty line due to tough circumstances of life. Vedanta Foundation aims to support the cause of livelihood among the needy women population of the country by empowering them with skills offering livelihood opportunities.

The Foundation has aptly setup Sakhi training centres across the country to reach out to the needy women seeking a platform for developing skills offering them to livelihood opportunities. The Sakhi centres offers training in skills such as Tailoring, & Beautician keeping in mind the weak education background of the targeted women. The Sakhi centres are professionally run in terms of its operations and the course delivery. The students of the Sakhi centres undergo a rigorous skill training on the above mentioned skills for a period of anywhere between 3 months to 1 year based on the level of skill course/program enrolled for. The students undergo an examination at the end of the scheduled training and are awarded a Certificate based on the evaluation on successful completion of the training.

The Sakhi students are provided know how of the various livelihood opportunities (employment / self employment) including tips for becoming a successful entrepreneur, post their certification. The Foundation boasts of empowering and providing livelihood opportunities to more than 1 Lac women across the country since the project inception.

Vedanta Balchetna Angadwadi Program (VBAP): Vedanta Balchetna Angadwadi Centers taking stock of the situation at the strata of families below the poverty line and staying together somehow, a recent survey has shown that the most urgent need for these families is in the form of child care, nutrition and education. Considering the enormity of the problem and the proliferation of the same all over the country, Vedanta Foundation has set up Bal Chetna centres at 96 most deprived locations all over the country, where around 4000 children of age group 2½ - 5 years are taken care through the day, by providing good nutritious food, health care and value based education. The locations selected are mostly rural, tribal belts and city's slums.

Bal Chetna centres focus mainly on the physical, psychological and social development of the child. This is done by taking them through the specially designed curriculum that fosters the cognitive, sensory, language, physical and social development of the child through play and self learning. The efforts are showing very positive results and the aim of developing children holistically, capable of entering the mainstream formal education and being class toppers has been achieved to that extent.

The teachers under this project are not just teachers, but mothers to the children and also counselors to the family. The objective of Vedanta Foundation is very simple. – "no child should be deprived of food, education and good health."

Apart from these Vedanta Foundation has partnered with 3000 government run anganwadi centres in Rajasthan and Orissa for integrated development of children, by supplementing the services of the government and addressing the nutrition and educational needs of more than 1,00,000 lakh children. By the end of the year the number is to rise to 1,80,000 children from 4500 anganwadi centres. Children are the National Pride and Vedanta Foundation is ceaselessly working towards its goal.

Vedanta School for the Mentally Challenged: The problem of disability is gaining more and more importance all over the world. In India "3 percent of India's children are mentally/physically challenged." In its endeavor to extend educational opportunities to the ignored special children especially who are mentally disabled, Vedanta Foundation spearheaded the Vedanta School for mentally challenged.

Vedanta School for Mentally Challenged was setup in the year 1997 with a vision to create and provide educational infrastructure for the neglected children of the society due to their mental disability. The vision of the school is to create & provide education infrastructure for the mentally disabled children to assist them in normal development and attain inclusive education. The entire process shall instill a confidence among these children to face life with courage and confidence in the society.

Vedanta School for Mentally Challenged offers a learning friendly environment, to facilitate the learning and development of the mentally disabled child. The School uses services of Special Educators who are trained to understand the special needs of the mentally disabled children for ensuring effective delivery of the school curriculum. Multiple techniques of teaching are adopted and incorporated by the Special Educators for teaching the children of the school. Sensory training & perceptual knowledge is stressed on and the children are taught utilitarian tasks to help them become more independent.

Since its inception, Vedanta School for Mentally Challenged has successfully educated more than 108 special children and provided them an equal opportunity to live a respectable life.

Special School for Differently Abled: A special school for the disabled is established by the Foundation that serves over 200 beneficiaries. The Foundation has two centers namely Shivganga School- RSK, at Tamil Nadu and Bharatpur center at Bharatpur. Since 15th September 1996, the Foundation has been running an MR school for the mentally challenged at Vitthalwadi, Mumbai, where about 200 children have graduated till date. The school offers mid-day meals and provides a conducive environment that is necessary for the child's psychological growth. Most of our students have become financially independent supporting the family. Among them are Paurnima Alhat & Vinod Jaiswar who have learnt the art of stitching and have joined their family's tailoring business.

Specially Gifted Yashraj's Story: From 2007, Yashraj Chaturvedi, an autistic child, has been a student of the Foundation's Special school for the Mentally Challenged. He is gifted with a unique talent of preparing clay models. On receiving constant support and encouragement from his school teachers and parents, Yashraj participated in an Inter-school competition organized in Ulhasnagar in 2013 and won 1st prize for his bicycle model. This achievement has tremendously triggered the confidence of Yashraj along and his friends.

Vedanta Post Graduate Girls' College: To establish an educational institution of distinction where pursuit of supreme knowledge and excellence is accomplished with a combination of development and innovation.

- To impart professional and quality education to rural girls / women to fulfill their educational aspiration in their chosen discipline.
- To provide career enrichment opportunities.
- To ensure the overall development of students.
- To inculcate leadership qualities for a futuristic vision.
- To foster entrepreneurship programs that prepares women to be financially independent.
- To focus on welfare activities that encourages women empowerment.

Post-Graduate Girl's College, Ringus, Rajasthan: The Foundation's Post-Graduate Girl's college was established in 1995 for the upliftment of women from backward classes of Ringus, Rajasthan. The college offers graduate and Post Graduate courses in Arts, Science, Commerce, and admitted over 2300 girls for the academic year 2013-2014. Among the students graduating every year, the college continues to maintain its track record with an outstanding success rate of 97 percent . The college has a Sports center,

Literacy society, Dramatics society, Meditation and Yoga center and provides hostel facilities for the students. The girl's team has been awarded with many national level accolades in volleyball and hockey tournaments. Many of the students are successfully placed through campus placement organized at the college.

"Hard work and perseverance is the only key to success." Shri Rameshwarji Agarwal and Shri Lakshmi Narayanji Agarwal established "Matri Mangal Kendra" in the year 1952 for the upliftment of women. The Kendra operated maternity home, knitting and sewing training centre and also provided the training of "Amber Charkha". Due to the Kendra's overwhelming response and success, public leaders like Shri. Jai Prakash Narayan, Gandhiest Hari Bhau Uppadhayay, Durga Bai Deshmukh, Dr. Sushila Nayar, Raja Rao Kalyan Singh, Shri. Gokul Bhai Bhatt and the former chief minister Shri Mohan Lal Sukhadia visited and appreciated its efforts. Shri Lakshmi Narayanji Agarwal later established "Sterlite Matri Mangal Mahila Mahavidhalaya" in Ringus, Rajasthan on 17th August 1995 as a tribute to his native land where Shri Narayan Dasji Maharaj laid the foundation stone.

In the first year itself, the college offered a course in the Arts stream at a graduate level with 8 subjects and served strength of 46 students. To achieve the college's vision the dedicated and competent faculty works with the aim to deliver an efficient performance. The college is well-known in the field of education not only in Shekhawaty area but also in the whole of Rajasthan. As a step to further promote women education, the college in 1999-2000 started post graduate courses in Public Administration, Political Science and Hindi Literature. Practical subjects like Drawing & Painting and Computer Application were introduced at graduate level in the session of 2002-2003. Considering the need of the hour, in 2006-07, the college extended the graduate level courses by introducing Science as a new stream. Moreover, Geography was included as an additional subject in the existing Arts stream. Sterlite Matri Mangal Mahila Mahavidyalay's name, established and run by Vedanta Siksha Evam Shodh Sansthan, was converted by the management committee in 2007.

The college is a miniature society, where the students are trained to perform their social responsibilities with discipline. The college alumni have been appointed on various Govt. and Non- Govt. positions across the state. A lot of them are appointed in administrative services, teaching in schools and colleges, police force, research and political leadership. Many of them participated at National and International level games.

Courses offered: The College offers undergraduate courses in Arts, Commerce and Science streams. There are in all twelve subjects offered in Arts, Science and Commerce.

B.A: Political Science, Public Adm., Geography, History, Hindi lit, Sanskrit, Economic, Home Sc. English lit, Sociology, Drawing and Painting

B.Sc.: Botany, Chemistry, Zoology, Maths, Physics.

B.Com: ABST, Business Administration, EAFM & Book Keeping (for non- commerce)

BCA: (Bachelor of computer Applications)

P.G Course

M.A: Political Science, Public Administration, Hindi Lit, Geography, English Lit, Drawing & Painting.

M.Sc.: Botany, Chemistry

M.Com: ABST

Life at Campus: The College conducts an Orientation Programme so that the students are familiarized with the College campus, the library, the staff and the traditions of the College. The Investiture Ceremony marks the beginning of the official functioning of the Council of Students. The Council then organizes a social function to welcome the new students that helps create a feeling of fraternity and comradeship among them.

The College organizes and rewards the achievements of students in the curricular and extra- curricular fields at the Annual Awards Day held towards the close of the session. Regular attendance in the classes is essential for the students to be considered for awards.

Industrial Visit: For students to get an exposure to the corporate environment and work culture, the College regularly organizes Industrial visits to various companies. In the past, the college organized industrial visits to companies like Hindustan Zinc Ltd, World's second largest Zinc producing company and Radico Kaithan Ltd wherein the entire processes of the manufacturing was explained in detail and practically illustrated. Industrial Visit is an effective learning tool for the student that bridges the gap between the various concepts and its application.

N.S.S: NSS is a voluntary activity for the students of all streams. It provides them with an insight to community service of the society. The main concepts of NSS are overall development of students through its service. The main motto is "Not me but you". Two NSS units each of 100 volunteers are functioned in the college. Respective units have adopted two back ward areas ward like no. 16 Harizan Basti and Lakhani Village as a part of their service. A seven days eye camp was organized at an adopted village from 26th Dec. 2013 to 1st Jan. 2014.

Scout Guide: As a part of our Scouts and Guide team, the College has 36 ranger girls & 4 rangers units. 18 of ranger girls have received Praveen Puraskar and 12 girls are nominated for the Neepun (Rajya) Puraskar as well as for Uprastrapati Shield. The rangers participate in state level events like March-past State Ranger Meet Programme held every year and are also actively involved in community service like conducting sanitation programmes, social awareness rallies etc. They also help to conduct the eye camps held by Vedanta Charitable Hospital and Research Center every year.

Sports: Sports and Games are necessary to maintain good health, foster team spirit and good behavior. Sports reduce mental exhaustion and offer a change from the monotony of daily life. Education without sports is incomplete, thus keeping these values in mind; sports have been an integral part of Vedanta College's co-curricular activities.

Infrastructure Facilities: To meet the demand of curricular as well as professional requirement, the college provides the following facilities.

Class Room: The College has 38 Classrooms having well-structured physical and intra structural facility to support sound process of teaching and learning. The Classrooms are well ventilated and spacious enough to accommodate at least 60 students at a time to facilitate proper teacher- student's interaction. The college also provides a well-equipped lab facility for practical knowledge.

Library: The College owns a well-stocked library which has a regular supply of latest books and journals on various subjects where student and faculty can keep themselves abreast with the recent developments in their respective subjects. There is no department specific library; there are separate reading rooms for Arts, Commerce and Science faculties where student can read books, journals, magazines and newspapers.

The college has a vast library with an area of about 5000 square feet and is partially computerized. Efforts are being made to make the library user friendly. The College has received a number of books through donation from individuals and different organizations.

The Book Bank is an important segment of the library. Students can borrow a maximum of three books at a time after depositing the amount mentioned on books. While returning the books, students are refunded the amount after deducting Rs. 15/- on each book.

Board Room: The College has a full air-conditioned board room for conducting important meetings and seminars where over a hundred people can be comfortably seated. It is well-equipped with modern audio-visual equipment's that facilitates interactive sessions.

Internet Facility: Internet facility is provided free of cost to the staff and students. Each staff room is equipped with a desktop and a computer lab with 30 computers is separately maintained for providing Internet access to students. Broadband access is provided by BSNL.

Seminar Hall: The College has a seminar or conference hall with a capacity to accommodate 2000 students at a time. It is well equipped with audio visual aids to provide quality ambience for different academic & cultural events.

Hostel: The Hostel accommodation is quite sufficient to meet the demand of the outstation students seeking admission at Ringus Post Graduate Girl's College. The hostel provides basic lodging and boarding facilities. Two students share a room, which is furnished with beds, electric lights, fan, a cupboard, table and chairs. There is a common kitchen and common sanitation facilities with 24-hours running water.

Faculty: The real strength of an institution lies in its strong team of highly qualified and dedicated faculty. The management is very supportive of its faculty, and has encouraged its teachers to pursue research and participate in seminars, workshops, and symposiums at the state and national levels.

Special Provisions for Financially Weaker Students under Caste & tribes categories: Under this scheme students can collect the prescribed application form from the college and submit the same for waiver of tuition fees, along with required documents. The college management decision will be final regarding the grant of these scholarships.

"Earn while you learn": The college management has provided a conducive earning opportunity through gainful employment of college students with the objective of ensuring continuity of education of financially weak students. The call center has been set up within the college campus to provide employment opportunity to the college students on part time basis post study hours. The students can avail this opportunity to support their education and gain experience and earn about Rs. 3500-4000 pm.

Placement Cell: The College provides job opportunities for the Under Graduate and Post Graduate final year students as well as college alumni. Companies like ICICI bank, Muthoot Fin. Corp and many others have participated in our campus drives and recruited students in large numbers.

Alumni Association: An Alumni meet was held in the 1st week of March 2012 wherein the Alumni were honored by College Managing Committee. The main aim of the association is to maintain a link between the Institute and alumni sharing details of mutual growth, achievement and advancement in various fields.

Vedanta College of Management and Information Technology (VCMIT): Established on August 2010, VCMIT, located in Ulhasnagar, Thane offers a range of degree courses in BMS, B.Com, B.Sc-IT, BBI, BAF, B.Sc-Com along with facilities like a library, laboratory and a gym. Livelihood training in Electronics, Mobile Repairing and Motor Driving is imparted to students which help them acquire the practical skills, necessary for employment in a particular occupation. "The college has an in-house BPO to facilitate financially underprivileged students under the Foundation's 'Earn while Learn' scheme."- Dr. Milind Vaidya, Principal, VCMIT.

Gurukul Public School: Vedanta Foundation has established a Gurukul Public School at Ringus, Rajasthan on 1st July 2008 with an aim to educate students from LKG to standard 12th. The school currently has strength of 1365 students. Special care is taken to impart education using various high-tech education aids such as China made play equipments, robots, interactive charts, etc. Besides, the Foundation also distributes school bags, uniforms, books and other variables to the students.

Child Care Centers and Balchetna Anganwadis: For improving the health status of over lakh children, Vedanta Foundation has established more than 75 Vedanta Child Care Centers across Chhattisgarh, Lanjigarh, Udaipur and Tamil Nadu. The Foundation in association with the State Governments and approval of Ministry of Women and Child Development has setup more than 3613 Balchetna Anganwadis for underprivileged children in the age group of 3-6 years in Karnataka, Odisha and Rajasthan.

Khushi Project: Khushi is a unique tri-partite Public–Private–People initiative aiming to reach 3055 Anganwadi centres (AWC) in select Blocks of Ajmer, Bhilwara, Chittorgarh, Rajsamand and Udaipur districts. The goal is to strengthen the efficacy of Government's Integrated Child Development Services (ICDS) Scheme to improve health and well-being of children below 6 years of age. The program was re-launched in 2295 (out of 3055) Anganwadi Centers in association with reputed NGO partners like CARE India, 'Gramin Evam Samajik Vikas Sanstha', 'Seva Mandir' and 'Jatan Sansthan'. Through this program they are reaching out to about 36,000 children in the 3 to 6 years age group, and another 63,000 children below 3 years of age. The intervention has resulted in an increase in attendance of children at the centers and in the level of preschool education at the centers.

Impact of the project in Rajasthan:

- More than 81 percent Anganwadi centres are opening regularly
- 721 Kitchen Gardens developed at these AWCs and at community households to supplement the hot meals of AWCs
- Khushi teams organised recipe trials at 499 AWCs using the Take Home Ration (THR) as the main ingredient and other food items. The idea was to teach mothers how the THR can be converted into a delicious meal also, and thus improving the health of the mother and child. About 10000 mothers participated in these recipe trials and were delighted at the outcomes.
- Continuously organising community meetings at the AWCs to strengthen community engagement in more than 2300 AWCs
- 1200 Anganwadi Workers were trained across 3 districts, strengthening their abilities in preschool education.
- Regular community contributions are happening in more than 1200 Anganwadis in terms of milk, fruits, infrastructure – repairs

& renovations, food, uniforms, sweaters etc. in order to bring communities closer these centers

Vedanta E-Shiksha @ Schools Program: While one considers the great strides taken by India in popularization and streamlining of education in the Country, the gap between knowledge levels of the urban and rural students is still large enough. All said and done the rural students across India have to still battle with non–availability of the minimum facilities for education. The quality of education is not even standalone not to say about the levels of the highly priced private education in the Country.

Although there is growth in all sectors in India, the most benefits accrue to a small percent age of populace who stays in the urban environments. The rural environments do not even get to have the basic infrastructure and reel under poverty naturally without even being cushioned.

The Government, the biggest player in rural education, is in-charge of running and managing around 80 percent of all recognized schools at the elementary stage. Over the years, it has launched many programs to combat negative statistics like 40 percent illiteracy rate and 85 percent dropout rate. Education has also been made free for children between 6 to 14 years of age or up to class VIII under the Right of Children to Free and Compulsory Education Act 2009. All these have brought certain small benefits to the rural population in some of the clusters, but the major part of the country does not seem to have been covered properly.

One of the most ambitious projects of the Government launched is aptly named 'Education for All' that is 'Sarva Shiksha Abhiyan'. The initiative has to be given full marks for being the largest of any such education initiatives in the World. Although a huge investment has gone in to this initiative one has to agree that the ambitious project has faltered somewhere along and has not been able to deliver any positive results leave alone the results desired.

One can understand the fallacies of an initiative of the Government due to inherent mechanism deterrent to its growth and functioning. At the same time the Government circles themselves have come up with an excellent method of combating the problems by going in to the Public Private Partnerships (PPP). The PPP has brought in miraculous positive results in sectors where it was thought that the initiatives would fail. PPP has an in-built mechanism of clearly identified partnership structures, sharing of objectives and have specified performance indicators for delivery.

One such success story worthy of the kudos is that of the PPP with Vedanta Foundation as one of the agencies.

Vedanta E-Shiksha@Schools is the flagship program of Vedanta Foundation. This is one of the largest projects undertaken under the Central Government's Sarva Shiksha Abhiyan scheme. The acceptability and assimilation in this project is increased as the project uses award-winning e-content for learning the core subjects and provides computer education in vernacular / local languages. The multimedia elements present in the e-content are compliant with the state government syllabus. Hence they help students to understand concepts easily and retain them for a longer period of time. In addition to the digital content, computer education books are provided to each school. At the end of the year these books are handed over to the school library for any further reference by the children. Once the students gain the necessary skills to manage work on a computer they automatically become confident and ready to refer to the books in the Library. The larger objective of the program is to create self sufficient skilled individuals. The training and skills make them independent.

Objectives of Vedanta E-Shiksha@Schools Project

- To impact 10,000 schools, benefiting over 1 million children with technology-led education
- To improve student performance in academics and facilitate their overall personality development
- To decrease the dropout rate and absenteeism
- To improve motivation level and knowledge of teachers with a scalable Teacher Training Program
- To implement an innovative and creative curriculum that enhances the learning process

The Public Private Partnership in this unique project envisages that the operational responsibilities of running the program further are handed over to the School authorities after a period of THREE years. As the school has been a consistent partner in the program, it has all the input necessary to implement the program further. Thus there is a smooth transition.

The continued effectiveness which is the most important factor of this whole process is organized through Teacher training and empowerment, identification of locally based suitable human resources, who will carry the program forward for newer children arriving. Thus the implementation of the project is complete and positive.

Vedanta E-Shiksha@Schools has made an indelible impact on the quality of education in some rural areas of the Country. At present 2933 Government schools across Maharashtra, Goa, Rajasthan, Karnataka, and Orissa have been receiving quality education through the ICT. The benefits have been accrued to more than 3 Lakh students across the board.

In order to assess the academic performance of the students as well as the qualitative improvement in the infrastructure of the School, a third party baseline survey is conducted in every state after the signing of the Memorandum of Understanding with that State Government.

Education as a right of every young citizen of India has been imbibed very deep in the governance of the country. The education need not be just held as a right but we must also ensure that the right type of education to every child making the future functionaries of India globally successful. A purposeful life is evolved in to a successful life through the kind of education we are providing at Vedanta E-Shiksha@Schools.

As an organization dedicated to the betterment of the downtrodden, we take pride in the fact that we are helping to steer the overburdened rural education system in the right direction by providing ample opportunities to the less privileged rural children.

Recent activities: On the 22nd November 2012, the Schedule Caste and Schedule Tribe Development Department, Odisha signed an MoU with Vedanta Foundation to implement the e-Shiksha program in 1000 Government run schools. About 2 lac students will be benefitting from this program.

E-Shiksha was commenced in 349 schools in Goa: A Memorandum of Understanding was signed between Vedanta Foundation and the Bihar Education Project Council, to make E-Shiksha available to 1000 Upper primary Government Schools in the state of Bihar.

Vedanta foundation along with Hindustan zinc distributed computer education books at Ransagar School District Dungarpur (Rajasthan); the event was attended by District Education Officer Mr. Bansilal Roth, Sarpanch Ms. Champa Devi Parmar.

Prison Program: "Hate the Crime and Not the Criminal" as said by Mahatma Gandhi holds true for Vedanta's core beliefs. India ranks 5th in prison population in the World. More than 4 lac prisoners are lodged in nearly 1336 prisons in India. The reforms and the rehabilitation of the people in prisons have been discussed on multiple platforms. However, the project set out by the VEDANTA Foundation really answers the call and tries to provide a solution to the impending concern of the country.

The Vedanta project for the prison inmates starts with understanding the mindset of the inmate and maps them to appropriate skill development training. The Vocational Training Programs for these inmates are majorly focused on developing Computer and Tailoring skills, keeping in mind the employment/ self employment opportunities it offers. The trainers for these have been pre-groomed to understand the difficulties faced by the inmates and hence the delivery of training is absolutely revered. The inmates are treated like any other students and undergo the usual process of evaluation and certification on completion of training. Ultimately this leads them to the mainstream of the society and with their skill levels the society is able to absorb them.

"I feel like I am going to college, which I could only dream" is a spontaneous response from one of the inmates after he started attending the VEDANTA program.

The entire process right from identification of the student to his certification takes place in such a way so as to boost the confidence of the student. VEDANTA Foundation is administering this vocational avenue to gainful employment opportunities for prison inmates at various prisons across the country. Around 12,000 inmates across 21 prisons in the country have undergone the courses and are ready for the mainstream, after their release.

Rehabilitation of inmates will be meaningful only if they are employed after release. In order to remove the social stigma attached to the prison inmates, VEDANTA Foundation is in discussion with various employers to explore opportunities for appropriate employment of the skilled inmates. Meanwhile the Foundation offers the required support on mainstream employment to the inmates in the form of its pioneering concept of Campus JOB Fairs, wherein the receptive Employers from the Industry participate to offer employment to the prison inmates.

Vedanta Foundation pioneered the concept of Prison Campus Job Fair and went on to become the country's first to organize a first of its kind JOB Fair for the inmates within the Campus of the world Famous Tihar Jail.

The success of the Campus Job Fair in the prison has been well received among the government / prison authorities and the prison inmates. The foundation has so far successfully launched the careers of more than 50 prison inmates across various prisons of the country through a series of Campus Job Fairs. Vedanta Prison Program is a small step towards liberating the country from the impending concern of rehabilitating the growing prison population of one of the worlds growing economy – India, and help the country grow inclusively.

National Super 100: The Foundation's 'Super 30' project is a 10 month intensive residential course that provides professional coaching for underprivileged meritorious students for securing admissions into leading IIT/ Medical institution. Mr. Abhayanand (IPS, Gold medalist in physics, DGP – Bihar), the founder of SUPER 30 concept supported two of Vedanta Super 30 centers. Vedanta's National Super 100 center in Jaipur was inaugurated on 18th July 2012 by former Hon'ble minister, Higher Education, Mr. O.P Sharma. Later, in October 2012, another center was established at Noida near New Delhi in which a total of 190 students were selected through a process of examination and interviews from the 1700 applications received. A provision was also made for sponsoring selected students as many of them could not afford the course fees for admission into these premier institutes.

CA Classes: In the hope of securing high grades at competitive exams in Chartered accountancy, a widely chosen profession, most of these students gets enrolled at prestigious institutes. The Foundation, in continuation of its pursuit for education has joined hands with the Institute of Chartered Accountants of India to support the underprivileged students aspiring to become Chartered Accountants. By facilitating their coaching, hostel needs, a fully equipped reading room, required study material and counseling, these students would be trained at centers across India.

Sakhi: Vedanta's Sakhi empowers women by training them in Makeup artistry, Tailoring and Mehendi design creations with its centers established at various locations in rural and semi-urban areas including jails like Tihar. To provide women with a suitable platform to showcase their creations, many departmental stores and hyper markets support this initiative. Over 2.5 lakh women have benefited from this training programme.

Call Center- Earn While Learn Program: 'Earn while you Learn' is a unique scheme in which students pay their educational expenses by working after study hours, for the call centers available at Ringus, Rajasthan and Vitthalwadi college premises. Each call center houses over 200 workstations and our college faculty in association with Enser Communications provides students with the necessary support and training.

"The Call Centers set up by Vedanta Foundation in association with Enser Communications Pvt. Ltd. offers an opportunity for "Earn while you learn".

Computer Training Centers: Vedanta Foundation has imparted basic computer training to over a million students through its Computer Training centers located Pan India. For over 250 centers, the Foundation provides all the required hardware, software, course material, teachers and certificates, however, local associations and NGO's often provide assistance with space and students enrollment.

Sushil Kumar, coming from a small town of Motihari in Bihar, is among Vedanta's alumni who successfully completed a 6 month Diploma course in Computer Application in 2003 and later worked as a computer operator with a salary of Rs. 6000/- pm. Today, Sushil Kumar is known as the first winner of Rs 5 crores on KBC season 5 and Vedanta Foundation is proud to be a part of his journey.

Umeed - Prison Programme: To rehabilitate and equip the jail inmates with a skill set that will enable them to get respectable jobs on their release, the Vedanta Foundation offers computer training at its centers located across 43 jails all over India that includes central jails like Tihar where more than 15,000 inmates have been placed with a suitable employment thereafter.

Mass Marriages: Many couples in rural India are unable to afford the cost of a marriage ceremony, which is why they do not get married officially. Likewise, the couples' children are also deprived of admission due to lack of parent's identity. Vedanta Foundation often organizes Mass Marriage Programs and ensures to issue an authentic marriage certificate to the couples, thus safeguarding them from being subject to social exclusion. The 1st event was organized by the Foundation on 25th May 2013 where Mr. Baliram Jadhav, Palghar MP blessed 101 tribal couples at Mokhada Taluka in Thane district, Maharashtra. Similar events were later organized at various other locations like Jawhar in Thane, Kumudabali village at Muniguda block in Odisha and many others. Chief Guest like Mrs. Reema Lagoo and G. R. Khairnar had attended the occasion to bless these couples. The marriage was solemnized in a traditional fashion without any exchange of dowry or ostentation and all the marriage necessities like mundavlya, mangalsutra, other pooja samagri along with gifts like cycles, silver ornaments, basic utensil set, rajai's, sarees, watch, goggles, sewing machines, mobile phones and a fixed deposit of Rs 5000/- at the Post Office were distributed to each of the tribal couples. This initiative envisions helping the tribal couples to join the mainstreams.

Rojgar Avsar: Vedanta Foundation initiated several employment drives for over 30,000 underprivileged unemployed youth across states where companies like Mc Donald's, Eureka Forbes, Pantaloons Retail, Cinemax, CCD and many others participated. "Vedanta Foundation's unconditional support in fulfilling our national manpower needs, speaks of their strong social and moral commitment towards addressing unemployment in India."

Vedanta Charitable Hospital and Research Center: With an aim to provide free medical services to the needy in Ringus, Rajasthan, the Foundation, on 8th December 2010 inaugurated the Vedanta Charitable Hospital and Research Center that has outpatients departments, and XRay, pathology, physiotherapy departments along with a maternity ward and often organizes many free health camps that benefits scores of people.

Rajai Distribution: With a noble intention to protect the underprivileged section from the severity of cold, Vedanta Foundation donated Rajais to the respective municipalities of the cold-struck areas like Delhi, Madhya Pradesh, Chhattisgarh, Uttar Pradesh and many others who in turn distributed the Rajais to the below poverty line sufferers.

Temple Project: To provide accommodation and basic amenities to lakhs of devotees, the Foundation has built Dharmashalas at various religious places in India like Kedarnath, Gangotri, Yamunotri, etc. The Vedanta Bhakt Nivas, near Vitthal- Rukmini temple in Pandharpur at a time houses over 400 underprivileged devotees called warkaris.

Other Projects: Vedanta Foundation has always been on the forefront of any Social activity, which needs to be taken up for the people of India under its various flagship projects as mentioned like Vedanta Super 30, Vocational training, Earn While learn etc as already mentioned earlier.

Hinduja Foundation

The Hinduja Foundation is the implementing agency for Rural Development Projects and programs mandated by respective Company Boards as part of their CSR projects u/135 of the Companies Act 2013. The objective of the Hinduja Foundation Rural Development Project in Jawhar is to farm based enhance the livelihood of the project participant communities through 360 interventions in the form of improved agriculture practices, Wadi tree based farming, support to landless & women headed families, and bring about improvement in their quality of life through income generation and development of model villages, enhanced health and sanitation facilities, water resource management, upgradation of educational facilities, empowerment of women and development of the village infrastructure. The upgradation of Primary Health Centres and the deployment of a fleet of Mobile Medical vans are other major initiatives undertaken by the Hinduja Foundation in Jawhar taluka with the support of Hinduja Group Companies.

The Hinduja Group is based in Mumbai. They are involved in a wide range of activities including foundries, import export, trading, motor vehicles, banking, call centres and healthcare.

The company was founded in 1914 by Parmanand Deepchandh Hinduja, who was from a Sindhi family based in India. Initially operating in Karachi and Mumbai, he set up the company's first international operation in Iran in 1919. The headquarters of the group moved to Iran where it remained until 1979, when the Islamic Revolution forced it to move to Europe.

Srichand Hinduja and his brother Gopichand moved to London in 1979 to develop the export business; Prakash manages the group's finances in Geneva, Switzerland while the youngest brother, Ashok, oversees the Indian interests. The brothers are all devout Hindu, vegetarian and teetotalers, and dress in similar ways, with a preference for black suits and round glasses.

Under the leadership of its chairman, Srichand, today the Hinduja Group has become one of the largest diversified groups in the world. The group employs over 70,000 people and has offices in cities of the world and all the major cities in India. In 2017, Srichand and Gopichand Hinduja were described as the wealthiest men in Britain with an estimated wealth of £16.2 billion in the Sunday Times Rich List 2017.

In 2015 at The Asian Awards, the Hinduja brothers were honoured with the Business Leader of the Year Award.

Ashok Leyland Ltd: Ashok Leyland, a flagship business of Hinduja group, is the 2nd largest manufacturer of commercial vehicles in India, 4th largest manufacturer of buses in the world and 10th largest manufacturer of trucks globally. The company has its footprints across 50 countries and is headquartered in Chennai. It has 9 manufacturing plants around the world with 7 manufacturing plants in India and one each in Ras Al Khaimah, UAE and Leeds, United Kingdom.

Achieving a record revenue of Rs. 26,248 Crores and a record profit of Rs. 1, 5 6 3 Crores together with sustaining the market share gains in a competitive environment is quite commendable.

Ashok Leyland Defence: The Hinduja group has formed as an independent company to spearhead its defence business. Ashok Leyland Defence

Systems, is the newly floated company by the Hinduja Group. Ashok Leyland, the flagship company of Hinduja group, holds 26 percent in the newly formed Ashok Leyland Defence Systems (ALDS), which has a mandate to design and develop defence logistics and tactical vehicles, defence communication and other systems. Dr V. Sumantran, executive vice chairman, Hinduja Automotive Limited, heads the new venture. Ashok Leyland is the largest supplier of logistics vehicles to the Indian Army. It has supplied over 60,000 of its Stallion vehicles which form the Army's logistics backbone.

Gulf Oil Corporation Ltd: The chemical hub of the Hinduja Group was strengthened by the merger of Gulf Oil India Limited with IDL Industries Limited, which became effective from 1 January 2002.

The company has four major operating divisions:

- Commercial Explosives - handling explosives, detonators, explosive bonded metal clads and special devices for defense and space applications. It has eight plants in India, its Hyderabad plant being the largest detonator manufacturing facility in the world (192 million per annum). It is the largest exporter of explosives and detonators to 21 countries, including the Philippines and countries in South East Asia, North Africa, the Persian Gulf, the Middle East, and Southern Europe.
- Lubricants - lubricants, greases, and car accessories. Set up in 1993, and now the second largest private sector lubricant oil manufacturer in India.
- Mining and Infrastructure - undertakes large scale mining services in coal and iron ore, plus services to the infrastructure sector such as underground metro railways and national highways. It is executing two large projects for Coal India Ltd. The division has a major presence in the iron ore mining sector where it is working in very large mines rich in iron ore.
- Speciality Chemicals - manufactures active pharmaceutical ingredients, intermediates, and finished forms such as tablets, capsules, injectables and liquids. Also undertakes contract research and development services. Manufacturing based in Hyderabad.

Gulf Oil International: Gulf Oil International, which operates from London offices, is one of the largest petroleum companies and petroleum product traders in the world, operating in more than 83 countries through a network of own companies, joint ventures, licensees, and distributors. It employs 3000 people directly worldwide, with indirect employment touching 30,000.

It has filling stations in most countries in Europe, parts of South America, and Indonesia. It markets car batteries, car care products, vehicle air filters, lubrication machinery, and speciality chemicals in many countries. The company operates its Gulf Express chain of car service centres in Saudi Arabia and is planning to expand into Bahrain and other countries in the Middle East.

Gulf Oil International is one of the biggest petroleum product traders in the world, with a large plant in China and expanding into the Middle East, Africa and the Asia Pacific Region, with entries announced into Indonesia, Sri Lanka, and China, and expansion projects in Dubai, Saudi Arabia and India.

IndusInd Bank Ltd: IndusInd Bank is a private sector bank, and is the only Indian bank to have been founded by NRIs (Non-resident Indians), and the only commercial bank in India to receive ISO-9001:2000certification for its branch network. It began its operation in 1994 with a capital of Rs.1 billion (US$14 million) and with a focus on corporate and SME lending, and following its merger with Ashok Leyland Finance Ltd (ALFL) in 2004, has had an increasing emphasis on retail banking, and has grown into a bank with capital of Rs.10 billion (US$140 million) and assets of around Rs.200 billion (US$2.8 billion). It has a customer base of 1.5 million and a network of 400 branches and 600 off-site ATMs (as on 31 March 2012) spread across 141 geographical locations pan India.

The bank has representative overseas offices in Dubai and London, and correspondent banking relationships with 335 banks worldwide. The bank has entered into strategic alliances with Union National Bank in the United Arab Emirates and Doha Bank in Qatar to enhance its NRI business. The bank's national reach is extended further through its marketing arrangements for loan products through an associate firm, IndusInd Marketing and Financial Services, which has 745 marketing outlets across the country. The bank has secured high domestic investment-grade ratings for its financial instruments from the local subsidiaries of S&P, Moody's and Fitch.

Hinduja Foundries Ltd: Hinduja Foundries is a five decades old company catering to the casting needs of the automobile OEMs in India. It has three manufacturing plants in operation in Southern India. Around 30 percent of the vehicles rolled out in India (cars, commercial vehicles and tractors) have major castings supplied by the company. A modern new green field foundry was set up in Sriperumbudur near Chennai with an R&D centre and started its production in 2007.

Hinduja Global Solutions Ltd.: Hinduja Global Solutions Limited (formerly HTMT Global Solutions) began as an IT consulting firm specializing in providing solutions centred on a mainframe platform, in partnership with IBM. In 1995, the company entered corporate training in mainframes.

The company has 40000 employees with offices in North America and London, and 65 "delivery centres" spread across Bangalore, Mysore, Mumbai, Nagercoil, Chennai, Durgapur, Noida, Siliguri and Hyderabad in India;

Lyndhurst, Peoria, Illinois, St Louis, Waterloo, and El Paso in the United States; Montreal, Nova Scotia, Prince Edward Island, Ontario in Canada,Cyber City in Mauritius, Manila in the Philippines and Dubai in UAE.

The Contact Centre and Back Office Services Division houses "international voice centres" and back office processing units for Health Insurance, Pharmaceuticals, Life Sciences, Telecom, Banking and Financial Services, Consumer Electronics / Products, Technology, Automotive, Government, Media and Entertainment, Energy and Utilities and Transportation and Logistics companies.

Its Mauritius centre supports the French-speaking population, and its Texas centre provides support in Spanish. In Cablenet is one of the companies which come under the umbrella of Hinduja TMT or HTMT. It is part of its foray into Media and Communications.

P. D. Hinduja National Hospital and Medical Research Centre: The P. D. Hinduja National Hospital and Medical Research Centre, Mumbai is a multi-speciality tertiary care hospital with a medical research centre set up in collaboration with Massachusetts General Hospital (MGH), Boston. The hospital has an inpatient capacity of 350 beds including of 53 critical care beds in the specialties. As a tertiary care hospital, it offers services covering investigations and diagnosis to therapy, surgery, and post-operative care. It is the first tertiary care hospital to have been awarded ISO 9002 certification from KEMA, Netherlands, for Quality management systems, and was awarded the "Golden Peacock Global Award" for philanthropy in emerging economies (2006).

The hospital has treated 1.5 million outpatients, and performed a million surgeries and 7.5 million lab investigations. Its laboratory is the first hospital laboratory to be accredited by the College of American Pathologists.

Hinduja Bank (Switzerland) Ltd: Hinduja Bank (Switzerland) Ltd was founded as a finance company in 1978 and became a Swiss regulated bank in 1994.

Hinduja Bank has its headquarters in Geneva and has a network in Switzerland including offices in Lucerne, Zurich, St Margrethen, Basel and Lugano. Additionally it has a global presence in London, Dubai, Paris, New York, Mauritius and Chennai. Over the years, its businesses expanded to include Wealth Management, Trade Finance Services, Global Investment Solutions and Corporate Finance Services.

Striving for Change: India has a rich cultural heritage and valued traditions, especially that of philanthropy and service to others. Powered by this strong value of paying one's debt to society, the Group's founder, Parmanand Deepchand Hinduja, earmarked a majority portion of their personal wealth for the benefit of the less-fortunate.

Yet, even as he lived by these precepts, little must he have imagined that the culture of giving that he had initiated would spread beyond the shores of India. But today, the Hinduja Foundation has done exactly that, spreading its wings and growing into a truly multi-cultural charitable organization with roots in India, and branches in the United Kingdom and the United States of America.

The Foundation has supported a number of initiatives to preserve the cultural heritage of the nation, particularly projects presenting and highlighting the everlasting progressive values of the Indian subcontinent. This includes projects that uphold social wellbeing and healthcare, like long-term social welfare measures, swift help in times of crises and undertaking rural development projects to enhance the livelihood of rural communities with planned initiatives, activities and village infrastructure development.

In the sphere of education, the Hinduja Foundations in India, UK and US have each set up endowments that support several Indian students each year in India and abroad in prestigious universities, such as Cambridge University, UK and Columbia University, US.

The Journey 2017:

- Phase II of the शाश्वत ग्राम – Sustainable Rural Development Program is led entirely by tribal women in a novel move. The 360 degrees farm-based interventions in the form of improved agriculture practices have brought large scale improvements in the quality of life of the tribal villagers. All farming in the project is now organic without use of chemical inputs.

2015:

- The Foundation introduces a comprehensive शाश्वत ग्राम - Rural Development Program, through involving activities that support income generation and tackles underemployment in tribal villages.
- The Hinduja Foundation Antiquity Collection was launched at a glittering function at the World Trade Centre, Mumbai on 15th October, 2015. Its first publication "Ancient Coins of India-The Lance Dane Bequest" was released on the occasion. Selected coins were exhibited at the Annual Philately Fair and later at the inauguration of Amravati City, Andhra Pradesh by the Prime Minister.

2013:

- The Foundation constructs winter shelters for the Rehabilitation of Disaster Affected Persons in Uttarakhand, in the Himalayan heights, after the massive flooding and destruction of lives and property in June 2013.

- Hinduja Foundation Antiquity Collection: The Collection comprises of coins, Indian art and artefacts including bronzes and stone sculptures, terracotta, wood carvings, textiles, beads, photo archives, rare books on the theme of the collection and paintings. The coin segment is a premier numismatic collection of the period 600BC ton 600AD, especially coins in copper and silver. Some coin series in the collection are very comprehensive like coinage of the Satavahana dynasty (150 BC to 250 AD) which is reputed to be the only collection of its kind worldwide. The Collection has many punch marked mudra series, the earliest coins of India.

2012:

Columbia University Medical School in New York establishes a fund for Alternative and Preventative Medical Research and Education at Columbia University Medical Center, through a bequest from the Hinduja Foundation.

- The Hinduja Foundation institutes Scholarships for Children of Needy Widows in order to provide succour to poor and disadvantaged widows.

2011:

- The Foundation establishes scholar selection through an endowment for the Dharam Hinduja Fellowship Fund, which supports the training of students from Indian Universities for PhD studies in Indian studies at South Asia Institute, Columbia University.
- The Foundation introduces Mobile Healthcare Units in the tribal areas of Jawhar in Maharashtra. The mobile vans are fully equipped with basic pathological facilities, doctors, nurses and technicians and operate in a scheduled program providing quality healthcare services in tribal villages of the region.

2010:

- An Ayurvedic Workshop is organized with Columbia University Medical College.

2009:

- The Foundation sets up the Dharam Hinduja Medicine and Education Fund at the College of Physicians and Surgeons at Columbia University Medical Center, with a donation of $1,000,000.

2007:

- The Foundation funds the publication of a catalogue of Sanskrit Manuscripts at Columbia University, the first detailed and scholarly catalogue of nearly 400 Sanskrit manuscripts at the University.

2000: The Foundation sponsors the Millennium World Peace Summit, a historic gathering of the world's pre-eminent Religious and Spiritual Leaders at the United Nations.

1999:

- The Foundation sets up the Dharam Hinduja Lectureship in Sanskrit Teaching and Indic Research at Columbia University.

1998:

- The Hinduja Foundation establishes the ASCI - Hinduja Institute of Healthcare Management, Hyderabad in collaboration with the Administrative Staff College of India (ASCI) and the Johns Hopkins University, USA. The institute was also supported by the P. D. Hinduja National Hospital as a 'Centre of Excellence'.
- The Foundation signs an agreement to provide financial assistance of £1,00,0000 to support the important Faith Zone in the huge Millennium Dome project in Greenwich.
- The Foundation donates to the International Society of Krishna Consciousness Temple in Hertfordshire, the Swami Narayan Temple in Northwest London and the Venkateswara Balaji temple outside Birmingham.
- The Foundation gives a Grant of £20,000 to the Leprosy Mission in memory of the late Lady Diana, Princess of Wales, to build vocational training centres in India.
- The Foundation in the UK aids various efforts such as a program for cancer research and sick children through the Indo-British Macmillan Appeal, the Cancer Research Campaign and the Great Ormond Street Hospital for Children.
- The Foundation signs an agreement with Cambridge University to become a significant donor to the Divinity Faculty's new building.
- The Foundation sponsors the ISKON Hinduja Glory of India Vedic Cultural Centre, a state-of-the-art experience-exhibition created on Indian Vedic Culture created in New Delhi.

1997:

- The Hinduja Foundation and Massachusetts General Hospital create an exchange fellowship program, the John E. Lawrence Fellowship Program, for the purpose of enhancing and promoting professional, educational and cultural exchange between India and US.

1996-97:

- The Foundation establishes the Hinduja Foundation Scholarships for Wards of Employees of Ashok Leyland & Hinduja Foundries. The Scheme offers 16 scholarships annually. The scholarship is available to students who secure admission to professional courses on merit.

1996:

- The Foundation establishes Indic Research Centres at the Dharam Hinduja International Centres for Indic Research in India and the University of Cambridge in the UK in 1996.

1995-96:

- The Foundation provides fifty Hinduja Foundation Scholarships for Wards of Employees of P. D. Hinduja National Hospital & Medical Research Centre for higher studies to meritorious children of the hospital staff, and one scholarship for a hospital employee desiring to pursue higher studies.

1995:

- The Foundation sponsors a three year program, known as South Asia Business & Economics Course, at the prestigious Georgetown University.

1994:

- The Foundation commissions the legendary Indian painter, MF Hussain, to create an inter-faith series of famous oil-on-canvas paintings titled 'Theorama'.
- The Dharam Hinduja Indic Research Center is established at Columbia University to support research on India's ancient wisdom and knowledge.
- The Hinduja Foundation consolidates its association with Cambridge University through two more programs and in a significant move, the Foundation establishes the Dharam Hinduja Institute of Indic Research within Cambridge University's Divinity Faculty.

1993 - 94:

- From academic year 1993-94, the Hinduja Foundation initiated a scholarship scheme, Hinduja Foundation Scholarships for Post Graduate Studies in Ayurveda, for a deserving Post Graduate student in Ayurvedic Medicine.

1993:

- The Hinduja Foundation, in collaboration with the All India Lawn Tennis Association (AITA), established the Dharam Hinduja

- AITA Tennis Academy in Delhi (1993-2000) with the aim of upgrading the skills of a number of promising tennis players, who subsequently made a mark at the national and international level.

- The Hinduja Foundation institutes a Grant to the University of Pennsylvania for Wharton School Athletics.
- The Dharam Hinduja International Centre of Indic Research for research into ancient Indian culture and its relevance to contemporary values is established in Delhi.

1992:

- The Hinduja Foundation introduced cash awards and monthly stipends for the medal winners at the Olympiad's/Asiad's on their kit to encourage adopted sportspersons and their coaches.

1991:

- The Hinduja Foundation joins forces with the Commonwealth Cambridge Trust, under the patronage of the Prince of Wales, to establish a seven year program with an endowment of £2,00,0000.
- The Centre for India-US Education is established in New York, in cooperation with Asia Society to strengthen India-US understanding through educational activities.
- The Hinduja Foundation (UK) establishes the Hinduja Cambridge Trust with an endowment fund of £2,00,0000 Sterling. The returns finance the Dharam Hinduja Cambridge Scholarships, instituted for Indian students desiring to pursue post graduate and doctoral studies at Cambridge University, U.K.
- The Hinduja Foundation begins the Dharam Hinduja Merit Cum Means Scholarships to provide deserving Indian students of proven merit but limited means, the resources and encouragement for personality growth.

1988:

- The Hinduja Foundation (US) co-founded the Harvard Hinduja Council in collaboration the Harvard School of Public Health. The Council aims to fund programs to develop innovative approaches to health issues in India.

1984:

- The Hinduja Foundation is set up in the United States of America.

1983:

- The Hinduja Foundation supports the start-up of the US Chapter of the Bharatiya Vidya Bhavan and donates premises for their activities in the memory of Shri P. D. Hinduja.

- The Hinduja Foundation donates US $2,00,0000 to set up the Hinduja Research Laboratory, Boston.This is a modern, fully equipped centre for research in Endocrinology, located in the Massachusetts General Hospital, Boston. This donation is on the US Congressional record.

1975:

- With donations from the Hinduja Foundation, the Sindhi Educational Society (Madras) establishes the Seth P. D. Hinduja Sindhi Model Secondary School in Chennai.

1972-73:

- The Hinduja Foundation takes a leading role in setting up and upgrading P. D. Hinduja Sindhi Hospital, Bangalore, in collaboration with the Sindhi Youth Association, Bangalore.

1971:

- Shri P. D. Hinduja, beloved Founder and philanthropist, passes away. He leaves behind a rich legacy of charitable service, a committed band of institutions and enterprises deeply conscious of their social responsibility, and a family brought up to believe that philanthropy is an honourable reward of business.

1969:

- P. D. Hinduja registers the Hinduja Foundation on 3rd April, 1969. It was a public charitable trust with a broad spectrum of charitable objectives. Gradually, Hinduja Foundations presence was also established in the United Kingdom and the United States.

1951:

- Shri P. D. Hinduja sets up an outdoor clinic in Mumbai, named the 'Seth Deepchand Gangaram Hinduja Health Care' catering for refugees. This small outpatient facility eventually develops into the P. D. Hinduja National Hospital and Medical Research Centre, an ultramodern non-profit tertiary healthcare centre of international repute.

1947:

- Witnessing the tragedy of partition of the Indian subcontinent, P. D. Hinduja pooled resources with his friends and led the way ahead by setting up relief centres, settlements, and medical care units for displaced and uprooted families.

1944:

- Shri P. D. Hinduja establishes a charitable educational trust, the Shrimati Pahunchbai Deepchand Hinduja Trust, in memory of his mother, marking the beginning of structured charity. Today, this trust runs the well-known K.P.B. Hinduja College of Commerce in Mumbai.

1914:

- Shri P. D. Hinduja takes the first steps in establishing the Hinduja Group as an Investment and Banking Group with a diversified global portfolio of holdings across manufacturing, services and banking sectors.

The Foundation

Vision: Transform the lives of the underprivileged in a self-sustaining manner.

Misssion:

- Enable the beneficiaries to breakout of the cycle of poverty and draw them into a cycle of growth, development and empowerment, whilst retaining ecological balance in the process.
- The focus of the Foundation will be to:
  - o Promote and catalyse education, health, and welfare among the underprivileged.
  - o Foster an environment which would bring the underprivileged into the mainstream.
  - o Encourage, promote and preserve Indian Heritage & Culture

Over half a century ago, Shri Parmanand Deepchand Hinduja, the founder of the Hinduja Group and Foundation, enunciated this philosophy and made a commitment to serve those less privileged than him.

Being a firm believer that he had to return to society what he gained from it, and in turn serve and help people better their existence, he developed the following five guiding principles, which continue to guide and inspire the Hinduja Family's philanthropic zeal.

Let your life be guided by Dharma (Duty): The greatest quality a human being can have is to be a true follower of Dharma.

When you have dharma with you, you have everything. For Dharma comes prosperity (Arth), fulfilment of all desires (Kama) and knowledge, wisdom (Gyana) and liberation (Moksha). You need not to be a Vedic (Book of Knowledge) scholar to follow Dharma.

Hinduja Foundation – UK: Like the Hinduja Foundation in India, in the UK its activities focus on education, healthcare, interfaith understanding and the arts.

The Hinduja Foundation in the UK has been operating for over thirty years during which time it had managed the Hinduja Cambridge Trust scholarship scheme for Asian students studying at the University of Cambridge, established Dharam Hinduja Indic Research Centre at Cambridge University's Faculty of Divinity, contributed to the UK's celebration of the new Millennium with the Faith Zone at the Millennium Dome, and supported the Duke of Edinburgh's Award.

Healthcare: Over the years in the UK, the Foundation has made donations to a number of healthcare charities, notably the Stroke Association, the Elton John Aids Foundation, Concerned for Mental Health, Clic Sergeant Cancer charity, the British Cardiac Research Trust and in 2015 King's College London's new Cancer Centre.

Furthermore, support has also been given to UK registered charities in healthcare operating outside the UK, notably the Leprosy Mission with the late Princess of Wales and its work in India and the Lebanese charity Give a Child a Toy which works to provide life-saving operations, the purchase of vital medical equipment, and the provision of essentials for various orphanages and children centres in Lebanon

Hinduja Foundation – USA: Education, healthcare and multicultural understanding form the cornerstone of the activities of the Hinduja Foundation in the United States.

The Foundation's quest to raise the quality of human life has resulted in various programs at leading universities and medical centers in addition to a wide range and variety of meaningful projects across the country.

The Hinduja Foundation supported the startup of the US Chapter of the Bharatiya Vidya Bhavan and donated the premises for their activities in the memory of the Parmanand D. Hinduja.

Rural Development: The Foundation aims to enrich the lives of those living in the rural areas of India. In the socio-economic landscape of the country, there is a lack of livelihood opportunities in the rural communities. Hinduja Foundation aims to correct this imbalance with its timely initiatives and programmes in the rural and remote areas of India.

Rural Development projects and initiatives: The Hinduja Foundation is the implementing agency for Rural Development Projects and programs mandated by respective Company Boards as part of their CSR projects u/135 of the Companies Act 2013. The CSR programs and activities are implemented on behalf of Ashok Leyland Ltd., Hinduja Group Ltd., Hinduja Realty Ventures Ltd., Hinduja Finance Ltd., Hinduja Ventures Ltd, Gulf Oil Lubricants India

Ltd., Gulf Oil Corporation Ltd., Hinduja Global Solutions Ltd., HGS International Services and Indusind Media & Communication.

The objective of the Hinduja Foundation Rural Development Project in Jawhar is to enhance the livelihood of the project participant communities through a 360 ° farm based interventions in the form of improved agriculture practices, Wadi tree based farming, support to landless & women headed families, and bring about improvement in their quality of life through income generation and development of model villages, enhanced health and sanitation facilities, water resource management, upgradation of educational facilities, empowerment of women and development of the village infrastructure. The upgradation of Primary Health Centres and the deployment of a fleet of Mobile Medical vans are other major initiatives undertaken by the Hinduja Foundation in Jawhar taluka with the support of Hinduja Group Companies. Over 90,000 patients have been treated in the period 2011-17 through the Mobile Medical Units of the Foundation. In 2016-17 11 specialty camps were conducted by the Hinduja Hospital consultants and doctors and OPDs have provided access to more than 300 padas (hamlets).

Criteria for selection of villages

- Low HDI index
- Tribal population and remoteness of village
- Villages where HF Mobile Medical Units are operating
- High Migration
- Malnourishment
- Limited livelihood opportunities
- Subsistence agriculture
- Percentage of BPL families

Challenges faced in Implementing

- To ascertain the needs of the tribal community through an accurate and participatory process.
- Partner empanelment after due diligence
- Project Management involving methodical and regular interventions.
- Project Design by aligning the project structure with the objectives laid out for the project.
- Knowledge Management by synthesizing learnings from the project and measuring the impact.

A 'Need Assessment Survey' exercise was undertaken in 28 villages of Jawhar taluka. After undertaking baseline survey and its analysis, a detailed

Project Report (DPR) was prepared for undertaking comprehensive development activities comprising of livelihood promotion, improvement in quality of life, women's empowerment, village infrastructure development and training of the community in relevant activities. The project titled as 'Hinduja Foundation Sustainable Rural Development Project, Jawhar' commenced from the month of June 2015 with expertise from BAIF. 5 villages were selected for implementation of the Project in the first phase from 2015-20 and another five villages in the second phase from 2017-22.

- Total Villages to date : 10
- Total Budget : Rs. 1899.52 Lakhs
- Project Period : 2015- 2025
- Population Covered : 16,544

Implementation Approach

- Participatory Planning Involving Women
- Collective Decision Making
- Transparency In Operations

The project continues to run smoothly owing to the coordination with the Govt. authorities, partner NGOs, Panchayats and villagers.

Rural Practices Underta: The Foundation works extensively to foster sustainable agricultural practices and inculcating the principles of farm management to the villagers, building their capacities to utilize better practices with better techniques.

Village Resource Mapping: A plan is created with the Gram Panchayat and the villagers to help identify the resources existing and help the community to realise its assets and then work forward from there on.

Improved Agriculture Practices: The Foundation has been working to improve the yields of rural areas by introducing Improved Agriculture Practices among the Project Participants and reduce the dependency on few crops by encouraging diversity of cropping for long-term sustainability.

The Project supports cultivation of finger millets, vegetable cultivation, Rabi crops and support for floriculture cultivation.

Tree Based Farming (Wadi): Soil conservation activities are undertaken in the Wadi plot to enhance soil fertility by the Foundation. Water management activities are also undertaken in the Wadi to ensure sustainability as availability of water for irrigation is critical.

Support to Landless & Woman-Headed Families: Landless families are unable to garner productive resources for their livelihood. The Foundation, through its projects, has extended its support to 3 landless and 5 women-headed families identified with the help of Panchayats and villagers to generate income. Suitable activities have been identified after the visit to families and the resources available to them.

Water Resource Management: Water is a critical component to sustain farming. Rain-fed agriculture is fraught with uncertainties because of the pattern of rainfall. Therefore, the Foundation strives to ensure availability of water both for irrigation and for meeting the drinking water needs of the community.

Water resource development through the deepening of wells: The Project undertook the deepening of the open wells to tap live underground sources of water and to increase storage capacity of the well. 9 wells were dug during the reporting period which benefitted about 41 families on 69 acres of land.

Water Lifting Devices in Groups: Group Water Lifting Device is a mobile unit that consists of a diesel pump set and pipes. Members of the Water-User-Groups use the set in rotation for irrigating vegetables in Rabi season. Fuel is provided by the farmers.

Water Lifting for Drinking Water: Water scarcity is a huge problem during the summers. A pilot project provided solar-powered lift from nearby wells for drinking in Shingarpada village. 115 families benefited from getting drinking water at their doorstep.

Training: Training in various skills involving agriculture and allied activities is provided to the participant community.

Activities Implemented

Need-based Training of Farmers: Specific trainings are organized based on the needs felt through 'Training Needs Assessment.'

Exposure Visit of Farmers: Exposure visits are organized so that participants learn by observing how specific activities are undertaken by farmers in developed areas. The visits provide a wonderful opportunity for farmer-to-farmer interaction and learning, which is most effective in convincing and development of confidence.

Training and Women's Empowerment: In India, women constitute half of the total population. A majority of women in rural areas are voiceless and depend on the men for their livelihood. The Foundation aims to bring a positive change in the lives of the women in the rural areas.

Capacity Building and Training of SHGs (Self Help Groups): SHGs play a key role in the empowerment of women so that they can effectively mobilize community in general and women in particular. It gives a platform to empower women through social development and financial independence. The Project is making efforts to build capacities of members of the women's SHGs through numerous need-based trainings.

Capacity Building and Training of SHG (Self Help Groups) Office Bearers: The office bearers are trained in various skills for the efficient functioning of the SHGs.

Support for Record Keeping: One of the vital functions of SHGs is regular saving and credit. The SHGs meet at a fixed interval of week, fortnight or a month to deposit their savings and for repayment or disbursement of loans. Apart from this, several community and development issues are discussed and numerous decisions are taken. It is essential to document and keep relevant records to maintain transparency. The project has provided support to purchase relevant records and printed stationary.

Training of Barefoot Accountants: Saving and Credit activity and financial linkages developed with banks and government schemes involve financial transactions. An accurate record has to be maintained for transparency of operations and for periodic auditing. Educated youth in the community are trained to maintain the record as per standard procedures and are affectionately called 'barefoot accountants'.

Exposure Visits: Exposure visits of the SHGs in the Project have been organized for outstanding and exemplary SHGs in the nearby areas.

Strengthening of People's Organization: Capacity building training was given to office bearers of existing POs.

Innovations: The Foundation has carried out several innovative schemes during the roll-out of the project.

Temporary Check Dam (TCD): TCDs have so far been constructed with sand bags in the taluka in support of the Rural Development program. These dams have helped in arresting monsoon flows and improving irrigation supply to the farmers for floriculture and vegetable growing for an additional 2-3 months.

Talia Drip Tray: Talia trays of Israeli design have been used for conjunctive use of water for irrigating horticulture plants by funneling available water like scattered rainfall and dew. Trial with 200 trays is being undertaken at Pimplashet and Kharonda.

Automated Agri Weather Stations (AWS): The Foundation's AWS located in Jawhar is telemetrically linked to servers to send weather information to the IMD which in turn provides daily, three-day weather forecasts for the project villages. It has the following features:

- Communication over GPRS
- Battery Charging by Solar Panel
- Offline data storage in micro SD Card
- Real-time data access on web and mobile
- NIST traceable sensors as under:
    - Wind speed
    - Wind direction
    - Rain collector

- o Air temperature
- o Humidity
- o Solar radiation
- o Leaf wetness
- o Soil moisture
- o Atmospheric pressure
- o Soil temperature

Education Upgradation: Several schools in the area are in great need of intervention. Development of two Ashram residential tribal schools and 15 Zila Parishad schools in five villages into holistic innovative learning centres with the aid of specialist NGO in Chambarshet and Ozar is being undertaken in 2017. Initial surveys have been completed. Transforming two Ashram residential tribal schools, an Ashram school for girls and 7 Zila Parishad schools in the Jawhar taluka villages into holistic innovative learning centres has been scuccessfully implemented. 3,875 students from the 10 schools, 10 principals, 69 teachers and 1542 community children from 50 adjoining hamlets have benefited.

Cataloging & Documentation: The Collection was received uncataloged. To systematically document and catalog the Collection, the Indian Institute of Research in Numismatics, Nashik, successfully carried out detailed documentation in respect of the coins at the Institute in Nashik. The other antiquities have been documented by object experts.

Curating: The curating of the Collection is being carried out by a leading archival services firm.

- We are utilizing state of the art Collection Management software to securely store the documented details of the collection and afford ease of documentation, viewing to researchers, and selective public web access through a virtual museum.
- Data center with high end servers has been established to host the software and collection data.

Display

- We envisage state of the art display fixtures, other modern interactive methods: touchscreen with individual items genealogy; audio (oral history); documents (letters, papers, records etc.); newsreel/movie/documentary; website; display of other arts and artefacts of the Collection.
- A library and archive for research and reference, for scholars, studentsestablished to host the software and collection data.

Roadmap: As a continuation of the Hinduja Foundation's longstanding commitment and endeavours across the globe in the promotion of arts and culture and particularly the advancement of knowledge in the cultural ethos of India, to:

- Display the Hinduja Foundation Antiquity Collections in public places and through the website for the benefit of the public.
- Partner with Universities and other bodies for research into numismatics, heritage and culture of India.
- Create catalogues and other publications to spread knowledge of this antiquity.
- Run programmes and events on antiquity, culture and history of India.

Education: Every child must have equal access to a quality education because it determines the quality of life in the nation.

Education is the key to change and progress in India. The Foundation strives to provide quality education to each and every section of the society.

Large scale educational initiatives need significant and sustained effort that can be achieved only through working at multiple levels and on several areas simultaneously.

The Foundation has been working for years now towards making deep and large-scale impact on the quality of education in India.

Rural education initiatives: Education is the mirror to society. The Foundation believes that quality education broadens horizons, creating choices for children to achieve their dreams.

Zilla Parishad and ashram residential schools, AWHAR: Several schools in the area are in abject need of intervention. The Foundation partnered with a specialist NGO and undertook the development of Zilla Parishad schools in Kundachapada, Chambharshet, Pimpalshet, Akre, Devgaon, Kharonda and Hedichapada, two Ashram (Residential) Schools in Chambarshet and Ozar and one girl's ashram school in Gorthan.

The schools also hold camps for summer and winter with crafts, street-play training, superstition eradication and games. The Foundation also provided a solar powered ICT bus on wheels, and continues to train teachers, while conducting regular community education surveys to further its cause in areas of need.

- **In-School Programs -** Since good education is dependent on the quality of teachers, the Foundation offered after-school support that helped 1242 children. The Foundation initiated in-school programs, providing learning support for children from the under privileged communities. The Foundation is helping 3,875 students from 10 schools over a period of 6 years to achieve better academic proficiency.

- **After-School Programs** - The Foundation holds after-school programs for 1542 community children from 10 villages and 50 hamlets.
- **Training for Teachers** - 69 teachers and 10 principals from 10 schools received extensive mentoring, professional development and training of curriculum delivery.
- **Skill Enhancement for Students** - The Foundation strengthened the cognitive skills and provided classes to improve the spoken English of the students for holistic development.
- **Wellness Sessions for Students** - The Foundation also ran programs on hygiene and sanitation, health and nutrition, physical and emotional development, and personality development.

Current Activities

- **ZP Kundachapada School** - The Foundation is currently over-seeing the renovation of the main classrooms, while additional classrooms, an assembly area and stage are still being built. The Aanganwadi located in the school premises is also being renovated as it is in poor condition. Toilets and water provisions have been completed.
- **ZP Pimpalshet School** - Renovations have been recently completed with the help of the Foundation, and an e-learning interactive board/smart board was also fitted.
- **Ashram School, Chambharshet, Jawhar** - The Foundation spent Rs. 1.86 lakhs to provide school text books to 435 students from class 9-12, as curriculum books are not provided by the government.

Worli School Upgradation: The Foundation is in the process of upgrading the Worli School, with two class rooms already redone – a Computer Lab and an E-Learning Lab with an interactive board/smart board for the benefit of the children. MCGM approval has been obtained for a 'Gyan Shakti Program'.

Dharam Hinduja merit-cum-Means scholarships: The scholarships were instituted in 1991, the International Year of the Girl Child. The scheme is based on an objective and transparent system of selection aimed to recognize and reward outstanding but needy school–leavers backed by the financial support of this scholarship, to pursue further studies. While the merit criteria are derived from pan-India State Board Merit lists, need is assessed on an objective basis on the basis of financial status of the family assessed through documents provided. Priority is given to orphans, children from women-headed families and marginalized families like labourer's etc. The Merit lists are forwarded by the State Education Boards and shortlisted students are informed to apply and include details of academic achievements and information of family income. Direct applications to the Foundation are not required.

Three Scholarships are awarded from each state annually of which at least one must be a girl. Scholars are awarded a continuing scholarship from Std XI till first Graduation whatever the field — engineering (4 years), medicine (4 1/2 years + 1 year of internship) or regular graduation (3 years). The Scholarship is continued subject to the scholar maintaining a laid down academic standard annually and character endorsement from the institution s/he is studying in.

There are about 340 Hinduja Scholars presently studying under the Programme covering 21 States including North-East states. Allied with the main Scholarship scheme are scholarship schemes run for Group companies, P.D. Hinduja National Hospital, Mumbai and K.P.B Hinduja College, Mumbai.

Various scholarships offered by the foundation: The Foundations supports talent and excellence in the field of education. It supports several scholarship schemes to help those individuals who are passionate about improving their knowledge and those living in constrained environments.

For Wards of Employees of Ashok Leyland & Ennore (Hinduja Foundries): The Foundation provides Hinduja Foundation Scholarships for Wards of Employees of Ashok Leyland and Ennore (Hinduja Foundries). The Scheme offers 16 scholarships every year. The scholarship is available to meritorious student for professional courses.

For Children of the Hinduja National Hospital Employees: The Foundation awards a total of 54 scholarships to meritorious school-going students studying in standards V, VI, VII, VIII, IX and Xth.

For Children of Needy Widows: A scholarship scheme in collaboration with Loomba Foundation was started in May 2012 to ensure assistance for the children of needy widows with verifiable need-based norms and parameters. Annually, a substantial contribution is made to provide scholarships to the affected children, who are monitored for scholastic progress.

- Scholars awarded a continuing scholarship of Rs.2,000/- p.m. from Std. XI till first Graduation in any subject.
- Scholarship continued for a minimum of five years and a maximum of seven years (for engineering or medical graduates).
- Scholarship continuance is contingent on maintaining specified high academic grades in each class.
- Presently there are 342 Hinduja Scholars under the Programme.

Nanhi Kali: Nanhi Kali is a project which endeavours to extend opportunities of quality education at school level to those disadvantaged girl children who do not have access to education. Hinduja Foundation supports this endeavour by sponsoring 30 Nanhi Kalis.

World Vision: The sponsorship under this programme creates a positive and enduring change in the lives of underprivileged children. Hinduja Foundation has adopted 25 boys and girls and supports their education.

Hinduja Foundation's School Scholarship Project: This scholarship is for the students of SOS Children's Villages of India in the cities of Chennai, Pune and Raipur catering to 215 boys and girls between Standards I to IX.

Hinduja Foundation's Employment Linked Education Scholarship Project: This scholarship is for the students of SOS Children's Villages of India in the cities of Chennai, Guwahati, Kolkatta, Pune and Raipur catering to 60 boys and girls studying in Standards X and above for vocational courses of their choice.

- In view of the large number of scholarship schemes supported, requests are generally not entertained for individual scholarships, scholarships for post graduate studies and scholarships abroad.

Smt. P.D. Hinduja Trust's

K.P.B Hinduja College of Commerce: In 1944, the Founder started a school at Charni Road in Mumbai, which over the years has developed into the renowned KPB Hinduja College of Commerce.

From student strength of 400 in 1974, it has reached an astronomical figure of 7100 while the number of teachers has increased from 12 up to 125, with 67 full-time and 58 visiting faculties. Today, besides being a Ph.D. Centre, the college offers 26 courses which include 25 professional courses.

- Ranked No.1 in Mumbai in India Today national survey.
- College adjudged the "Best College in Commerce" by the University of Mumbai 2012-13.
- The college has been re-accredited with 'A+' Grade by the National Assessment and Accreditation Council in March, 2017.
- UGC has certified it as a "College with Potential for Excellence".
- The college is preparing for autonomous status.

Seth P.D. Hinduja Sindhi Model Secondary School: The Foundation donated generously towards building the Seth P. D. Hinduja Sindhi Model Secondary School in Chennai.

Educational Initiatives: The Foundation endeavours to broaden and enrich the educational experiences of children in India and abroad both. The Foundation makes a number of donations to deserving institutions and NGOs annually. It has played an increasingly influential role in education in India and abroad, and has also supported the following educational related endeavours.

- Hinduja Technological Institute, Aurangabad
- Hinduja Prataprudra Planetarium, Warangal (AP)
- ASCI – Hinduja Institute of Healthcare Management, Hyderabad
- Swaminarayan Hindu Mission School (UK) Scholarship Scheme for Indian students attending the school.
- Duke of Edinburgh's Award Programme: Supports young people in their self-development and recognises their achievements.
- Dharam Hinduja Cambridge Trust Scholarships: This scheme awards Dharam Hinduja Cambridge Scholarships through an endowment from Hinduja Foundation, UK, for Indian students for studies at Cambridge University.
- Dharam Hinduja Lectureship in Sanskrit Teaching and Indic Research at the University of Columbia

The Dharam Hinduja International Centres of Indic Research were established at the Columbia University in USA in 1994, New Delhi in 1996 and at the University of Cambridge in 1996. It donated 222 books on Sanskrit and Oriental Studies including interpretation of India's ancient texts to the Bhandarkar Oriental Research Institute, Pune, which is the world's premier institution on Oriental Studies besides on-going research in Indic studies.

- The India center donated 222 books on Sanskrit and Oriental Studies including interpretation of India's ancient texts to the Bhandarkar Oriental Research Institute, Pune, which is the world's premier institution on Oriental Studies besides on-going research in Indic studies.

Educational resources: The Foundation offers educational resources for students to support education for the nation's progress. It has donated 8500 books valued at US $ 425,000 to educational institutions in Tier II and Tier III cities to provide access to educational content and bridge the woefully inadequate library and internet resources in majority of our universities.

More than 90 percent of the books are new text-books at the university levels by well-known US publishers covering all disciplines.

The Foundation has also supported the following publications:

- Encyclopaedia of Nobel Laureates; Encyclopaedia of Hinduism
- Encyclopaedia of Sports & Games
- Encyclopedia of Nobel Laureates
- Kautilya's Arthashastra

Arts & Culture: India is a land of diverse cultures. It is of utmost importance to protect and promote its rich art, culture and heritage.

The Foundation strives to maintain the glorious heritage and composite culture of India. It works towards the protection, conservation and preservation of the country's tangible heritage. A current flagship program undertaken by the foundation is the development of the Hinduja Antiquity Collection.

Antiquity collection: The Foundation's prized Antiquity Collection includes a large number of coins of ancient India, paintings, bronzes and stone sculptures, terracotta's, wood carvings, erotica, textile, beads, photo archives and rare books.

The Antiquity Collection was formally launched on 15th October 2015 at the World Trade Centre, Mumbai in the presence of the Governor, Maharashtra and other distinguished guests.

The objective of the Antiquity Collection is to provide opportunities for research and education, while advancing the knowledge of India's glorious culture and heritage.

Coin Collection: The Foundation's Coin Collection is a premier numismatic collection of the period 600 BC to 600 AD. The Collection's world renowned coins were on display for the public from 16th-18th October, 2015 at World Trade Centre. The Satavahana collection was showcased at Amravati in the presence of Prime Minister, CM of A.P. and other dignitaries.

Coins play a significant role in understanding and reconstructing history. They also confirm and substantiate the history known from other sources. This Collection is claimed to be better than the coin collection of the National Museum for the said period in copper and silver. Some coin series are probably the most comprehensive known anywhere like Satavahana dynasty (150 BC to 250 AD).

The Collection has punch-marked Mudras, the earliest known coins of India, and is amongst the best known in India. Most of the coins from 600 BC to 600 AD are in silver, copper, lead, potin (a mixture of cobalt, tin and arsenic) and gold fanams.

It also highlights another dynasty Western Kshatrapas (1st to 5th AD) which is known through its coinage only and is amongst the earliest dated coins of India. There are local, tribal, monarchical and city issues in large numbers. Some dynasties represented in the collection are Magadha, Kasi, Kosala, Kuru, Panchala, Surasena, Avanti, Gandhara, Chandraketugadh, Sakyas, Mauryas, Hunas, Abhiras, Anandas, Pandyas, Gauda, Valabhi, the later Guptas, Yadavas of Devagiri, Kalachuris etc.

Artifacts: Figurines in bronze and sculptures in stone of gods and goddesses and animals in the Collection represent other aspects of the ancient art of India, along with terracottas and wood carvings.

Photo Archives: The photo archives in the Collection are a valuable record of Indian art and coinage with photographs from private collections, museums, temples and archeological sites taken painstakingly over decades. Together, they provide a rich documentary archive for researchers and practitioners of art history and heritage preservation. This has been subject matter of continuing PhD research.

Books: The Collection comprises of more than 5000 rare books that include periodicals, journals and catalogues on all aspects of ancient and modern Indian Art. There are books on History, Archaeology, Art and Architecture, Epigraphy, Numismatics, Religion, Philosophy, Sociology, Iconography, Sculptural Art, Modern Art, Performing Arts, Heritage and Erotica available that are well-preserved.

The objective of the Hinduja Foundation in developing its Antiquity Collection is to advance knowledge of India's glorious cultural heritage and to provide opportunities for research and education to historians and students from across the world.

Programmes at the Smithsonian institute: Through the years the Foundation has given a number of grants to the Smithsonian Institute in Washington DC to support its international cultural exhibits and learning programmes.

Nehru gallery at Victoria and albert museum: In the early 1990s, the Foundation contributed and supported the establishment of the Nehru Gallery at the Victoria and Albert Museum in London.

Persia exhibition at the British museum: In 2005, the Foundation was a major donor to the Persia Exhibition with the Iran Heritage Foundation at the British Museum – this brought together the largest number of Persian artefacts and paintings ever assembled outside Iran.

Theorama: The Foundation commissioned the legendary Indian painter, MF Hussain, to create a series of paintings titled 'Theorama' in 1994.

Encyclopedia of Hinduism: The Hinduja Foundation sponsored the publication of the first Encyclopedia of Hinduism which was launched by His Holiness, the Dalai Lama.The encyclopaedia, prepared over 25 years by 2,000 scholars, gives a comprehensive perspective of our ancient way of life and culture that has its roots going back thousands of years.

Millennium pledge (UK): The Hinduja Foundation launched the Millennium Pledge in a series of initiatives to celebrate the new Millennium. It aimed to bring about greater understanding and the removal of prejudices amongst communities, religions, sects and nations.

Promoting arts & culture around the globe: ISKCON Hinduja Glory of India Vedic Cultural Centre, New Delhi, a state-of-the-art multimedia exhibition on Indian Vedic culture.

International Society for Krishna Consciousness (ISKCON): The Foundation donated to the International Society of Krishna Consciousness

Temple in Hertfordshire, the Swami Narayan Temple in Northwest London and the Venkateswara Balaji temple outside Birmingham.

Other initiatives of note include

- Nehru Art Gallery of Indian Art at the Victoria and Albert Museum
- Bharatiya Vidya Bhavan (UK)
- Women's India Association and the Sindhi Association

The Asia Society: The Centre for India-US Education was established in New York, in cooperation with Asia Society to strengthen India-US understanding through educational activities.

Bharatiya Vidya Bhavan: The Hinduja Foundation supported the start-up of the US Chapter of the Bharatiya Vidya Bhavan and donated premises for their activities in the memory of Shri P. D. Hinduja.

Supporting the performing arts: The Foundation has taken a keen interest in encouraging creative and performing arts, especially efforts which help improve multicultural understanding.

The Mahabharata: Peter Brook's renowned theatrical production on the famous Indian epic by the same name.

The Millennium pledge (UK): Encouraging greater interfaith understanding at the time of Diwali at Alexandra Palace, 1999, with former British Prime Minister, Tony Blair.

Prince Albert II of Monaco Foundation: The Hinduja Foundation is a founder member of Prince Albert II of Monaco Foundation and has donated over 1 million Euros over four years.

The saga of the Hinduja Group started in Sindh, the cradle of the Indus Valley Civilisation, where more than 5,000 years ago, the human race learnt its first lessons in organized business and banking.

Parmanand Deepchand Hinduja, a young entrepreneur from the fabled town of Shikarpur in Sindh district (now in Pakistan) realised early in life that business was all about spotting opportunities and seizing them, wherever they surfaced.

In 1914, he travelled to the trade and financial capital, Bombay (later changed to Mumbai) where he quickly learnt the ropes of business. In 1919, the business journey, which began in Sindh, entered the international arena with an office in Iran (the first outside India).

Merchant Banking and Trade were the twin pillars of the Group's business. The Group remained headquartered in Iran till 1979. It then moved to Europe.

In the past 100+years, the Group has expanded and diversified its businesses with significant social and charitable contributions, under the present leadership of Chairman, Srichand Hinduja and ably supported by his brothers, Gopichand, Prakash and Ashok Hinduja.

Today, the Hinduja Group has become one of the largest diversified groups in the world spanning all the continents. The Group employs over 150,000+ people and has offices in many key cities of the world and all the major cities in India.

The Hinduja Family has always adapted to free-market reforms, moving quickly in new markets that have opened and capitalizing on new economic opportunities. As a result, Hinduja Group is now strategically positioned to contribute to old economy sectors, such as Banking & Finance, Transport and Energy, as well as the new economy sectors of Technology, Media and Renewables.

Firm believers in traditional family values, the Hindujas have all along striven to inculcate the family concept in their business enterprises while following the core philosophy of the Founder.

Every member of the Group is encouraged to practice the Vedic principles of work: 'Service with devotion' and 'willingness to see fulfilment of one's self-interest in the active promotion of the interest of the collective'.

Mutual trust, respect, cohesion and co-operation are emphasized as key organizational guidelines. At the same time, sound modern management practices are given primacy within individual companies of the Group and also at the corporate level.

Professionals are allocated independent charge of diversified activities. There is a high premium on healthy internal competition. Executives and Employees are appreciated and incentivized for performance excellence.

The Group, throughout its history, has demonstrated a strong commitment to creating better understanding between the people and the governments of the world. Building amity and co-operation between their host country and their mother country, India, has been an article of faith for the Hindujas.

As a responsible corporate citizen, Hinduja Group believes that the sole purpose of our existence is enhancing the shareholders' value. All the internal processes at the Group are focused towards achieving this objective. Hinduja Group's external communication efforts are also focused in the same direction.

We regularly update the website with the quarterly results about various Group companies. We also share with our investors and public at large, any significant developments in the business through media releases.

The Group has set high standards for ourselves in terms of disclosure and corporate governance and are committed to achieve them, in fact, surpass them.

Business verticals: The Hinduja Group is one of the largest diversified groups in the world with direct presence in 38 countries and activities spanning across a 100 countries. Operating globally in 10 business verticals that range from Banking and Finance to Information Technology Enabled Services, the Group enjoys flagship presence through leading companies, some of which are global and national icons.

Ashok Leyland is the 2nd largest manufacturer of commercial vehicles in India, the 4th largest manufacturer of buses in the world and the 16th largest manufacturer of trucks all around the world.

Headquartered in Chennai, India, Ashok Leyland's manufacturing footprint is spread across the globe with 8 plants including one at Ras Al Khaimah (UAE). An industry leader in automotive solutions, Ashok Leyland recorded record revenues of INR 26,248 crores (2017-18).

Ashok Leyland's Joint Venture partners include Continental AG (Germany) for Automotive Infotronics and the Alteams Group for the manufacture of high-press die-casting extruded aluminium components for automotive and telecommunications sectors.

Ashok Leyland is the largest supplier of mobility solutions to the Indian Army and is their logistics backbone, a segment where the company boasts core competence. With a major presence across 50 countries, Ashok Leyland is one of the most fully-integrated manufacturing companies.

Hinduja Tech is a premier engineering and digital technologies services provider focused on the automotive manufacturing industry using global delivery model. We have inherited decades of automotive product development expertise in our DNA and we offer full vehicle and powertrain development services from concept through SOP.

Optare designs, manufactures and sells advanced single deck and double deck buses for a global market place with the support of its parent company, Ashok Leyland. With over a century of expertise in the latest technologies, Optare's buses operate in United Kingdom, Continental Europe, North America and further. The Company also offers comprehensive after-sales service and supplies complete vehicles, CKD or SKD kits, technology transfer and licensing agreements around the world.

With the help of enhanced diesel technology, alternative fuel options and hybrid systems, Optare has developed a range of low-carbon buses and full electric drivelines which are available across entire product ranges. Optare has set the benchmark for fuel economy and CO2 reduction with reduced weight designs and optimised drive systems.

The Gulf brand is one of the most famous brands in the Oil and Lubricants industry and is a proud member of Hinduja Group. Gulf Oil International is one of the largest independent downstream lubricants companies in the world with sales made in over 100 countries. It owns and operates blending plants in Argentina, China, India, Philippines, and the United Arab Emirates.

Gulf products are also manufactured, under license, in several other countries via third party blending plants using Gulf formulations. The most visible presence the brand has is through its ever-growing number of Gulf branded petrol stations. Gulf is always looking for new partners to take the brand into new territories and new product markets.

The Gulf brand and the Gulf racing colours go hand in hand with motor racing. The light blue and orange racing colours of the Gulf brand that are loved by motorsport enthusiasts the world over, celebrated their 50th anniversary in 2017. Gulf is synonymous with sports and its sponsorship activities further demonstrate the quality, performance and power of the products, delivering results in the greatest tests of endurance.

Gulf has many famous motor racing victories to its name from all corners of the world. In 2008, Gulf first sponsored the Aston Martin Racing team. The team, that year (2008) secured the GT1 Category at the Le Mans 24 Hours race, 40 years after Gulf's first outright win. The team won the 2009 Le Mans Series for both the drivers and the team. In 2011, at the Laguna Seca round of the American Le Mans series, Gulf and Aston Martin Racing returned to winning ways, running almost faultlessly enroute to victory. The car took a podium place at the final round of the Intercontinental Le Mans Cup, the 'Petit Le Mans'. In 2013, the season saw Aston Martin Racing continue in its winning ways in the World Endurance Championship, in both the GTE Pro and GTE Categories.

Gulf is proud to be an Official Partner of the world's number 1 football team, Manchester United. This is a ground-breaking partnership initiative for the sport, in what is an initial three and a half year deal with the most famous of English Premier League Clubs.

Gulf has two partner teams in the World Superbike Championship series, the first with the Milwaukee Aprilia team and the second with the Althea BMW team. Gulf also sponsors Gulf Racing, competing in the World Endurance Championships in the Porsche 911 RSR.

Gulf Oil Marine: Gulf also has a separate venture, Gulf Oil Marine. Based in Hong Kong, Gulf Oil Marine specializes in the delivery of bulk marine lubricants for ocean going vessels. The company began operations in 2009 and already boasts one of the widest port supply networks in the industry with more than 1,000 seaports worldwide.

Gulf Oil Marine's plans include a continued focus on the Far East markets for additional opportunities and coverage, together with further expansion in the Middle East and onwards into Africa. The aim is for Gulf Oil Marine to be firmly established in the top ten lubricant brands globally, by the end of 2020.

Hinduja Global Solutions (HGS) is a service provider headquartered in Bangalore, India, operating on a global level with over four decades of experience working with some of the world's most popular brands.

HGS delivers localized solutions and takes customer interaction and satisfaction to a higher level through deep domain and process expertise. It operates a global network of 69 customer experience centres with around 45,900 employees across the U.S., Canada, the UK, India, the Netherlands, France, Germany, Italy, Jamaica, UAE, and the Philippines, making a difference to more than 600 of the world's top brands across nine key verticals. For the year ended (31st March 2017), HGS had revenues of US$ 555 million.

CyQureX is a 360 degree cyber security services company: Along with its partners, CyQureX provides an array of products and services that will secure your business so you can drive innovation and growth. The products and services are designed to secure a company's value chain end-to-end.

Hinduja Group has entered into the Renewable Energy sector with a long-term commitment to be an integral part of India's vision to be a leader in Sustainability. Hinduja Renewables Energy Private Limited (HREPL) is an independent power producer with a vision to grow through both organic and inorganic means.

With innovative business models to adopt in both, the rooftop and utility segment, the Group began its initiation into the solar sector in 2016, now operating a portfolio of 125 MW. With immense growth opportunities in Private PPA, Commercial and Industrial rooftop markets, Hinduja Group aims to lead in tapping these projects through HREPL.

HREPL's solar portfolio, as of 2018, comprises of Ground Mounted Solar Plants and Rooftop Solar Plants all over India, with 3 plants in Rajasthan, 2 plants in Maharashtra, 2 plants in Tamil Nadu and 1 plant in Gujarat.

HREPL's projects are currently consistently generating PLF upwards of 22 percent on fixed tilt and were instrumental in setting up India's first 5 MW single axis tracking project.

HREPL is constantly looking at opportunities in charging infrastructure, alternative battery power storage with battery management, as replacement to Genset based power, and many other opportunities for the C&I segment.

Philanthropy: India has a rich cultural heritage and valued traditions, especially that of philanthropy and service to others. Powered by this strong value of paying one's debt to society, the Group's founder, Parmanand Deepchand Hinduja, earmarked a majority portion of their personal wealth for the benefit of the less-fortunate.

Healthcare: Every individual, no matter rich or poor deserves quality and holistic healthcare. The Foundation has been striving towards building a healthier nation by making healthcare within the reach of every individual for the benefit of the whole of humanity.

Education: Every child must have equal access to a quality education because it determines the quality of life in the nation. Education is the key to change and progress in India. The Foundation strives to provide quality education to each and every section of society.

Large scale educational initiatives need significant and sustained effort that can be achieved only through working at multiple levels and on several areas simultaneously. The Foundation has been working for years now towards making deep and large-scale impact on the quality of education in India.

Art & Culture: India is a land of diverse cultures. It is of utmost importance to rotect and promote its rich art, culture and heritage. The Foundation strives to maintain the glorious heritage and composite culture of India. It works towards the protection, conservation and preservation of the country's tangible heritage. A current flagship program undertaken by the foundation is the development of the Hinduja Antiquity Collection.

Social Welfare: The upliftment of society is an ethical duty with the philosophy of oneness at its core. Be it carefully planned long term welfare measures or swift help in times of crises, Hinduja Foundation has done its bit to bring smiles back to helpless faces. Consciously aware of their social responsibility, Hinduja Foundation has played its role in upholding social wellbeing with carefully planned long-term social welfare measures, prompt aid in times of crises and by undertaking a number of Rural Development schemes in underdeveloped areas.

Hinduja Foundation adopts 13 Villages to uplift rural India: Hinduja Foundation, a part of the 100-year-old Hinduja Group has adopted 13 new villages under the Model Village Project, in India to develop rural areas. The 13 villages are from the State of Maharashtra which has seen the highest distress on account of drought and heat wave.

These developmental projects will be executed between 2017 to 2022. The 13 new villages adopted in Maharshtra, Palghar District include – Akre, Sakod, Deogaon, Aalyachimet, Barwadpada, Jagda, Dajese, Pimparna, Khambale, Talasari, Kirmire, Sakharshet, and Umbarkheda.

"With the ongoing distress among farmers in India, particularly in Maharashtra which was affected by the worst drought, Hinduja Foundation as a part of its Model Village Project has adopted 13 new villages in India to develop rural areas in the country. It will focus on enhancing livelihood opportunities, develop sanitation & clean water drinking facility, promote the use of alternate energy like solar power, improving health & hygiene facilities, build educational facilities, undertake training programmes for women empowerment and infrastructural development in the village," said Brig. Chukerbuti, Executive Vice President of the Hinduja Foundation.

The Foundation under the Rural Development Project (Gramin Vikas Prakalp) in 2015 had adopted five villages and based on its success and experience, they have decided to adopt more villages. Under the existing programme the Foundation has adopted Pimpalshet, Ojhar, Kharonda, Tilondhe and Chambharshet for the period June 2015 – 2027.

Also, a total of five schools viz. Kranti Jyoti Madhyamik Ashram School, Chanjarshet, Sarkari Ashram School, Ojhar, Jilha Parishad schools from Pimpalshet, Chambharshet and one school from Khundachapada have been adopted.

Key developmental activity conducted by Hinduja Foundation, under the model village project in Jawhar, Pimpalshet, Ojhar, Tilonde and Chambharshet in Maharashtra.

Solar based water lifting project*:* The foundation has set up a potable water project powered by solar power to ensure drinking water is made available to locals.

Hinduja's water lifting project was powered by solar power where water is lifted from the nearby river and stored in tanks built on hills, making water available for locals/ villagers. They also built a solar drinking water project for domestic use like cooking, drinking, etc. This project has impacted nearly 104 families. Recently, with an aim to save water and provide it to the villagers of Jawhar, students from Hinduja College took an initiative to construct check dams and soak pits in the taluka. The Foundation has constructed a water tank at Shingarpada, and construction for water tanks is ongoing in Kharonda Gavthan, Hedicha Pada and Ojhar Gavthan.

Tree based farming programme: Wadi is typically 1 acre plot of fruit plants surrounded by one or two rows of forestry plantation and inter-cultivation with crops, between the rows of horticulture plants. Wadi can provide sustainable income to the farmers from sale of fruits and timber. Cropping undertaken as inter-cultivation ensures food security of the family. Wadis are generally planted on wasteland. Establishment of Wadi on such lands helps it to turn it into productive land due to addition of bio-mass and development of water resources. Wadi, thus is a great tool for wasteland development. Hinduja foundation till date has planted 90,000 trees on waste lands with 95 percent survival rate, bringing such lands under cultivation.

Agri-based programme*:* Deepening of the open wells is being undertaken by the Project to tap live underground sources of water and to increase storage capacity of the well. To help farmers in their vegetable cultivation and floriculture activities, Hinduja foundation has dug 9 wells in Jawahar taluka.

The vegetable cultivation programme was conducted to help farmers get additional income. Also this programme added advantage in improving the nutritional status of the families through home level consumption. The Potential of Vegetable Cultivation as an income generation activity was recognized by Hinduja Foundation. Cultivation of vegetables such as Bitter gourd in Kharif & Chilli, onion, Cowpea, Cluster bean, Gram Cucumber & watermelon in Rabi was promoted.

India CSR News Network: Hinduja Foundation, the Corporate Social Responsibility (CSR) wing of the 100-year-old plus Hinduja Group that works on sustainable rural development projects in rural Maharashtra. The Hinduja Foundation's key activities over the last 60 years encompass Healthcare, Education, Sustainable Rural Development, Preservation and Promotion of Arts & Culture, and Social welfare.

The objective of the Hinduja Foundation's Sustainable Rural Development Project, presently being run in Jawhar taluka, Palghar dist. of North Maharashtra, is to improve the quality of life of the beneficiaries through development of model villages. Enhancement of the livelihood of the participant communities through farm based interventions coupled with enhanced health and sanitation facilities, water resource management and upgraded educational facilities is the primary aim of the project. In concert with these initiatives training is being carried out for empowerment of women through self-help groups and setting up of peoples organisations.

Hinduja Foundation through its rural development project in Jawhar has touched the lives of 2008 families so far with a population of 11,172 individuals. In the second phase the Foundation has adopted 13 more villages. Ultimately, the Foundation intends to cover 6,000 families with an estimated 30,000 individuals under this programme.

Hinduja Foundation had initially identified 28 backward tribal villages in the tribal Jawhar belt by conducting a comprehensive Need Assessment Survey of which five villages with thirty hamlets were initially selected for the Rural Development Project. A report was thereafter prepared for undertaking comprehensive developmental activities in the area. The foundation has a PPP Agreement with the Additional Collector of Jawhar for smooth running of the project.

The outlay for the integrated developmental activities being conducted in Jawhar including sustainable rural development, healthcare and education is in the region of Rs. 29 crores. The Sustainable Rural Development project commenced in June 2015 with phase 2 of the program being completed by 2022.

Corporate Social Responsibility: Our fundamental approach to business is to create long-term sustainable value for our customers, employees, shareholders and society. We recognize our social, economic, and environmental responsibility to the communities in which we operate.

Hinduja Global Solutions (HGS): HGS is an Indianpure play business and service provider headquartered in Bangalore, and part of theHinduja Group.[1] Formerly known as HTMT Global, the company re-branded itself as HGS in line with the group policy. It has over 44000 employees worldwide with a large employee base in India. It has presence in 7 countries including Philippines, USA, UK, Canada, UAE and Jamaica. In India, it has "delivery centers" in major cities like Bangalore, Chennai, Hyderabad, Mumbai, and growing cities like Mysore, Nagercoil, Durgapur, Siliguri, and Guntur.

The history of Hinduja Global Solutions began in 1993 under the name Ashok Leyland Information Technology, providing information technology services. In 2000, it merged with Hinduja Finance Corporation to form HGS. 2003 marked a milestone with the acquisition of Customer Contact Center Inc., a call center company located in the Philippines. In 2007, it acquired AFFINA LLC, a US-based contact center and database management and marketing research company and in 2010, UK-based Careline Services, another contact center management services provider, was acquired. In 2011, it acquired Canadian-based On-line Support Inc. to further strengthen its presence in North America.

On 30 June 2015, it announced the signing of a definitive agreement to take over a significant portion of Mphasis Emerging Markets business. With this acquisition, the firm expanded its presence in Bangalore, Noida, Raipur, Chennai, Pune, Mumbai, Vadodara, Indore, Puducherry, Ahmedabad, Bhubaneswar and Mangalore, and also entered the competitive BPO market in terms of employment with its only centre in North India in Noida.

At HGS, we echo and advance the ideologies of Parmanand Deepchand Hinduja, the founder of the Hinduja Group. In 1944, he set up The Hinduja Foundation, a public charitable trust, borne from a life-long conviction that philanthropy is a sacred social responsibility of all enterprise. The Foundation has a broad spectrum of objectives and conducts its activities across offices in India, the USA and the UK. It is associated with a number of philanthropic activities in areas of healthcare, education, and social welfare.

Local Relevance: HGS believes in being locally relevant and is committed to making a positive contribution to the communities in which we operate and thrive. Across the globe, our regional offices play an important role in designing, implementing and monitoring community outreach programs through active collaboration with universities, charities, NGOs and clients to promote education, fund cancer research, stimulate entrepreneurship, provide disaster relief or improve life for under privileged children.

Our community engagement programs also reflect elements of our global sustainability strategy which maintain a firm focus on carbon footprint reduction, local sourcing and elimination of energy/water wastage.

HGS Veterans Program: We run a highly successful employment program for military veterans and their families in the USA. The program, which runs in partnership with several US universities, offers tuition reimbursements, competitive salaries and benefits packages to military veterans and their families. To date, the program continues to support and nurture the career growth and development of men and women who have dedicated their lives to protecting their nation. It has empowered thousands of veterans and their families to better their lives through education and advance their life prospects at HGS.

HGS Recruits Success and Drives Efficiency with Military Employment: We at HGS have immense respect for our military forces and the employment initiative is an effort to offer them better job opportunities in the civilian sector. Our vision is to help make our clients more competitive by engaging the unparalleled people skills, work ethic, and customer service abilities of military hires. As part of our partnership with our clients, HGS leverages this partnership program in our recruitment efforts offering clients excellent brand representatives providing great customer support services. Incorporating an employment program for the military, who risk their lives on the frontlines, makes not only good business sense, it also adds to your Corporate Social Responsibility (CSR) activities.

Committed to Veteran-Friendly Recruitment, Training and Retention As part of our commitment to our military recruitment program, HGS has taken the pledge and been accepted as a member of the Hires Heroes Consortium (HHC) and we are committed to military and veteran friendly recruitment, training, and retention practices. Through our partnership with the military at Fort Bliss, HGS is able to staff active and veteran military personnel and their spouses bringing extensive benefits to both the military community and our clients.

About HGS HGS is a leader in optimizing the customer experience and helping our clients to become more competitive. HGS provides a full suite of business process management (BPM) services from traditional voice contact center services and transformational DigiCX services that are unifying customer engagement to platform-based, back-office services and digital marketing solutions. By applying analytics, automation, and interaction expertise to deliver innovation and thought leadership, HGS increases revenue, improves operating efficiency, and helps retain valuable customers. HGS expertise spans the telecommunications and media, healthcare, insurance, banking, consumer electronics and technology, retail, and consumer packaged goods industries, as well as the public sector. HGS operates on a global landscape with 40,000 employees in 66 worldwide locations delivering localized solutions. For the year ended 31st March 2016, HGS had revenues of US$ 507 million. HGS, part of the multi-billion dollar Hinduja Group, has more than four decades of experience working with some of the world's most recognized brands.

Bibliography

- Angela Kail, Tris Lumley, "Theory of Change: The Beginning of Making a Difference," New Philanthropy Capital.
- Arulampalam, W., & Stoneham, P. An Investigation into the Givings by Large Corporate Donors to UK Charities,
- Bain & Company India Philanthropy Report: various issues
- CAF-India Annual Report. New Delhi: Charities Aid Foundation-India.
- CECP. *Giving in numbers*. New York, NY: Committee Encouraging Corporate Philanthropy.
- Charities Aid Foundation, CAF World Giving Index
- "Collaborative Giving," Rockefeller Philanthropy Advisors,
- Dadrawala, Noshir. Management of Philanthropic Organizations. Bombay: Center for Advancement of Philanthropy.
- Dasra. *Beyond philanthropy: Towards a collaborative approach in India*.
- Drèze, Jean & Amartya Sen. India: Development and Participation. New Delhi: Oxford University Press.
- Eikenberry, A. M. *Giving circles: Philanthropy, voluntary association, and democracy*. Bloomington, IN: Indiana University Press.
- Eckhart-Queenan, J., & Etzel, M., Three Cases of Better Corporate Philanthropy. Harvard Business Review.
- "Finding Your Focus in Philanthropy," Rockefeller Philanthropy Advisors,
- FICCI. n.d. FICC's Initiatives in Corporate Social Responsibility and Social Development. New Delhi: FICCI.
- Fontela, J., The Difference between Corporate Philanthropy and Corporate Responsibility. Chron.
- Fooks, G. J., & Gilmore, A. B., Corporate Philanthropy, Political Influence, and Health Policy. PLoSONE 8(11).

- Gore, M. S. 'Historical background of social work in India', in Sumitra Gupta, ed., Social Welfare in India. n.p.: Chugh.
- Government of India (Planning Commission), National Human Development Report. New Delhi: Oxford University Press.
- Hari Menon, senior advisor, Philanthropic Partnerships and Government Relations – South and South-east Asia, Gates Foundation India
- Heasman, M. Corporate Philanthropy: Recent Examples from Kellogg and Coca-Cola. Food for Good Blog.
- Hopkins, E. *Collaborative philanthropies: What groups of foundations can do that individual funders cannot*, Oxford, United Kingdom: Lexington Books.
- ITC Limited. n.d. The Social Side of Enterprise. Calcutta: ITC Limited.
- Johnson, Paula. Global Social Investing: A Preliminary Overview. The Philanthropy Initiative.
- John, R. *Beyond the cheque: How venture philanthropists add value*. Oxford, United Kingdom: Skoll Centre for Social Entrepreneurship, Said Business School, University of Oxford.
- JP Morgan Chase, Corporate Responsibility.
- Kabongo, J. D., Chang, K., & Li, Y. The Impact of Operational Diversity on Corporate Philanthropy: An Empirical Study of U.S. Companies.
- Koh, H., Karamchandani, A., & Katz, R. *From blueprint to scale: The case for philanthropy in impact investing*. Mumbai, India: Monitor Inclusive Markets.
- Lala. R.M. The Heartbeat of a Trust. New Delhi: Tata McGraw-Hill.
- Lim, T. Measuring the Value of Corporate Philanthropy. New York: CECP.
- MacArthur Foundation and Intellecap, "Strengthening Philanthropic Giving and Impact Investing for Development in India"
- Ochs, K., Social Innovation and Education: Examining the Venture Philanthropy Model of International Development.
- "Peer to Peer: At the Heart of Influencing More Effective Philanthropy," William and Flora Hewlett Foundation.
- Sasse, C. M., & Trahan, R. T. Rethinking the New Corporate Philanthropy. Business Horizons,

- Wells, R. A. (ed.), The Honor of Giving Philanthropy in Native America. Indianapolis: Center on Philanthropy at Indiana University

Appendix

Schedule VII of Companies Act

Activities which may be included by companies in their Corporate Social Responsibility Policies Activities relating to:—

(i) Eradicating hunger, poverty and malnutrition, ["promoting health care including preventive health care"] and sanitation [including contribution to the Swach Bharat Kosh set-up by the Central Government for the promotion of sanitation] and making available safe drinking water.

(ii) Promoting education, including special education and employment enhancing vocation skills especially among children, women, elderly and the differently abled and livelihood enhancement projects.

(iii) Promoting gender equality, empowering women, setting up homes and hostels for women and orphans; setting up old age homes, day care centres and such other facilities for senior citizens and measures for reducing inequalities faced by socially and economi-cally backward groups.

(iv) Ensuring environmental sustainability, ecological balance, protec-tion of flora and fauna, animal welfare, agroforestry, conservation of natural resources and maintaining quality of soil, air and water [including contribution to the Clean Ganga Fund set-up by the Central Government for rejuvenation of river Ganga].

(v) Protection of national heritage, art and culture including restoration of buildings and sites of historical importance and works of art; setting up public libraries; promotion and development of traditional art and handicrafts;

(vi) Measures for the benefit of armed forces veterans, war widows and their dependents;

(vii) Training to promote rural sports, nationally recognised sports, paralympic sports and olympic sports

(viii) Contribution to the prime minister's national relief fund or any other fund set up by the central govt. for socio economic development and relief and welfare of the schedule caste, tribes, other backward classes, minorities and women;

(ix) Contributions or funds provided to technology incubators located within academic institutions which are approved by the central govt.

(x) Rural development projects

(xi) Slum area development.

[Explanation.- For the purposes of this item, the term 'slum area' shall mean any area declared as such by the Central Government or any State Government or any other competent authority under any law for the time being in force.]

(xii) Disaster management, including relief, rehabilitation and reconstruction activities.

Index

E

H

M

Q

R

U

Y

Z